Fod

The U.S. &

British Virgin Islands

Fodor's Travel Publications, Inc.
New York • Toronto • London • Sydney • Auckland

Fodor's The U.S. & British Virgin Islands

Editor: Jillian L. Magalaner
Editorial Contributors: Pamela Acheson, Echo Garrett, Gary Goodlander, Bevin McLaughlin, Mary Ellen Schultz, Jordan Simon, Nancy van Itallie
Creative Director: Fabrizio La Rocca
Map Editor: Robert Blake
Cartographer: David Lindroth
Cover Photograph: Dee Scarr/Touch the Sea
Illustrator: Karl Tanner

Design: Vignelli Associates

Special Sales

Contents

Maps

Foreword

A special thanks is extended to the British Virgin Islands Tourist Board; the U.S.V.I. Government Tourist Offices; American Airlines; Peter Island Resort and Yacht Harbour; Long Bay Hotel; Leverick Bay Resort; the Bitterend Yacht Club; Robinson, Yesawich & Pepperdine, Inc., especially Dan Higgins and Mariska Elia; Development Counsellors International; and Barker, Campbell & Farley.

While every care has been taken to ensure the accuracy of the information in this guide, the passage of time will always bring change, and consequently, the publisher cannot accept responsibility for errors that may occur.

All prices and opening times quoted here are based on information supplied to us at press time. Hours and admission charges may change, however, and the prudent traveler will avoid inconvenience by calling ahead.

Fodor's wants to hear about your travel experiences, both pleasant and unpleasant. When a hotel or restaurant fails to live up to its billing, let us know and we will investigate the complaint and revise our entries where the facts warrant it.

Send your letters to the editors of Fodor's Travel Publications, 201 East 50th Street, New York, NY 10022.

Highlights'95 and Fodor's Choice

Highlights '95

The U.S. Virgin Islands
St. Thomas Private Jet Airline, soon to be known as **National Airlines** (they've purchased the name from the former Florida-based company) now offers service from Chicago, Atlanta, Miami, Dallas, and Las Vegas to St. Thomas and St. Croix. Fares are among the lowest. The island's newest attraction, the **Estate St. Peter Greathouse Botanical Gardens,** offers gorgeous views of more than 20 other islands and islets, plus a gallery of local art and a nature trail through nearly 200 varieties of tropical trees and plants.

There is now another hotel right near the airport. The **Carib Beach Hotel,** badly damaged by Hurricane Hugo, has finally reopened. A sister to Best Western Emerald Beach, it offers slightly lower rates.

St. Croix The **Tamarind Reef Hotel** completed renovations and reopened in early 1994. This affordable North shore property offers high-end motel lodging. The 46 units contain air-conditioning, hair dryer, safe, private terrace or balcony, and kitchenette or minifridge, and coffeemaker. The hotel includes a restaurant, bar, and pool, as well as a water-sports center on the small rough beach and use of the marina facilities next door.

St. John The big news on St. John is the opening of **Harmony,** on a bluff overlooking Maho Bay, under the same ownership as the popular Maho Bay campground. The eight units (another eight and a pool are scheduled to come on line by mid-1995) are completely solar powered; 70% of the construction material is recycled plastic, including the remarkably authentic-looking tile floors. The handsome bungalows have such politically correct artwork as Andean shawls and wood carvings from the Brazilian rain forest on the walls (most of it for sale). Each unit contains a kitchenette, private bath, and terrace with sweeping views of Maho Bay.

The British Virgin Islands
Tortola Tortola's controversial **cruise ship dock** is finished but may never be used. Tortola is not entirely without visitors from cruise ships, however; in a given week, one or two small cruise ships make a day-long stop in Road Town harbor, usually on different days.

Landscapers and stonemasons have been working around **Road Town,** planting trees and tropical flowers and crafting walkways and small malls. The town is getting prettier and less dusty every day.

Virgin Gorda The island's first **desalinization plant** went into operation in March 1994, prompting the **Olde Yard Inn** to begin construction of a **swimming pool,** which is due to be completed by fall 1994. The lack of a pool has been the one drawback of this charming property.

Anegada Anegada's first and only **gas station** opened in January 1994. But don't worry. Other than making life more convenient, it hasn't changed a thing on this supremely peaceful island.

Fodor's Choice

No two people will agree on what makes a perfect vacation, but it's fun and helpful to know what others think. We hope you'll have the chance to experience some of Fodor's Choices yourself while visiting the Virgin Islands. For detailed information about each entry, refer to the appropriate chapter in this guidebook.

Scenic Views

Moonrise over Sapphire Bay, St. Thomas

Sailing into Red Hook from St. John at sunset

Observation Tower, Skyworld, Tortola

Beaches

Magens Bay, St. Thomas

Trunk Bay, St. John

Smuggler's Cove, Tortola

Spring Bay & The Baths, Virgin Gorda

Deadman's Bay, Peter Island

Hotels

Carambola Beach Resort, St. Croix (*$$$$*)

Drake's Anchorage, Virgin Gorda (*$$$$*)

Little Dix Bay, Virgin Gorda (*$$$$*)

Peter Island Hotel and Yacht Club, Peter Island (*$$$$*)

Point Pleasant Resort, St. Thomas (*$$$*)

Fort Recovery, Tortola (*$$*)

Hilty House, St. Croix (*$*)

Restaurants

Kendricks, St. Croix (*$$$$*)

Tradewinds, Peter Island (*$$$$*)

Virgilio's, St. Thomas (*$$$$*)

Le Château de Bordeaux, St. John (*$$$–$$$$*)

Brandywine Bay,Tortola (*$$$*)

Pangaea, St. Croix (*$$$*)

Paradiso, St. John (*$$$*)

Upstairs, Tortola (*$$$*)

East Coast Bar and Grill, St. Thomas (*$$–$$$*)

Etta's, St. John (*$*)

Special Moments

Watching the pelicans dive for supper at twilight on Cruz Bay, St. John.

The parade of cruise ships out of Charlotte Amalie harbor at sunset.

Hearing Quito Rhymer's love songs drift across the water at Cane Garden Bay.

Watching the phosphorous light up the water's edge at night at Savannah Bay.

Music, Nightlife, Bars

Barnacle Bill's, St. Thomas

Any bar on Jost van Dyke

Bomba Shack, Tortola

Blue Moon, St. Croix

Blackbeard's Castle, St. Thomas

Quito's Gazebo, Tortola

Bath and Turtle, Virgin Gorda

The Virgin Islands

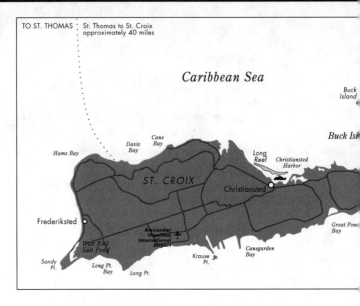

TO ST. THOMAS · St. Thomas to St. Croix
approximately 40 miles

Caribbean Sea

Buck Island

Buck Isl

Davis Bay

Cane Bay

Hams Bay

Long Reef

Christiansted Harbor

ST. CROIX

Christiansted

Frederiksted

Great Pon Bay

Alexander Hamilton International Airport

West End Salt Pond

Sandy Pt.

Long Pt. Bay

Long Pt.

Krause Pt.

Canegarden Bay

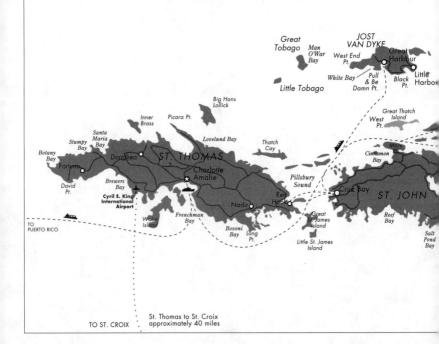

A T L A N T I C   *O C E A N*

Great Tobago

Man O'War Bay

JOST VAN DYKE

West End Pt.

Great Harbour

White Bay

Pull & Be Damn Pt.

Little Harbo

Black Pt.

Little Tobago

Big Hans Lollick

Inner Brass

Picara Pt.

Lovelund Bay

Great Thatch Island

West Pt.

Santa Maria Bay

Stumpy Bay

Botany Bay

Dorothea

ST. THOMAS

Thatch Cay

Man

Cinnamon Bay

Charlotte Amalie

Pillsbury Sound

Cruz Bay

ST. JOHN

Fortuna

Brewers Bay

David Pt.

Cyril E. King International Airport

Frenchman Bay

Nadir

Red Hook

Reef Bay

Water Island

Bovoni Bay

Long Pt.

Great St. James Island

Little St. James Island

Salt Pond Bay

TO PUERTO RICO

TO ST. CROIX · St. Thomas to St. Croix
approximately 40 miles

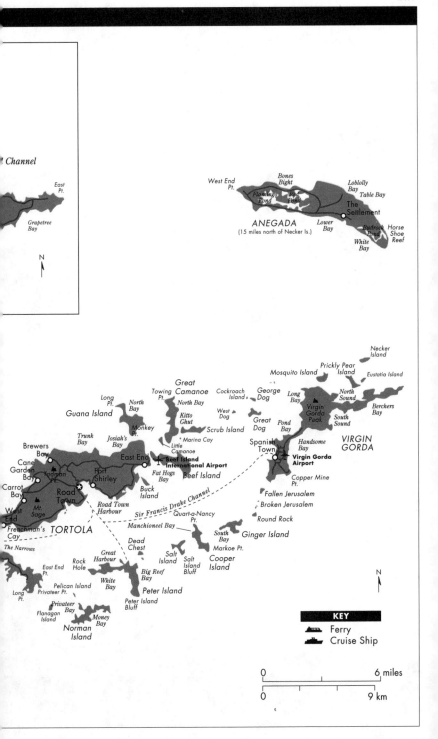

Channel

East Pt.

Grapetree Bay

N

West End Pt.

Bones Bight

Loblolly Bay

Table Bay

Flamingo Pond

Red Pond

The Settlement

ANEGADA
(15 miles north of Necker Is.)

Lower Bay

Budrock Pond

Horse Shoe Reef

White Bay

Necker Island

Prickly Pear Island

Mosquito Island

Eustatia Island

Great Camanoe

Cockroach Island

George Dog

Long Bay

North Sound

Berchers Bay

Long Pt.

Towing Pt.

North Bay

Virgin Gorda Peak

South Sound

Guana Island

North Bay

Kitto Ghut

West Dog

VIRGIN GORDA

Trunk Bay

Josiah's Bay

Monkey Pt.

Scrub Island

Great Dog

Pond Bay

Handsome Bay

Brewers Bay

* Marina Cay

Little Camanoe

Spanish Town

Cane Garden Bay

East End

Beef Island International Airport

Virgin Gorda Airport

Copper Mine Pt.

Tedman Pt.

Fort Shirley

Fat Hogs Bay

Beef Island

Carrot Bay

Road Town

Mt. Sage

Buck Island

Fallen Jerusalem

Broken Jerusalem

West End

Road Town Harbour

Sir Francis Drake Channel

Quart-a-Nancy Pt.

Round Rock

Frenchman's Cay

TORTOLA

Manchioneel Bay

South Bay

Ginger Island

The Narrows

Dead Chest

Markoe Pt.

East End Pt.

Rock Hole

Great Harbour

Salt Island

Salt Island Bluff

Cooper Island

Pelican Island

White Bay

Big Reef Bay

Long Pt.

Privateer Pt.

Peter Island

N

Privateer Bay

Money Bay

Peter Island Bluff

Flanagan Island

Norman Island

KEY

🚗 Ferry

🚢 Cruise Ship

0   6 miles

0   9 km

The Caribbean

U.S.A. ○ Miami

Havana ✪

Cuba

CUBA

Little Cayman

Cayman Brac

Grand Cayman

Montego Bay ○

G R E A T E R

Jamaica

THE BAHAMAS

Turks and Caicos Islands

HAITI

Hispaniola

✪ Port-au-Prince

Caribbean

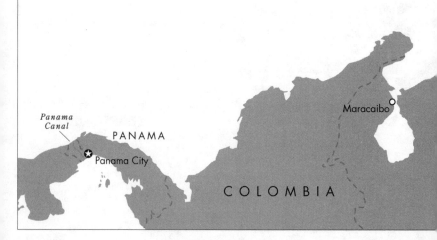

Panama Canal

PANAMA

✪ Panama City

Maracaibo ○

COLOMBIA

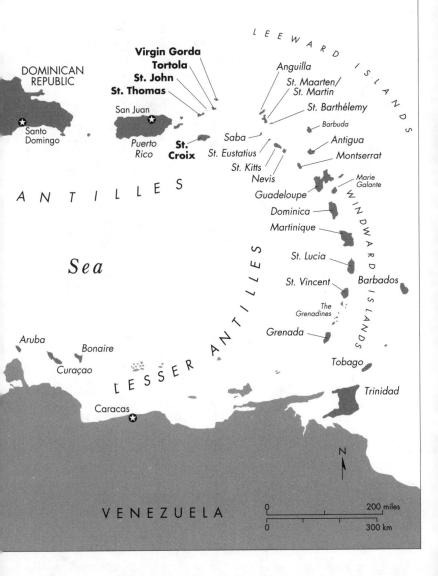

xvi

World Time Zones

Numbers below vertical bands relate each zone to Greenwich Mean Time (0 hrs.).
Local times frequently differ from these general indications,
as indicated by light-face numbers on map.

Algiers, **29**	Berlin, **34**	Delhi, **48**	Istanbul, **40**
Anchorage, **3**	Bogotá, **19**	Denver, **8**	Jerusalem, **42**
Athens, **41**	Budapest, **37**	Djakarta, **53**	Johannesburg, **44**
Auckland, **1**	Buenos Aires, **24**	Dublin, **26**	Lima, **20**
Baghdad, **46**	Caracas, **22**	Edmonton, **7**	Lisbon, **28**
Bangkok, **50**	Chicago, **9**	Hong Kong, **56**	London (Greenwich), **27**
Beijing, **54**	Copenhagen, **33**	Honolulu, **2**	Los Angeles, **6**
	Dallas, **10**		Madrid, **38**
			Manila, **57**

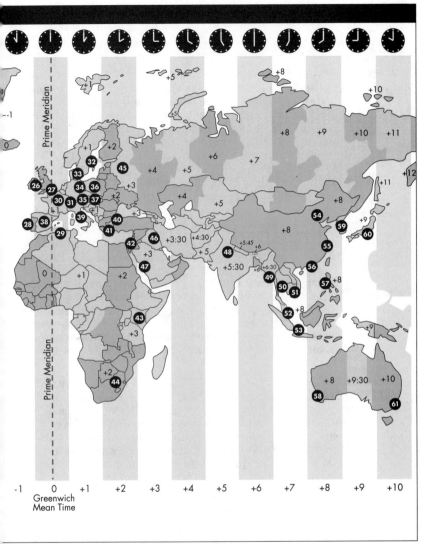

-1   0   +1   +2   +3   +4   +5   +6   +7   +8   +9   +10

Greenwich
Mean Time

Mecca, **47**
Mexico City, **12**
Miami, **18**
Montréal, **15**
Moscow, **45**
Nairobi, **43**
New York City, **16**

Ottawa, **14**
Paris, **30**
Perth, **58**
Reykjavík, **25**
Rio de Janeiro, **23**
Rome, **39**
Saigon (Ho Chi Minh City), **51**

San Francisco, **5**
Santiago, **21**
Seoul, **59**
Shanghai, **55**
Singapore, **52**
Stockholm, **32**
Sydney, **61**
Tokyo, **60**

Toronto, **13**
Vancouver, **4**
Vienna, **35**
Warsaw, **36**
Washington, D.C., **17**
Yangon, **49**
Zürich, **31**

Introduction

By Jordan Simon

A freelance writer who has traveled throughout the Caribbean, Jordan Simon has written for Elle, Travel & Leisure, Modern Bride, *and* Fodor's Caribbean.

Separated by only a narrow channel of shimmering water patrolled by flotillas of pelicans and pleasure craft, the United States and British Virgin Island groups are nevertheless a world apart. It isn't just the obvious: a tale of two traditions and governments. Indeed, clearing customs is usually a formality, and the U.S. dollar is the official currency on both sides of the "border." Rather it's the individual look and feel that set them apart, the atmosphere they determinedly cultivate—and the differing breeds of visitors this attracts—an atmosphere perhaps too glibly defined as American verve versus British reserve.

Though the islands are closely grouped, the vegetation and terrain vary widely. The U.S.V.I. are largely lush and tropical. On St. John, where two thirds of the land is under U.S. National Park Service protection, there are more than 250 species of trees, vines, shrubs, flowers, and other plant life. Each of the three major U.S. Virgin Islands—St. John, St. Thomas, and St. Croix—is really a collection of ecosystems, ranging from tropical seacoast to mountain, rainforest to desert. The flowering trees are particularly superb: Frangipani and flamboyant, hibiscus, and lignum vitae blanket the hills and rolling fields with a dainty blue, pink, yellow, and white quilt.

In contrast, Tortola and Virgin Gorda, the largest two islands in the B.V.I., have a ravishing, desertlike dryness found only on the eastern extremes of St. Thomas and St. Croix. Tortola is the more verdant of the two, whereas Virgin Gorda is fringed with monumental boulders whose exact origins are still shrouded in mystery. These are the "cactus tropics," embroidered with agave and other spiny plants, and enlivened by the vibrant colors of an occasional wild hibiscus or bougainvillea tree.

Both island groups are steeped in history. The U.S.V.I. are graced with the rich architectural legacy of the original Danish settlers, including the picturesque ruins of their sugar plantations. St. Croix is particularly notable. Christiansted and Frederiksted, the two main towns on St. Croix, feature delightful red-roofed gingerbreads in coral and canary yellow, fronted by shaded galleries and stately colonnades. The old sugar estates on St. Croix are the islands' best-preserved and most elegant. Caribbean ghost towns unto themselves, they are crawling and cracked with undergrowth, the haunting grandeur of their double stairways eloquently attesting to St. Croix's former prosperity.

If their architectural remains are not as spectacular, the B.V.I. boast an incomparable *air* of history. In the 17th and 18th centuries the islands' numerous cays, rocks, secret coves, and treacherous reefs formed the perfect headquarters for raiding corsairs and privateers, among them the infamous Edward

"Blackbeard" Teach, Captain Kidd, and Sir Francis Drake. Norman Island is the reputed locale of Robert Louis Stevenson's classic *Treasure Island*. The tiny island, Dead Chest, is said to have inspired the chantey of the same name: "Fifteen men on a dead man's chest, yo ho ho and a bottle of rum."

The nautical spirit lives on, and today these pirate hideaways attract legions of "yachties." The calm, iridescent waters of the B.V.I. are one of the world's most popular sailing destinations. In fact, the islands, forested by masts and flecked with sails, are perhaps best experienced by boat—what better way to explore every rainbow-colored coral reef or gleaming scimitar of white sand (replete with beach bar)? The favorite sport may well be motoring to a private sheltered cove, waving if it's occupied, and cruising to the next.

But ultimately the greatest differences between the U.S.V.I. and the B.V.I. are man-made. Step off the plane in St. Thomas and you know you're in a consumer society where bigger is better. There are more hotels per square mile here than anywhere else in the Caribbean. Posters hawking products and fast-food franchises dominate the lush surroundings. Charlotte Amalie, the bustling capital, pulsates with legendary duty-free shopping and by far the most active nightlife in the area. You'll discover more pristine pockets on pastoral St. Croix, which by comparison resembles a friendly small town. The odd isle out in the U.S.V.I. equation is tranquil, sleepy St. John, the closest American island to the B.V.I. in distance and temperament. But even here the development and pace often exceed that of her British cousins.

With so many options for the tourist dollar, competition between U.S.V.I. properties is fierce. The constant upgrading of facilities, added amenities, and attractive package rates translate into tremendous value for vacationers. If you want all the comforts, conveniences (and convenience stores) of home—with tropical sun and exotic accent—head for the U.S.V.I.

Although tourism is as much the number one industry on the B.V.I. as it is on the U.S.V.I., you'd never know it in these quiet, unhurried islands, where there are few major developments and where the largest hotel has only 140 rooms. There are no high rises here, no traffic lights, and few cruise ships disgorging hordes of shoppers and sightseers. Though there are repeated promises (viewed more as threats by locals) from the Tourist Office to deepen the harbor and lengthen the airport runways to allow more visitors, there is a tacit understanding that it is precisely their comparatively undeveloped state that makes the B.V.I. such a desirable vacation spot.

By many tourism standards, the B.V.I. are *not* a bargain. The hotels tend to be small and exclusive; many were built by industrial barons and shipping magnates as hideaways for themselves and friends. But true luxury is often understated. It isn't necessarily blow dryers and satellite TVs in every room. Rather, it's

the privacy, the relaxed, easygoing pace, the personalized service, and the ambience.

Expatriates on both the U.S.V.I. and the B.V.I. often delight in
taking potshots at their neighbors. You'll find many passionate
devotees and repeat visitors who wouldn't dream of crossing the
border. U.S.V.I. detractors point to the swarming crowds and
comparatively high crime rate on St. Thomas and St. Croix.
B.V.I. critics cite the boring lifestyle and difficulty of getting
top-notch goods even on Tortola. The U.S.V.I. have been dis-
paraged as "entry-level Caribbean" and "Detroit with palm
trees." Their aficionados will counter, "There's a reason the
British Home Office once called the B.V.I. 'the least important
part of the Empire.'"

It only demonstrates how popular the islands are with their
fans. Luckily, whichever you prefer, there's always the advantage of proximity. In the Virgin Islands you can truly have the
best of both worlds.

1 Essential Information

Before You Go

Government Tourist Offices

The U.S. Virgin Islands Information about the United States Virgin Islands is available through the following **U.S.V.I. Government Tourist Offices:** 225 Peachtree St., Suite 760, Atlanta, GA 30303, tel. 404/688–0906, fax 404/525–1102; 599 Michigan Ave., Suite 2030, Chicago, IL 60611, tel. 312/670–8784, fax 312/670–8788; 3460 Wilshire Blvd., Suite 412, Los Angeles, CA 90010, tel. 213/739–0138, fax 213/739–2005; 2655 Le Jeune Rd., Suite 907, Coral Gables, FL 33134, tel. 305/442–7200, fax 305/445–9044; 1270 6th Ave., New York, NY 10020, tel. 212/332–2222, fax 212/332–2223; 900 17th Ave. NW, Suite 500, Washington, DC 20006, tel. 202/293–3707, fax 202/785–2542; 1300 Ashford Ave., Condado, Santurce, Puerto Rico 00907, tel. 809/724–3816, fax 809/724–7223; 33 Niagara St., Toronto M5V 1C2, tel. 416/362–8784, fax 416/362–9841; and 2 Cinnamon Row, Plantation Wharf, York Pl., London SW11 3TW, tel. 071/978–5262, fax 071/924–3171.

You can also call the Division of Tourism's toll-free number (tel. 800/USVI–INFO).

The U.S. Department of State's **Overseas Citizens Emergency Center** (Room 4811, Washington, DC 20520; enclose S.A.S.E.) issues Consular Information Sheets, which cover crime, security, political climate, and health risks as well as embassy locations, entry requirements, currency regulations, and other routine matters. For the latest information, stop in at any U.S. passport office, consulate, or embassy; call the interactive hot line (tel. 202/647–5225; fax 202/647–3000); or, with your PC's modem, tap into the Bureau of Consular Affairs' computer bulletin board (tel. 202/647–9225).

The British Virgin Islands Information about the British Virgin Islands is available through the **British Virgin Islands Tourist Board** (370 Lexington Ave., Suite 330, New York, NY 10017, tel. 212/696–0400 or 800/835–8530, fax 212/949–8254) or at **British Virgin Islands Information Offices** (1686 Union St., Suite 305, San Francisco, CA 94123, tel. 415/775–0344 or 800/232–7770, fax 415/775–2554). British travelers can contact the **B.V.I. Tourist Board** (110 St. Martins La., London WC2N 4AZ, tel. 071/240–4259).

Tours and Packages

Should you buy your travel arrangements to the Virgin Islands packaged or do it yourself? There are advantages either way. Buying packaged arrangements saves you money, particularly if you can find a program that includes exactly the features you want. You also get a pretty good idea of what your trip will cost from the outset. Generally, you have two options: escorted tours and independent packages. However, escorted tours are virtually nonexistent in the Virgin Islands. Most travelers to this paradise of sun and sand explore the islands on their own, using independent packages. A range of special-interest programs is also available.

Whatever program you ultimately choose, be sure to find out exactly what is included: taxes, tips, transfers, meals, baggage handling, ground transportation, entertainment, excursions, sports or recreation (and rental equipment for any sports you may pursue). Ask about the hotel, its location, the size of its rooms, the kind of beds, and its facilities and amenities, such as pool, room service, or programs for children, if they're important to you. Be sure to inquire about the hotel's proximity to the beach: The term "beach nearby" can mean many things.

Find out cancellation penalties, which are charged by nearly all operators. The only way to avoid them is to buy trip-cancellation insurance (*see* Trip Insurance, *below*). Also ask about the single supplement, a surcharge assessed to solo travelers. Some operators do not make you pay it if you agree to be matched up with a roommate of the same sex, even if one is not found by departure time. Remember if many of the activities in a program don't interest you, that particular package probably isn't the most cost-effective choice.

Look into **American Airlines Fly AAway Vacations** (tel. 800/321–2121); **Certified Vacations** (Box 1525, Ft. Lauderdale, FL 33302, tel. 305/522–1414 or 800/233–7260); **Club Med** (40 W. 57th St., New York, NY 10019, tel. 800/258–2633; **Continental Airlines' Grand Destinations** (tel. 800/634–5555); **Delta Dream Vacations** (tel. 800/872–7786); **TWA Getaway Vacations** (tel. 800/438–2929); and programs from **Liberty Travel**, a consortium of travel agents (consult your telephone directory for the information on the one nearest you), and **Friendly Holidays** (1983 Marcus Ave., Suite C130, Lake Success, NY 11042, tel. 516/358–1200), a major tour operator that sells its wide variety of packages only through travel agents.

Tips for British Travelers

Tourist Information The **B.V.I. Tourist Board** (*see* Government Tourist Offices, *above*) can provide brochures and information on the British Virgin Islands.

For the United States Virgin Islands, contact the **U.S.V.I. Tourist Office** (*see* Government Tourist Offices, *above*).

Insurance Most tour operators, travel agents, and insurance agents sell specialized policies covering accident, medical expenses, personal liability, trip cancellation, and loss or theft of personal property. You can also buy an annual travel-insurance policy valid for every trip (usually of less than 90 days) you make during the year in which it's purchased. Make sure you will be covered if you have a preexisting medical condition or are pregnant.

The **Association of British Insurers,** a trade association representing 450 insurance companies, advises extra medical coverage for visitors to the United States.

For advice by phone or a free booklet, "Holiday Insurance," that sets out what to expect from a holiday-insurance policy and gives price guidelines, contact the Association of British Insurers (51 Gresham St., London EC2V 7HQ, tel. 071/600–3333; 30 Gordon St., Glasgow G1 3PU, tel. 041/226–3905; Scottish Provincial Bldg., Donegall Sq. W, Belfast BT1 6JE, tel. 0232/249176; call for other locations).

Tour Operators Flights and accommodations can be booked individually or as a package through **British Virgin Islands Holidays** (Wingjet Travel Ltd., 26 Hockerill St., Bishop's Stortford, Herts. CM23 2DW, tel. 0279/656111), which acts as agents for all major airlines and hotels in the B.V.I. They can arrange multicenter holiday stays, bare-boat charters and crewed-yacht charters, and inclusive package holidays. Also look into **Caribbean Connection** (Concorde House, Forest St., Chester CH1 1QR, tel. 0244/341131), **Caribtours** (161 Fulham Rd., London SW3 6SN, tel. 071/581–3517), **Harlequin Worldwide** (2

North Rd., South Ockendon, Essex RN15 6QJ, tel. 0708/852780), and **Hayes and Jarvis Ltd.** (Hayes House, 152 King St., London W6 0QU, tel. 081/748–5050).

Passports Britons need a valid 10-year passport to enter both the B.V.I. and the U.S.V.I. A British Visitors Passport is not acceptable. You do not need a visa for the U.S.V.I. if you are visiting either on business or pleasure, are staying less than 90 days, have a return ticket or onward ticket, are traveling with a major airline (in effect, any airline that flies from the United Kingdom to the United States), and complete visa waiver I-94W, which is supplied either at the airport of departure or on the plane. If you fail to comply with any one of these requirements or are entering the United States by land, you will need a visa. Although it is not officially required, it is recommended that Britons entering the U.S.V.I. by ship obtain a visa to avoid delays. Apply to a travel agent or the United States Embassy Visa and Immigration Department (5 Upper Grosvenor St., London W1A 2JB, tel. 071/499–3443 for a recorded message or 071/499–7010). Visa applications to the U.S. Embassy must be made by mail, not in person. Visas can be given only to holders of 10-year passports, although visas in expired passports remain valid. If you think you might stay longer than three months, you must apply for a visa before you travel.

Travelers with Disabilities Main sources include the **Royal Association for Disability and Rehabilitation** (RADAR, 25 Mortimer St., London W1N 8AB, tel. 071/637–5400), which publishes travel information for people with disabilities in Britain, and **Mobility International** (228 Borough High St., London SE1 1JX, tel. 071/403–5688), the headquarters of an international membership organization that serves as a clearinghouse of travel information for people with disabilities.

Customs and Duties
The U.S. Virgin Islands Entering the U.S.V.I., a British visitor 21 or older can bring in 200 cigarettes or 50 cigars or 2 kilograms smoking tobacco; 1 liter of alcohol; and duty-free gifts to a value of $100. You may not bring in meat or meat products, seeds, plants, or fruit. Never carry illegal drugs.

The British Virgin Islands The following duty-free allowances apply for Britons age 17 or older both on entering the B.V.I. and on returning to the United Kingdom: (1) 200 cigarettes or 100 cigarillos or 50 cigars or 250 grams of tobacco; (2) 2 liters of still table wine and (3) 1 liter of alcohol over 22% volume or 2 liters of alcohol under 22% volume (fortified or sparkling wine) or 2 more liters of table wine; (4) 60 cc of perfume and 250 ml of toilet water; (5) other goods to a value of £32, but no more than 50 liters of beer or 25 mechanical lighters.

When to Go

Traditionally high season in the Virgin Islands has been in the winter, from about December 15 to the week after Carnival, usually the last week in April. This is the most fashionable, the most expensive, and the most popular time for cruising or lazing on the beaches, far from the icy north, and most hotels fill up. You have to make your reservations at least two or three months in advance for the very best places.

Climate Weather in the Virgin Islands is a year-round wonder. The average daily temperature is about 80°F, and there isn't much variation from the coolest to the warmest months. Unlike stateside coastal areas, the nights, even on the beach, are warm, so don't bother to pack bulky sweaters.

Rainfall averages 40–44 inches per year. Rainfall doesn't mean the same thing in the tropics as it does in the temperate zone farther north. Rainstorms tend to be sudden and brief, often erupting early in the morning and at dusk.

One of life's pleasures in the Virgin Islands is taking shelter under a sea-grape tree at seaside, watching a rain shower move across the ocean, over your head and onward, leaving behind a sky washed clean and blue.

Although the Virgin Islands are traditionally considered a winter-resort escape, summer is one of the prettiest times of the year. The bright-orange flamboyant trees are in full bloom by July; the sea is even calmer; the summer rains, never very long, turn the island to its greenest; and things generally move at a slower pace. (It's cheaper, too).

Toward the end of summer, of course, hurricane season begins in earnest with the first tropical wave passing by in August. Since the advent of Hurricane Hugo, islanders have paid closer attention to the tropical waves as they form and travel up from Africa. In an odd paradox, tropical storms passing by leave behind the sunniest and clearest days you will see year-round. (And that's saying something in the land of zero air pollution.)

In May and June what's known as the Sahara Dust sometimes moves through. That's dust that literally blows across the oceans from the African desert, making for hazy spring days and spectacular sunsets.

What follows are average daily maximum and minimum temperatures for the Virgin Islands.

Jan.	86F	25C	May	88F	31C	Sept.	92F	33C
	74	23		75	24		76	24
Feb.	86F	25C	June	88F	31C	Oct.	92F	33C
	74	23		75	24		76	24
Mar.	87F	30C	July	95F	35C	Nov.	86F	25C
	71	22		77	25		72	22
Apr.	87F	30C	Aug.	95F	35C	Dec.	86F	25C
	71	22		77	25		72	22

Information Sources   For current weather conditions and forecasts for cities in the United States and abroad, plus the local time and helpful travel tips, call the **Weather Channel Connection** (tel. 900/932–8437; 95¢ per minute) from a touch-tone phone.

Festivals and Seasonal Events

January U.S.V.I.   **Martin Luther King, Jr. Day** is observed on all three U.S. Virgin Islands.

February B.V.I.   There is an annual **art show at the Botanical Gardens** (tel. 809/494–4557).

March B.V.I.   **Annual Charity Fishing Tournament.** The B.V.I. Yacht Club (tel. 809/494–3286) hosts this event in which anglers compete in bringing in wahoo, marlin, kingfish, and other Caribbean fish.
Horticultural Society Show. The Botanical Gardens (tel. 809/494–4557) displays breathtaking examples of the local foliage.
Virgin Gorda Festival. Calypso music, a parade, and a beauty pageant are the highlights of this local festival.

April
U.S.V.I. **St. Croix's International Triathalon.** Athletes from around the world head for St. Croix to participate in this grueling annual swimming, biking, and running race.

Rolex Cup Regatta. This is part of the three-race Caribbean Ocean Racing Triangle (CORT) that pulls in yachters and their pals from all over.

St. Thomas Carnival. A week-long, major-league blowout of parades, parties, and island-wide events. The date changes from year to year but always follows Easter.

B.V.I. **B.V.I. Spring Regatta.** For more than 20 years this internationally known race has drawn sailing enthusiasts from all over the world.

Pusser's Rum Run. The B.V.I. Yacht Club (tel. 809/494–3286) organizes this annual 10-mile race from Road Town to Pusser's Landing.

May
U.S.V.I. **Sportfishing tournaments.** Throughout the month of May, several locally sponsored fishing events are held (St. Thomas is home to seven world sport-fishing records), kicking off the summer-long fishing season.

June
U.S.V.I. **Organic Act Day** commemorates U.S. Virgin Islanders' equivalent of a constitution (drawn up in 1945), which allows them to elect a legislature and enact laws.

Hurricane Supplication Day. Virgin Islanders gather in churches on June 15 to pray for deliverance from the ravages of storms.

July
U.S.V.I. **St. John Carnival.** A small but colorful carnival, complete with bands and parades in characteristically laid-back St. John style.

July 4th Tournament. St. Thomas Gamefishing Club sponsors this Independence Day fishing tournament.

Bastille Day. Descendants of the French settlers on St. Thomas celebrate the French Revolution with a minicarnival in Frenchtown.

V.I. Open Atlantic Blue Marlin Tournament. Marlin anglers from around the world compete for big-money prizes for landing the biggest marlin.

August
U.S.V.I. **Texas Society Chili Cook-Off.** That's right, a Texas-style chili contest in the Virgin Islands. It's a beach party with country music, dancing, chili tasting, and a variety of fun and games.

B.V.I. **B.V.I. Summer Festival** (tel. 809/494–2875). This two-week free-for-all celebrates the season with local music, arts, and crafts, as well as a beauty pageant and parade.

September
B.V.I. **B.V.I. International Rugby Festival.** If rugby's not your thing, something in the whirlwind of social events surrounding this competition surely will be.

Foxy's Wooden Boat Regatta. This attracts sailors the world over, who come to Jost van Dyke for several days of racing and carousing.

October
U.S.V.I. **Columbus Day/V.I.–Puerto Rico Friendship Day.** Parades and festivities commemorate both at once.

Hurricane Thanksgiving Day. A legal holiday (usually, but not always, in October) during which residents give thanks for being spared.

B.V.I. **Bacardi Rum Beach Party** (tel. 809/495–4639). Cane Garden Bay Beach hosts this day filled with seaside activities, from a tug-of-war to a bikini contest.

November
U.S.V.I. **Liberty Day.** A legal holiday honoring Judge David Hamilton Jackson, who secured freedom of assembly and freedom of the press for the Danish Virgin Islands in 1915.

St. Croix Regatta, and **St. John Coral Bay Regatta.** Around Thanksgiving time, charter boats show their stuff in these regattas.

B.V.I. **B.V.I. Boat Show** (tel. 809/494–3286). Boat dealers from around the world assemble in the British Virgin Islands to display and sell boats.

Fast Tacks. Hosted by the Bitter End Yacht Club, this is a six-week series of races, games, and special events, including the world-class Bitter End Invitational Regatta.

December **St. Croix Christmas Fiesta.** Christmas and the day after (Christmas
U.S.V.I. Second Day) are legal holidays and mark the start of 12 days of celebrations in St. Croix.

What to Pack

Clothing Pack anything you want to. You won't need a suit and tie or a cocktail dress, but if you want to get all dressed up, you can most certainly find someplace to go. And, of course, the reverse is also true. Some hotels require jackets (no tie necessary) for men, but casual clothes are appropriate (and more comfortable) for almost everywhere. You may want to bring a lightweight sweater or long-sleeve T-shirt for breezy nights (or overly air-conditioned restaurants) or the ferry ride home after a day in the sun.

One clothing tip that will go a long way in tourist-local relations: Men, keep your shirts on, and women, get your tan on the beach, not in town. Road Town, Spanish Town, Charlotte Amalie, Christiansted, Frederiksted, and even casual Cruz Bay are not Florida beach towns, and you'll receive a much kinder reception from the prim Virgin Islanders if you are fully, albeit casually, dressed.

Luggage Free airline baggage allowances depend on the airline, the route,
Regulations and the class of your ticket. In general, on domestic flights and on international flights between the United States and foreign destinations, you are entitled to check two bags—neither exceeding 62 inches, or 158 centimeters (length + width + height), nor weighing more than 70 pounds (32 kilograms). A third piece may be brought aboard as a carryon; its total dimensions are generally limited to less than 45 inches (114 centimeters), so it will fit easily under the seat in front of you or in the overhead compartment. In the United States the Federal Aviation Administration (FAA) gives airlines broad latitude to limit carry-on allowances and tailor them to different aircraft and operational conditions. Charges for excess, oversize, or overweight pieces vary.

Safeguarding Before leaving home, itemize your bags' contents and their worth;
Your Luggage this list will help you estimate the extent of your loss if your bags go astray. To minimize that risk, tag them inside and out with your name, address, and phone number. (If you use your home address, cover it so that potential thieves can't see it.) Put a copy of your itinerary inside each bag, so that you can easily be tracked. At check-in, make sure that the tag attached by baggage handlers bears the correct three-letter code for your destination. If your bags do not arrive with you, or if you detect damage, do not leave the airport until you've filed a written report with the airline.

Miscellaneous If you have a health problem that may require you to purchase a prescription drug, take enough to last the duration of the trip. Pack a list of the offices that supply refunds for lost or stolen traveler's checks.

Traveler's Checks

Traveler's checks are preferable in metropolitan centers, although you'll need cash in rural areas and small towns. The most widely recognized are **American Express, Citicorp, Diners Club, Thomas Cook,** and **Visa,** which are sold by major commercial banks. Both American Express and Thomas Cook issue checks that can be countersigned and used by you or your traveling companion. Typically the issuing company or the bank at which you make your purchase charges 1% to 3% of the checks' face value as a fee. Record the numbers of checks as you spend them, and keep this list separate from the checks.

Cash Machines

Many automated-teller machines (ATMs) are tied to international networks such as **Cirrus** and **Plus.** You can use your bank card at ATMs away from home to withdraw money from your checking account and get cash advances on a credit-card account if your card has been programmed with a personal identification number, or PIN. Check in advance on limits on withdrawals and cash advances within specified periods. On cash advances you are charged interest from the day you receive the money from ATMs as well as from tellers. Note that transaction fees for ATM withdrawals outside your home turf will probably be higher than for withdrawals at home.

For specific Cirrus locations in the United States and Canada, call 800/424–7787 (for U.S. Plus locations, 800/843–7587), and press the area code and first three digits of the number you're calling from (or the calling area where you want an ATM).

Currency

The U.S. dollar is the medium of exchange in both the B.V.I. and the U.S.V.I.

What It Will Cost

In both the U.S.V.I. and the B.V.I., a cup of coffee goes for 70¢–$1, a beer costs $2–$5, and a cocktail runs $3–$5.

The U.S. Virgin Islands A 7.5% tax is added to hotel rates. Departure tax for the U.S.V.I. is included in the cost of your airplane ticket. Some hotels and restaurants add a 10% or 15% service charge to your bill, generally only if you are part of a group of 15 or more. There is no sales tax in the U.S.V.I.

The British Virgin Islands Hotels collect a 7% accommodations tax, which they will add to your bill along with a 10% service charge. Restaurants may put a similar service charge on the bill, or they may leave it up to you. For those leaving the B.V.I. by air, the departure tax is $5; by sea it is $4. A tourist information card must also be filled out by visitors. There is no sales tax in the B.V.I.

Passports and Visas

Upon entering either the B.V.I. or the U.S.V.I., U.S. and Canadian citizens are required to present some proof of citizenship, if not a passport then a birth certificate or driver's license. If you are arriving from the U.S. mainland or Puerto Rico, you need no inoculation or health certificate.

Customs and Duties

The U.S.
Virgin Islands
Before you leave the U.S.V.I. to return to the U.S. mainland, your baggage will be subject to inspection by U.S. Customs in St. Thomas or St. Croix; however, if you are making a connecting flight in San Juan, you will go through Customs in Puerto Rico.

A U.S. resident may bring back up to $1,200 worth of duty-free imports (goods not made in the U.S.V.I. or United States) every 30 days, twice the limit allowed for those coming from other Caribbean islands, and three times that allowed for those coming from most foreign nations. This includes an allowance of 200 cigarettes and 100 cigars (non-Cuban). Residents 21 years or older may bring back five bottles of liquor duty-free, or six bottles if one bottle was produced in the U.S.V.I. If you exceed your $1,200 exemption in foreign-made goods brought home, you will pay a duty of 5% for the next $1,000 (rather than the normal 10%); above that articles will be subject to various rates of duty. Apart from the $1,200 exemption, you can mail home $100 worth of gifts to friends or relatives on any one day. Anything island-made, including fashions, perfume, straw products, and jewelry are customs-exempt, but anything valued over $25 must have a certificate of origin. Original paintings and unset precious gems are also duty-free. Returning to the United States with plants and fruits is strictly controlled, but not impossible. You may need a certificate from the Department of Agriculture (tel. 809/776–2787), for example.

For returning Canadians, the same exemptions apply as described in the British Virgin Islands, *see below.*

The British
Virgin Islands
The British Virgin Islands are included in the Caribbean Basin Initiative's beneficiary countries and, therefore, the customs exemption for returning U.S. citizens is raised from $400 to $600. You may bring home duty-free up to $600 of foreign goods, as long as you have been out of the country for at least 48 hours and you haven't made an international trip in the past 30 days. Each member of the family is entitled to the same exemption, regardless of age, and exemptions may be pooled. For the next $1,000 worth of goods, a flat 10% rate is assessed; above $1,600, duties vary with the merchandise. Included in the allowances for travelers 21 or older are one liter of alcohol, 100 cigars (non-Cuban), and 200 cigarettes. Only one bottle of perfume trademarked in the United States may be imported. There is no duty on antiques or works of art over 100 years old. Anything exceeding these limits will be taxed at the port of entry and may be taxed additionally in the traveler's home state. Gifts valued at under $50 may be mailed duty-free to friends or relatives at home, but you may not send more than one package per day to a single addressee and packages may not include perfumes costing more than $5, tobacco, or liquor.

Exemptions for returning Canadians range from $20 to $300, depending on length of stay out of the country. For the $300 exemption, you must have been out of the country for one week. In any given year, you are only allowed one $300 exemption. You may bring in duty-free up to 50 cigars, 200 cigarettes, 2.2 pounds of tobacco, and 40 ounces of liquor, provided these are declared in writing to customs on arrival and accompany you in hand or check-through baggage. Personal gifts should be mailed labeled "Unsolicited Gift—Value under $40." Obtain a copy of the Canadian Customs brochure "I Declare" for further details.

Traveling with Cameras, Camcorders, and Laptops

About Film and Cameras If your camera is new or if you haven't used it for a while, shoot and develop a few rolls of film before leaving home. Store film in a cool, dry place—never in the car's glove compartment or on the shelf under the rear window.

Airport security X-rays generally aren't harmful to film with ISO below 400. To protect your film, carry it with you in a clear plastic bag and ask for a hand inspection. Such requests are honored at U.S. airports, up to the inspector abroad. Don't depend on a lead-lined bag to protect film in checked luggage—the airline may increase the radiation to see what's inside. Call the Kodak Information Center (tel. 800/242–2424) for details.

About Camcorders Before your trip, put camcorders through their paces, invest in a skylight filter to protect the lens, and check all the batteries.

About Videotape Videotape is not damaged by X-rays, but it may be harmed by the magnetic field of a walk-through metal detector, so ask for a hand check. Airport security personnel may ask you to turn on the camcorder to prove that it's what it appears to be, so make sure the battery is charged.

About Laptops Security X-rays do not harm hard-disk or floppy-disk storage, but you may request a hand check, at which point you may be asked to turn on the computer to prove that it is what it appears to be. (Check your battery before departure.) Most airlines allow you to use your laptop aloft except during takeoff and landing (so as not to interfere with navigation equipment). For international travel, register your foreign-made laptop with U.S. Customs as you leave the country. If your laptop is U.S.-made, call the consulate of the country you'll be visiting to find out whether it should be registered with customs upon arrival. Before departure, find out about repair facilities at your destination.

Language

In both the U.S.V.I. and the B.V.I., English is the language spoken. Be aware, though, that there's English and there's West Indian English. The two are like "chalk and cheese," as the saying goes, and you won't catch half of what is being said if the speaker doesn't want you to.

The local variation in vocabulary and intonation comes from a mixture of African, Spanish, Danish, English (American and British), and French. You'll pick up on a reversal in syntax ("what it is," instead of "what is it"), and a rearrangement of pronouns ("me son," and "the party's for we") with a generous helping of local slang.

Staying Healthy

If you have a health problem that may require the purchase of prescription drugs, have your doctor write a prescription using the drug's generic name, as brand names vary from country to country. The International Association for Medical Assistance to Travelers (IAMAT) is a worldwide association that offers a list of approved physicians and clinics whose training meets British and American standards. For a list of physicians and clinics in the Virgin Islands that are part of this network, contact IAMAT (417 Center St., Lewiston, NY 14092, tel. 716/754–4883; in Canada, 40 Regal Rd.,

Guelph, Ont. N1K 1B5; in Europe, 57 Voirets, 1212 Grand-Lancy, Geneva, Switzerland). Membership is free.

There's hardly a more effective way to ruin a vacation in the tropics than to get a sunburn on your first day out, and to have to sit inside for the next three. Even if you've never been sunburned in your life, it's possible that you may also have never been so close to the equator, so believe all the rhetoric and warnings and use a sunscreen. If you're dark-skinned start with at least an SPF 14 and keep it on. If you are fair-skinned use a sunscreen with a higher SPF. Midday is obviously the time of the most intense rays, so move under a sea-grape tree or take a lunch break. You'll get plenty of sun during the rest of the day.

Another surefire way to ruin your vacation: sitting on the beach or on the seaside rocks at sunset with exposed skin and no insect repellent. Mosquitoes can be a problem here. Off insect repellent is readily available but you may want to bring something stronger. Also a nuisance are the little varmints from the sand-flea family known as no-see-ums. You don't realize you're being had for dinner until it's too late, and, unfortunately, these bites stay, and itch, and itch, and itch. No-see-ums start getting hungry around 3 PM and are out in force by sunset. They are always more numerous in shady and woodsy areas (such as the campgrounds on St. John). So watch the sunset, and take all the moonlit-beach walks you want, but take a towel along for sitting on the beach, and keep reapplying the repellent.

Another health tip—to avoid suffering shock at the high drug-store prices in the Virgin Islands—is to buy creams, lotions, insect repellents, sunscreens, and sunburn remedies before you leave home.

In the water, look out for the black spiny creatures (sea urchins) on the bottom. However, since they are found most often in reef areas where you'll be snorkeling and you'll have on fins, you aren't liable to step on one by accident.

Familiarize yourself with the various types of coral before you go out. There's one particularly nasty type, the fire coral, which can give you a bad burn if you scrape against it. If you do get burned, apply ammonia to the spot as soon as possible.

Virgin Islands waters lack major hazards and are so clear that you can see down to the sea floor at 30 feet so you shouldn't have any surprises.

Scuba divers take note: Professional Association of Diving Instructors (PADI) recommends that you not scuba dive and fly within a 24-hour period.

Insurance

For U.S. Residents Most tour operators, travel agents, and insurance agents sell specialized health-and-accident, flight, trip-cancellation, and luggage insurance as well as comprehensive policies with some or all of these features. But before you make any purchase, review your existing health and homeowner policies to find out whether they cover expenses incurred while traveling.

Health-and-Accident Insurance Specific policy provisions of supplemental health-and-accident insurance for travelers include reimbursement for $1,000 to $150,000 worth of medical and/or dental expenses caused by an accident or illness during a trip. The personal-accident, or death-and-dismemberment, provision pays a lump sum to your beneficiaries if you die or to you if you lose one or both limbs or your eyesight; the lump sum awarded can range from $15,000 to $500,000. The medical-assistance provision may reimburse you for the cost of referrals, evacuation, or repatriation and other services, or it may automatically enroll you as a member of a particular medical-assistance company.

Flight Insurance Often bought as a last-minute impulse at the airport, flight insurance pays a lump sum when a plane crashes either to a beneficiary if the insured dies or sometimes to a surviving passenger who loses eyesight or a limb. Like most impulse buys, flight insurance is expensive and basically unnecessary. It supplements the airlines' coverage described in the limits-of-liability paragraphs on your ticket. Charging an airline ticket to a major credit card often automatically entitles you to coverage and may also embrace travel by bus, train, and ship.

Baggage Insurance In the event of loss, damage, or theft on international flights, airlines' liability is $20 per kilogram for checked baggage (roughly about $640 per 70-pound bag) and $400 per passenger for unchecked baggage. On domestic flights, the ceiling is $1,250 per passenger. Excess-valuation insurance can be bought directly from the airline at check-in for about $10 per $1,000 worth of coverage. However, you cannot buy it at any price for the rather extensive list of excluded items shown on your airline ticket.

Trip Insurance **Trip-cancellation-and-interruption insurance** protects you in the event you are unable to undertake or finish your trip, especially if your airline ticket, cruise, or package tour does not allow changes or cancellations. The amount of coverage you purchase should equal the cost of your trip should you, a traveling companion, or a family member fall ill, forcing you to stay home, plus the nondiscounted one-way airline ticket you would need to buy if you had to return home early. Read the fine print carefully; especially sections defining "family member" and "preexisting medical conditions." **Default** or **bankruptcy insurance** protects you against a supplier's failure to deliver. Such policies often do not cover default by a travel agency, tour operator, airline, or cruise line if you bought your tour and the coverage directly from the firm in question. Tours packaged by one of the 33 members of the United States Tour Operators Association (USTOA, 211 E. 51 St., Suite 12B, New York, NY 10022, tel. 212/750–7371), which requires members to maintain $1 million each in an account to reimburse clients in case of default, are likely to present the fewest difficulties. Even better, pay for travel arrangements with a major credit card, so that you can refuse to pay the bill if services have not been rendered—and let the card company fight your battles.

Comprehensive Policies Companies supplying comprehensive policies with some or all of the above features include **Access America, Inc.** (Box 90315, Richmond, VA 23230, tel. 800/284–8300); **Carefree Travel Insurance** (Box 310, 120 Mineola Blvd., Mineola, NY 11501, tel. 516/294–0220 or 800/323–3149); **Tele-Trip** (Mutual of Omaha Plaza, Box 31762, Omaha, NE 68131, tel. 800/228–9792); **The Travelers Companies** (1 Tower Sq., Hartford, CT 06183, tel. 203/277–0111 or 800/243–3174); **Travel Guard International** (1145 Clark St., Stevens Point, WI 54481, tel. 715/345–0505 or 800/782–5151); and **Wallach and Company, Inc.** (107 W. Federal St., Box 480, Middleburg, VA 22117, tel. 703/687–3166 or 800/237–6615).

Student and Youth Travel

Travel Agencies **Council Travel Services (CTS),** a subsidiary of the nonprofit Council on International Educational Exchange (CIEE), specializes in low-cost travel arrangements abroad for students and is the exclusive

U.S. agent for several discount cards. Also newly available from CTS are domestic air passes for bargain travel within the United States. CIEE's twice-yearly *Student Travels* magazine is available at the CTS office at CIEE headquarters (205 E. 42nd St., 16th Floor, New York, NY 10017, tel. 212/661–1450) and in Boston (tel. 617/266–1926), Miami (tel. 305/670–9261), Los Angeles (tel. 310/208–3551), and at 43 branches in college towns nationwide (free in person, $1 by mail). **Campus Connections** (1100 E. Marlton Pike, Cherry Hill, NJ 08034, tel. 800/428–3235) specializes in discounted accommodations and airfares for students. The **Educational Travel Centre** (438 N. Frances St., Madison, WI 53703, tel. 608/256–5551) offers low-cost domestic and international airline tickets mostly for flights departing from Chicago, and rail passes. Other travel agencies catering to students include **TMI Student Travel** (1146 Pleasant St., Watertown, MA 02172, tel. 617/661–8187 or 800/245–3672) and **Travel Cuts** (187 College St., Toronto, Ont. M5T 1P7, tel. 416/979–2406).

Discount Cards For discounts on transportation and on museum and attractions admissions, buy the **International Student Identity Card** (ISIC) if you're a bona fide student, or the **International Youth Card** (IYC) if you're under 26. In the United States the ISIC and IYC cards cost $16 each and include basic travel accident and sickness coverage. Apply to **CIEE** (*see* address *above*, tel. 212/661–1414; the application is in *Student Travels*). In Canada the cards are available for $15 each from **Travel Cuts** (*see above*). In the United Kingdom they cost £5 and £4 respectively at student unions and student travel companies, including Council Travel's London office (28A Poland St., London W1V 3DB, tel. 071/437–7767).

Traveling with Children

Publications
Newsletter *Family Travel Times,* published 10 times a year by **Travel With Your Children** (TWYCH, 45 W. 18th St., 7th Floor Tower, New York, NY 10011, tel. 212/206–0688; annual subscription $55), covers destinations, types of vacations, and modes of travel.

Books *Traveling with Children—And Enjoying It,* by Arlene K. Butler ($11.95 plus $3 shipping; Globe Pequot Press, Box 833, Old Saybrook, CT 06475, tel. 800/243–0495, or 800/962–0973 in CT) helps you plan your trip with children, from toddlers to teens. From the same publisher is *Recommended Family Resorts in the United States, Canada, and the Caribbean,* by Jane Wilford with Janet Tice ($12.95), which describes 100 resorts at length and includes a "Children's World" section describing activities and facilities as part of each entry.

Tour Operators **Grandtravel** (6900 Wisconsin Ave., Suite 706, Chevy Chase, MD 20815, tel. 301/986–0790 or 800/247–7651) offers international and domestic tours for people traveling with their grandchildren. The catalogue, as charmingly written and illustrated as a children's book, positively invites armchair traveling with lap-sitters aboard. **Rascals in Paradise** (650 5th St., Suite 505, San Francisco, CA 94107, tel. 415/978–9800, or 800/872–7225) specializes in programs for families.

Getting There *Air Fares* On domestic flights, children under 2 not occupying a seat travel free, and older children currently travel on the "lowest applicable" adult fare.

Baggage The adult baggage allowance applies for children paying half or more of the adult fare.

Safety Seats   The FAA recommends the use of safety seats aloft and details approved models in the free leaflet **"Child/Infant Safety Seats Recommended for Use in Aircraft"** (available from the Federal Aviation Administration, APA–200, 800 Independence Ave. SW, Washington, DC 20591, tel. 202/267–3479). Airline policy varies. U.S. carriers allow FAA-approved models bearing a sticker declaring their FAA approval. Because these seats are strapped into a regular passenger seat, they may require that parents buy a ticket even for an infant under 2 who would otherwise ride free. Foreign carriers may not allow infant seats, may charge the child's rather than the infant's fare for their use, or may require you to hold your baby during take-off and landing, thus defeating the seat's purpose.

Facilities Aloft   Some airlines provide other services for children, such as children's meals and freestanding bassinets (only to those with seats at the bulkhead, where there's enough legroom). Make your request when reserving. The annual February/March issue of **Family Travel Times** gives details of the children's services for dozens of airlines (*see above*). "Kids and Teens in Flight" (free from the U.S. Department of Transportation, tel. 202/366–2220) offers tips for children flying alone.

Lodging   The **Hyatt Regency** on St. John (tel. 800/233–1234) offers profession-
The U.S.   ally supervised day and evening activity programs for children ages
Virgin Islands   3–15. The programs, which include sports, games, and crafts, are available during weekends and holiday periods. On St. Thomas, the **Stouffer Grand Beach Resort** (tel. 809/775–1510 or 800/468–3571) offers family room rates, and a kids club (ages 4–12) that provides counselor-supervised activities such as kite flying, sand-castle building, and limbo lessons. The **Sapphire Beach Resort and Marina** (tel. 809/775–6100 or 800/524–2090) offers a program in which children under 12 stay free. Meals for guests' children are also free provided a parent buys a full meal. Daily supervised programs are also offered.

The British   While children are welcome at most hotels in the B.V.I., a number of
Virgin Islands   large resorts offer family-discount packages with a special emphasis on children's activities. **The Bitter End Yacht Club** (tel. 800/872–2392), on Virgin Gorda, is a family resort offering organized boating, snorkeling, and sightseeing for children ages 6–16. A special Family Plan provides parents and children with two connecting rooms for the price of one. Another dollar-wise option for families is the **Biras Creek Resort** (tel. 800/621–1270), also on Virgin Gorda. Its Ultimate Family Break package provides a separate room at a discounted price and includes supervised recreational activities for children ages six and older.

Guest Houses   Budget-minded families may also want to consider bed-and-breakfast or guest-house accommodations on the islands. For an up-to-date list of families offering these, contact the U.S.V.I. Tourist Office and the B.V.I. Tourist Board.

Campgrounds   **Cinnamon Bay Campground** (tel. 809/776–6330) and **Maho Bay**
The U.S.   **Campground** (tel. 809/776–6226), both on St. John, offer a variety of
Virgin Islands   facilities, including cottages, tents, and bare campsites, suitable for budget-minded families.

The British   The **Brewers Bay Campground** (tel. 809/494–3463) on Tortola, and
Virgin Islands   **Tula's N&N Campground** (tel. 809/774–0774) on Jost Van Dyke, offer facilities for individual and family camping.

Home   You can find a house, apartment, or other vacation property to ex-
Exchange   change for your own by becoming a member of a home-exchange or-

ganization, which then sends you its annual directories listing available exchanges and includes your own listing in at least one of them. Arrangements for the actual exchange are made by the two parties to it, not by the organization. For more information contact **International Home Exchange Association** (IHEA, 41 Sutter St., Suite 1090, San Francisco, CA 94104, tel. 415/673–0347 or 800/788–2489). **HomeLink International** (Box 650, Key West, FL 33041, tel. 800/ 638–3841), with thousands of foreign and domestic listings, publishes four annual directories plus updates; the $50 membership includes your listing in one book. **Loan-a-Home** (2 Park La., Apt. 6E, Mount Vernon, NY 10552, tel. 914/664–7640) specializes in long-term exchanges; there is no charge to list your home, but the directories cost $35 or $45 depending on the number you receive.

Apartment and Villa Rentals If you want a home base that's roomy enough for a family and comes with cooking facilities, a furnished rental may be the solution. It's generally cost-wise, too, although not always—some rentals are luxury properties (economical only when your party is large). Home-exchange directories do list rentals—often second homes owned by prospective house swappers—and there are services that can not only look for a house or apartment for you (even a castle if that's your fancy) but also handle the paperwork. Some send an illustrated catalogue and others send photographs of specific properties, sometimes at a charge; up-front registration fees may apply.

Among the companies are **At Home Abroad** (405 E. 56th St., Suite 6H, New York, NY 10022, tel. 212/421–9165); **Europa-Let** (92 North Main St., Ashland, OR 97520, tel. 503/482–5806 or 800/462–4486); **Interhome Inc.** (124 Little Falls Rd., Fairfield, NJ 07004, tel. 201/ 882–6864); **Overseas Connection** (31 North Harbor Dr., Sag Harbor, NY 11963, tel. 516/725–9308); **Property Rentals International** (1 Park West Circle, Suite 108, Midlothian, VA 23113, tel. 804/378–6054 or 800/220–3332); **Rent a Home International** (7200 34th Ave. NW, Seattle, WA 98117, tel. 206/789–9377 or 800/488–7368); **Vacation Home Rentals Worldwide** (235 Kensington Ave., Norwood, NJ 07648, tel. 201/767–9393 or 800/633–3284); **Villas and Apartments Abroad** (420 Madison Ave., Suite 1105, New York, NY 10017, tel. 212/759–1025 or 800/433–3020); and **Villas International** (605 Market St., Suite 510, San Francisco, CA 94105, tel. 415/281–0910 or 800/221–2260). **Hideaways International** (15 Goldsmith St., Box 1270, Littleton, MA 01460, tel. 508/486–8955 or 800/843–4433) functions as a travel club. Membership ($99 yearly per person or family at the same address) includes two annual guides plus quarterly newsletters; rentals are arranged directly between members, not by the club staff.

For villa rentals on Tortola, try **Rockview HolidayHomes** (Box 263, Road Town, Tortola, B.V.I., tel. 809/494–2550) or **Best Vacations Imaginable** (Box 306, Road Town, Tortola, B.V.I., tel. 809/494–6186). The best choice on Virgin Gorda is **Virgin Gorda Villa Rentals** (Box 63, Virgin Gorda, B.V.I., tel. 809/495–7421).

Baby-sitting Services For information, inquire at the local tourist office or at any of the larger hotels.

Hints for Travelers with Disabilities

The Virgin Islands are a difficult destination for travelers with disabilities. Some hotels feature ramps and moderately accessible facilities, but arrangements should be made in advance to ensure that ground-floor rooms are available. Taxis or specially adapted rental cars are the most practical option for island sightseeing. **The Virgin**

Island Commission on the Handicapped (tel. 809/776–1277) offers information on an islandwide Dial-A-Ride service and special parking permits.

The major airlines are prepared to assist travelers using wheelchairs and others who need special assistance, particularly if they are notified in advance as to what type of assistance is needed. Hotels and resorts will usually accommodate requests for ground-floor rooms, but it is wise to inquire ahead of time as to whether access to the beach, pool, lobby, and dining room requires the use of stairs and whether alternative ramps or elevators are available.

All new construction in the U.S.V.I. is required to comply with federal standards (Braille numbers in the elevators, ramps on curbs, etc.).

Hotels On St. Croix, **Hibiscus Beach Resort** (tel. 809/773–4042 or 800/442–
The U. S. 0121) has two rooms accessible to wheelchair users, and the **Club St.**
Virgin Islands **Croix** (tel. 809/773–4800 or 800/635–1533) has limited facilities for people who use wheelchairs. On St. John, the **Caneel Bay Resort** (tel. 809/776–6111 or 800/223–7637) has one room that's wheelchair-accessible. Hotels on St. Thomas that accommodate travelers using wheelchairs include **Marriott's Frenchman's Reef and Morning Star Beach Resort** (tel. 809/776–8500 or 800/524–7100) and the **Stouffer Grand Beach Resort** (tel. 809/775–1510 or 800/468–3571).

The British While hilly terrain makes the B.V.I. a difficult destination for visi-
Virgin Islands tors with mobility problems, many resorts offer ground-floor rooms with easy access to beaches and other facilities. However, it is best to inquire in advance about availability. Two wheelchair-accessible properties are **Fischer's Cove Beach Hotel** on Virgin Gorda (tel. 809/ 495–5252 or 800/621–1270) and **Prospect Reef** on Tortola (tel. 809/ 494–2512 or 800/356–8937).

Getting Taxis—generally large safari vans with ample room for a wheel-
Around chair—are probably the best option for visitors who use wheelchairs. They are plentiful and relatively inexpensive. All ferries running between the islands can be fitted with roll-up ramps.

Organizations Several organizations provide travel information for people with disabilities, usually for a membership fee, and some publish newsletters and bulletins. Among them are the **Information Center for Individuals with Disabilities** (Fort Point Pl., 27–43 Wormwood St., Boston, MA 02210, tel. 617/727–5540 or 800/462–5015 in MA between 11 and 4, or leave message; TTY 617/345–9743); **Mobility International USA** (Box 10767, Eugene, OR 97440, tel. and TTY 503/ 343–1284, fax 503/343–6812), the U.S. branch of an international organizatin based in Britain (*see* Tips for British Travelers, *above*) that has affiliates in 30 countries; **MossRehab Hospital Travel Information Service** (tel. 215/456–9603, TTY 215/456–9602); the **Travel Industry and Disabled Exchange** (TIDE, 5435 Donna Ave., Tarzana, CA 91356, tel. 818/344–3640, fax 818/344–0078); and **Travelin' Talk** (Box 3534, Clarksville, TN 37043, tel. 615/552–6670, fax 615/552– 1182).

Travel **Accessible Journeys** (35 West Sellers Ave., Ridley Park, PA 19078,
Agencies and tel. 610/521–0339 or 800/846–4537, fax 610/521–6959) arranges es-
Tour corted trips for travelers with disabilities and provides licensed
Operators caregivers to accompany those who require aid. **Flying Wheels Travel** (143 W. Bridge St., Box 382, Owatonna, MN 55060, tel. 507/451– 5005 or 800/535–6790) is a travel agency specializing in domestic and worldwide cruises, tours, and independent travel itineraries for people with mobility problems.

Publications In addition to the fact sheets, newsletters, and books mentioned above are several free publications available from the Consumer Information Center (Pueblo, CO 81009): "New Horizons for the Air Traveler with a Disability," a U.S. Department of Transportation booklet describing changes resulting from the 1986 Air Carrier Access Act and those still to come from the 1990 Americans with Disabilities Act (include Department 608Y in the address), and the Airport Operators Council's *Access Travel: Airports* (Dept. 5804), which describes facilities and services for people with disabilities at more than 500 airports worldwide.

The 500-page *Travelin' Talk Directory* (*see* Organizations, *above*; $35 check or money order with a money-back guarantee) lists names and addresses of people and organizations who offer help for travelers with disabilities. Twin Peaks Press (Box 129, Vancouver, WA 98666, tel. 206/694–2462 or 800/637–2256) publishes the *Directory of Travel Agencies for the Disabled* ($19.95, plus $2 for shipping), listing more than 370 agencies worldwide. The Sierra Club publishes *Easy Access to National Parks* ($16, plus $3 shipping; 730 Polk St., San Francisco, CA 94109, tel. 415/776–2211).

Hints for Older Travelers

During the off-season (April 15 to December 15), many hotels in the Virgin Islands offer substantial rate reductions for senior citizens. For a list of participating hotels, contact the U.S. Virgin Islands Tourist Board.

Organizations The **American Association of Retired Persons** (AARP, 601 E St. NW, Washington, DC 20049, tel. 202/434–2277) provides independent travelers who are members of the AARP (open to those age 50 or older; $8 per person or couple annually) with the Purchase Privilege Program, which offers discounts on hotels, car rentals, and sightseeing. AARP also arranges group tours, cruises, and apartment living through AARP Travel Experience from American Express (400 Pinnacle Way, Suite 450, Norcross, GA 30071, tel. 800/927–0111 or 800/745–4567).

Two other organizations offer discounts on lodgings, car rentals, and other travel perks, along with such nontravel perks as magazines and newsletters: The **National Council of Senior Citizens** (1331 F St. NW, Washington, DC 20004, tel. 202/347–8800; membership $12 annually) and **Mature Outlook** (6001 N. Clark St., Chicago, IL 60660, tel. 800/336–6330; $9.95 annually).

Note: Mention your senior-citizen identification card when booking hotel reservations for reduced rates, not when checking out. At restaurants, show your card before you're seated; discounts may be limited to certain menus, days, or hours. If you are renting a car, ask about promotional rates that might improve on your senior-citizen discount.

Educational Travel The nonprofit **Elderhostel** (75 Federal St., 3rd Floor, Boston, MA 02110, tel. 617/426–7788) has offered inexpensive study programs for people 60 and older since 1975. Held at more than 1,800 educational institutions, courses cover everything from marine science to Greek myths and cowboy poetry. Participants usually attend lectures in the morning and spend the afternoon sightseeing or on field trips; they live in dorms on the host campuses. Fees for two- to three-week international trips—including room, board, and transportation from the United States—range from $1,800 to $4,500.

Tour Operators	**Saga International Holidays** (222 Berkeley St., Boston, MA 02116, tel. 800/343–0273), which specializes in group travel for people over 60, offers a selection of variously priced tours and cruises covering five continents. If you want to take your grandchildren, look into Grandtravel (*see* Traveling with Children, *above*).
Publications	*The 50+ Traveler's Guidebook: Where to Go, Where to Stay, What to Do* by Anita Williams and Merrimac Dillon ($12.95; St. Martin's Press, 175 5th Ave., New York, NY 10010) is available in bookstores and offers many useful tips. "The Mature Traveler" (Box 50820, Reno, NV 89513, tel. 702/786–7419; $29.95), a monthly newsletter, contains many travel deals for older travelers.

Hints for Gay and Lesbian Travelers

Organizations	The **International Gay Travel Association** (Box 4974, Key West, FL 33041, tel. 305/292–0217, 800/999–7925, or 800/448–8550), which has 700 members, will provide you with names of travel agents and tour operators who specialize in gay travel. The **Gay and Lesbian Visitors Center of New York Inc.** (135 W. 20th St., 3rd Floor, New York, NY 10011, tel. 212/463–9030 or 800/395–2315; $100 annually) mails a monthly newsletter, valuable coupons, and more to its members.
Travel Agencies and Tour Operators	The dominant travel agency in the market is **Above and Beyond** (3568 Sacramento St., San Francisco, CA 94118, tel. 415/922–2683 or 800/397–2681). Tour operator **Olympus Vacations** (8424 Santa Monica Blvd., Suite 721, West Hollywood, CA 90069, tel. 310/657–2220 or 800/965–9678) offers gay and lesbian resort holidays. **Skylink Women's Travel** (746 Ashland Ave., Santa Monica, CA 90405, tel. 310/452–0506 or 800/225–5759) handles individual travel for lesbians all over the world and conducts two international and five domestic group trips annually.
Publications	The premiere international travel magazine for gays and lesbians is *Our World* (1104 N. Nova Rd., Suite 251, Daytona Beach, FL 32117, tel. 904/441–5367; $35 for 10 issues). "Out & About" (tel. 203/789–8518 or 800/929–2268; $49 for 10 issues) is a 16-page monthly newsletter with extensive information on resorts, hotels, and airlines that are gay-friendly.

Further Reading

If you have the time before your trip, read James Michener's *Caribbean*; it will enhance your visit. *Don't Stop the Carnival* by Herman Wouk is a classic Caribbean book, though some of its 1950s perspectives seem rather dated now.

Once you get to the Virgin Islands, take time to book-shop; there are some prolific U.S.V.I. writers and artists publishing on every subject from pirates to architecture. Look for books, art prints, and cards by Mapes de Monde, published by Virgin Islands native son Michael Paiewonsky, who splits his time between Rome and the U.S.V.I. Mapes de Monde also publishes *The Three Quarters of the Town of Charlotte Amalie* by local historian Edith Woods. It is richly printed and illustrated with Woods's fine pen-and-ink drawings. Photography buffs will want to look for the book of internationally known St. Croix photographer Fritz Henle. For B.V.I. history buffs, Vernon Pickering's *Concise History of the British Virgin Islands* is a wordy but worthy guide to the events and personalities that shaped the region. Pickering also produces the *Official Tourist Handbook* for the B.V.I. Pick up a copy of *A Place Like This: Hugh Benjamin's Peter Island*, the charming and eloquent personal account of the Kittitian's past two decades in the British Virgin Islands. The book was written in collaboration with Richard Myers, a New York writer.

For children there's *Up Mountain One Time* by Willie Wilson, and a *St. John Historical Coloring Book*.

For linguists, *What a Pistarckle!* by Lito Valls gives the origins of the many expressions you'll be hearing, and historians will enjoy *St. John Backtime* by Ruth Hull Low and Rafael Valls, and *Eyewitness Accounts of Slavery in the Danish West Indies* by Isidor Paiewonsky. For sailors, Simon Scott has written a *Cruising Guide to the Virgin Islands*.

The major newspapers in the U.S.V.I. are the *Virgin Islands Daily News*, a Gannett newspaper, published in St. Thomas, and the *St. Croix Avis*, published in Christiansted. *Tradewinds* is the weekly St. John paper.

Keep your eyes open for two locally published magazines: *Pride* and *V.I. Voice. Pride* will give you a look at local politics; *V.I. Voice* offers creative writing and frank discussions of local culture.

There are several visitor-oriented publications distributed free in hotel lobbies, visitor centers, and shops. For St. Thomas, the most current is *St. Thomas This Week* (check the cruiseship schedule on the front cover and you'll know when to avoid Charlotte Amalie) for that island, and *St. Croix This Week* for St. Croix. *Here's How* and *V.I. Playground* are good comprehensive guides, too.

For the real inside scoop on St. John, get hold of Linda Smith-Palmer's *St. John Guide Book* and detailed "St. John Map." Smith-Palmer is also the creator of the character Max the Mongoose, whose sage observations in the comic pages of the *Daily News* keep local politicians looking over their shoulders.

On the B.V.I., the *Island Sun* is the best local paper for everything from entertainment listings to local gossip. The *Welcome Tourist Guide* is comprehensive and available free at airports and larger hotels.

Credit Cards

The following credit-card abbreviations have been used: AE, American Express; D, Discover; DC, Diners Club; MC, MasterCard; V, Visa. It's always a good idea to call ahead and confirm an establishment's credit-card policy.

Arriving and Departing

From the United States by Plane

Flights are either nonstop, direct, or connecting. A **nonstop** flight requires no change of plane and makes no stops. A **direct** flight stops at least once and can involve a change of plane, although the flight number remains the same; if the first leg is late, the second waits. This is not the case with a **connecting** flight, which involves a different plane and a different flight number.

Many flights make a stop in Puerto Rico. If you do fly through San Juan give yourself enough time to be at the boarding gate at least a half hour before departure. If you cut it too short, you may find yourself running up to the counter, reservation in hand, only to find that the small planes have been filled.

Airlines
The U.S.
Virgin Islands You may fly into the U.S.V.I. direct via **Continental** (tel. 800/231–0856), **Delta** (tel. 800/221–1212), **American** (tel. 800/433–7300), or **USAir** (tel. 800/428–4322), or you may fly via San Juan on all the above plus **Sunaire Express** (tel. 809/495–2480 or 800/524–2094), **TWA** (tel. 800/221–2000), or **United** (tel. 800/328–6877).

The British
Virgin Islands There is no nonstop service available from the United States to the B.V.I.; connections are usually made through San Juan, Puerto Rico, or St. Thomas, U.S.V.I. Airlines serving San Juan include **American** (tel. 800/433–7300), **Continental** (tel. 800/231–0856), and **Delta** (tel. 800/323–2323). From San Juan, **American Eagle** (tel. 800/327–8376) flies to Beef Island/Tortola. Also, **Sunaire Express** (tel. 809/495–2480 or 800/524–2094) flies to Beef Island/Tortola and Virgin Gorda, via San Juan and St. Thomas. Sunaire Express also flies between St. Croix and Beef Island/Tortola. Service between the B.V.I. and the is lands of Anguilla, Antigua, St. Kitts, and St. Maarten is provided by **Leeward Island Air Transport (LIAT),** (tel. 809/462–0701). These and other islands can also be reached via **Gorda Aero Service** (Tortola, tel. 809/495–2271), a charter service.

Cutting Flight
Costs The Sunday travel section of most newspapers is a good source of deals. When booking, particularly through an unfamiliar company, call the Better Business Bureau and your local or state Consumer Protection Bureau to find out whether any complaints have been registered against the company, pay with a credit card if you can, and consider trip-cancellation and default insurance (*see* Insurance, *above*).

Promotional
Airfares Less expensive fares, called promotional or discount fares, are round-trip and involve restrictions, which vary according to the route and season. You must usually buy the ticket—commonly called an APEX (advance purchase excursion) when it's for international travel—in advance (seven, 14, or 21 days are usual), although some of the major airlines have added no-frills, cheap flights to compete with new bargain airlines on certain routes.

With the major airlines the cheaper fares generally require minimum and maximum stays (for instance, over a Saturday night or at least seven and no more than 30 days). Airlines generally allow some return date changes for a $25 to $50 fee, but most low-fare tickets are nonrefundable. Only a death in the family would prompt the airline to return any of your money if you cancel a nonrefundable ticket. However, you can apply an unused nonrefundable ticket toward a new ticket, again with a small fee. The lowest fare is subject to availability, and only a small percentage of the plane's total seats will be sold at that price. Contact the U.S. Department of Transportation's Office of Consumer Affairs (I–25, Washington, DC 20590, tel. 202/366–2220) for a copy of "Fly-Rights: A Guide to Air Travel in the U.S." *The Official Frequent Flyer Guidebook* by Randy Petersen ($14.99 plus $3 shipping; 4715-C Town Center Dr., Colorado Springs, CO 80916, tel. 719/597–8899, 800/487–8893, or 800/485–8893) yields valuable hints on getting the most for your air travel dollars.

Consolidators Consolidators or bulk-fare operators—"bucket shops"—buy blocks of seats on scheduled flights that airlines anticipate they won't be able to sell. They pay wholesale prices, add a markup, and resell the seats to travel agents or directly to the public at prices that still undercut the airline's promotional or discount fares (higher than a charter ticket but lower than an APEX ticket, and usually without the advance-purchase restriction). Moreover, some consolidators sometimes give you your money back. Carefully read the fine print detailing penalties for changes and cancellations. If you doubt the reliability of a company, call the airline once you've made your booking and confirm that you do, indeed, have a reservation on the flight.

Charter Flights Charter operators may offer flights alone or with ground arrangements that constitute a charter package. You typically must book charters through your travel agent. One well-known company is **Private Jet** (tel. 800/949–9400). Another good source is **Charterlink** (988 Sing Sing Rd., Horseheads, NY 14845, tel. 607/739–7148 or 800/221–1802), a no-fee charter broker that operates 24 hours a day.

Discount Travel Clubs Travel clubs offer members unsold space on airplanes, cruise ships, and package tours at as much as 50% below regular prices. Membership may include a regular bulletin or access to a toll-free hot line giving details of available trips departing anywhere from three or four days to several months in the future. Most also offer 50% discounts off hotel rack rates, but double check with the hotel to make sure it isn't offering a better promotional rate independent of the club. Clubs include **Discount Travel International** (114 Forrest Ave., Suite 203, Narberth, PA 19072, tel. 215/668–7184; $45 annually, single or family), **Entertainment Travel Editions** (Box 1014, Trumbull, CT 06611, tel. 800/445–4137; $28–$48 annually), **Great American Traveler** (Box 27965, Salt Lake City, UT 84127, tel. 800/548–2812; $29.95 annually), **Moment's Notice Discount Travel Club** (425 Madison Ave., New York, NY 10017, tel. 212/486–0503; $45 annually, single or family), **Privilege Card** (3391 Peachtree Rd. NE, Suite 110, Atlanta, GA 30326, tel. 404/262–0222 or 800/236–9732; domestic annual membership $49.95, international, $74.95), **Travelers Advantage** (CUC Travel Service, 49 Music Sq. W, Nashville, TN 37203, tel. 800/548–1116; $49 annually, single or family), and **Worldwide Discount Travel Club** (1674 Meridian Ave., Miami Beach, FL 33139, tel. 305/534–2082; $50 annually for family, $40 single).

Smoking Since February 1990, smoking has been banned on all domestic flights of less than six hours duration; the ban also applies to domestic segments of international flights aboard U.S. and foreign carriers. On U.S. carriers flying overseas, a seat in a no-smoking section must be provided for every passenger who requests one, and the section must be enlarged to accommodate such passengers if necessary as long as they have complied with the airline's deadline for check-in and seat assignment. If smoking bothers you, request a seat far from the smoking section.

From the United Kingdom by Plane

No airline flies directly from the United Kingdom to the B.V.I. or U.S.V.I. However, **British Airways** (tel. 081/897–4000 or 800/247–9297) flies from London directly to San Juan, Puerto Rico, twice weekly, Saturdays and Sundays. In San Juan you can connect with one of the several regional airlines that fly into the Virgin Islands (*see* From the United States by Plane, *above*).

2 Portrait of the Virgin Islands

Beach Picnic

By Calvin Trillin

As the boat from St. Thomas neared St. John, it occurred to me again that I might have made a serious mistake leaving behind my ham. You could say, after all, that our entire trip had been based on that ham. In our family, the possibility of renting a house for a week on St. John had been kicking around for years; Abigail and Sarah were so strongly for it that I sometimes referred to them as "the St. John lobby." We had been on St. John briefly during the week we'd spent on St. Thomas, only a short ferry ride away. St. Thomas is known mainly for recreational shopping—its principal town, Charlotte Amalie, had already been a tax-free port for a century and a half when the United States bought St. Thomas and St. John and St. Croix from Denmark toward the end of the five or six thousand years of human history now thought of as the pre-credit-card era—and what I remember most vividly about our week there was trying to explain to Abigail and Sarah that the mere existence of a customs exemption of $800 per person does not mean that each person is actually required to spend $800.* ("I happen to know of a man who was permitted to leave even though he had purchased only $68.50 worth of goods. He is now living happily in Metuchen, New Jersey.") I was rather intent on getting the point across because according to what I could see from the shopping patterns on St. Thomas, our family would ordinarily have been expected to buy $3,200 worth of perfume—enough perfume, I figured, to neutralize the aroma of a fair-sized cattle feedlot.

What Abigail and Sarah remembered most vividly were rumless piña coladas—it was their first crack at rumless piña coladas—and the spectacular beaches on St. John. The beaches are accessible to everyone through inclusion in the Virgin Islands National Park, which covers nearly three quarters of the island, and, just as important, going to the beach is pretty much all there is to do—a state of affairs that Abigail and Sarah would think of as what ham purveyors call Hog Heaven. We had talked about it a lot, but the conversation usually ended with a simple question: What would we eat?

The question went beyond the dismal food we had come to expect in Virgin Islands restaurants. (On St. Thomas, the restaurants had seemed to specialize in that old Caribbean standby, Miami frozen fish covered with Number 22 sunblock, and my attempts to find some native cooking had resulted mainly in the discovery of bullfoot soup.) In a house on St. John, we would presumably have our own kitchen, but we'd be dependent on the ingredients available in the island stores. Our only previous experience in that line—in the British Virgin Islands, where we had once

---

*The individual customs exemption has been increased from $800 to $1,200.

rented a house when Abigail was a baby—had produced the shopping incident that I have alluded to ever since when the subject of Caribbean eating comes up. On a shopping trip to Roadtown, the capital, Alice ordered a chicken and asked that it be cut up. When we returned from our other errands, we found that the butcher had taken a frozen chicken and run it through a band saw, producing what looked like some grotesque new form of lunchmeat.

The memory of that chicken caused a lot of conversations about St. John rentals to fizzle and die. Then, during one of the conversations, my eye happened to fall on a country ham that was hanging in our living room. Maybe I'd better explain the presence of a ham in our living room; Abigail and Sarah seem to think it requires an explanation whenever they bring friends home for the first time. Now and then, we have arranged to buy a country ham from Kentucky. The ham often arrives with a wire attached to it, and since we have a couple of stalking cats, I put the ham out of their reach by attaching the wire to a living room beam in what seems to be a natural hanging place—a spot where we once briefly considered hanging a philodendron. The first time I hung a ham in the living room, Alice pointed out that some of the people expected at a sort of PTA gathering about to be held at our house didn't know us well enough to see the clear logic involved in the ham's presence, so I put a three-by-five card of the sort used in art galleries on a post next to the ham. The card said, "Country ham. 1983. J. T. Mitchum. Meat and wire composition." Since then, I've found that even without the card many guests tend to take the country ham as a work of art, which, at least in the view of people who have eaten one of Mr. Mitchum's, it is.

Contemplating that ham, I found my resistance to renting a house in St. John melting away. We could take the ham along to sustain us, in the way a band of Plains Indians, living in happier times, would have brought their newly killed buffalo to the next camp site. We would bring other provisions from the neighborhood. We would not be dependent on frozen chicken lunchmeat. We made arrangements to rent a house for a week on St. John.

Then I left the ham at home. Not because it slipped my mind. A country ham is not the sort of thing you simply forget. Alice had argued that it was terribly heavy, that it was more than we needed, that she didn't feel like making biscuits on St. John (because the American Virgin Islands are U.S. territory, the federal law against eating country ham without biscuits applies). I finally agreed, although I couldn't resist pointing out that the remark about its being more than we needed was directly contradicted by the number of times I've heard people who have just finished off a plateful of country ham and biscuits say, "That's exactly what I needed."

I don't mean we arrived in St. John empty-handed. I had brought along an extra suitcase full of provisions. There were some breakfast necessities—tea and the seven-grain bread that

Alice likes in the mornings and, of course, a dozen New York bagels. We also had smoked chicken breasts, a package of a Tuscan grain called farro, a couple of packages of spaghetti, sun-dried tomatoes, a package of pignolia nuts, an Italian salami, several slices of the flat Italian bread called focaccia that a man near our house makes every morning, a jar of olive paste, and what Alice usually refers to as her risotto kit—arborio rice, fresh parmesan cheese, olive oil, wild mushrooms, a head of garlic, a large onion, and a can of chicken broth. Better safe than sorry.

Finding a place to rent had turned out to be relatively simple. St. John is organized on the premise that a lot of visitors will want to rent a house. The only hotels of any size on the island are Caneel Bay, one of the first of the resorts that the Rockefellers built for those who feel the need of being cosseted for a few days in reassuringly conventional luxury, and a new resort called the Virgin Grand, a touch of flash that is always mentioned in the first thirty seconds of any discussion about whether the island is in danger of being ruined by development.

The de facto concierges of St. John are a dozen or so property managers, each of whom presides over a small array of houses that seem to have been built with renting in mind—which is to say that you can usually count on your towels being of a uniform color and you don't have to toss somebody else's teddy bears off the bed to go to sleep. Most of the houses are tacked onto the side of a hill—the side of a hill is about the only place to build a house on St. John, which has so many ups and downs that its old Indian name was probably Place Where You're Always in First Gear—and have decks whose expansive views are measured by how many bays are visible. Our house was a simple but cheery two-bedroom place with what I would call a one-and-a-sliver-bay view. It had a kitchen more than adequate for the preparation of an arrival supper of grilled smoked-chicken sandwiches on focaccia. As I ate one, I tried to keep in mind that out there in the dark somewhere people were probably eating Miami frozen fish with sunblock. We weren't safe yet.

I think it was the phrase "fresh fish" that gave me the first hint that sustaining life on St. John might be easier than I had anticipated. For years, the American Virgin Islands have been known for being surrounded by fish that never seem to make it onto a plate. The first sunny news about fresh fish came accompanied by a small black cloud: local fishermen, I was told, showed up on Tuesday and Thursday mornings on a dock behind the customs shed in Cruz Bay, the one place on St. John that more or less passes as a town, but some of the coral-feeding fish they catch had lately been carrying a disease called ciguatera, which attacks your central nervous system. There was conflicting information around on the subject of ciguatera. I met people in St. John who said that they don't hesitate to eat coral-feeders, and I met someone who said she had been horribly ill from eating one kingfish. I met someone who said that in Japan ciguatera, which isn't detectable by taste or smell, is avoided by putting the fish in a bucket of water with a quarter and discarding it if the quarter tarnishes. I decided to pass. The phrase "attacks your central nervous system" tends to dull my appetite; also, I kept wondering what all those American quarters were doing in Japan.

It turned out, though, that a store in Cruz Bay called Caribbean Natural Foods sold fresh deep-water fish like tuna—not to speak of soy sauce and rice wine and sesame oil for the marinade. Caribbean Natural Foods was one of two or three small but ambitious food stores that had opened since our previous visit to St. John, and among them the island had available California wine and Tsingtao beer and Silver Palate chocolate sauce and Ben & Jerry's ice cream (including my daughters' favorite flavor, Dastardly Mash) and New York bagels and real pastrami and a salad identified as "tortellini with walnut pesto sauce and sour cream." I suppose there are old St. John hands who grumble that the world of exotic beers and gourmet ice cream was what they were trying to get away from, but there must be a lot of regular visitors who feel like celebrating the expansion of available foodstuffs with an appropriately catered parade.

L eading the parade would be people serious about picnics. On St. John, the pleasantness of beaches tends to vary roughly in direct proportion to how hard it is to get there. Anyone who chooses a beach on St. John because it has a convenient parking lot or a commissary or a marked underwater trail or plenty of changing rooms may find himself thinking at some point in the afternoon that he should have paid more attention to what his mother said about the rewards that come to those willing to make a little extra effort. (A difficult road, though, is not an absolute guarantee of peacefulness: someone who has been reading a novel on what seemed like an out-of-the-way beach may look up from his book and find that twenty boats of one sort or another have materialized in a line across the bay, prepared to disgorge a small but expensively outfitted invasion force.) Once you're settled in at the beach, the prospect of going back to Cruz Bay for lunch can provoke the great bicultural moan: "*Quel schlep!*" I don't know what people used to do about lunch at a beach like Francis Bay, where a beach-lounger can watch pelicans as they have a go at the flying fish and a snorkler with a little patience can usually spot a giant sea turtle. By the time we got there, you could reach into the ice chest for a seafood-salad sandwich and a bottle of Dos Equis.

At Salt Pond, a spectacular beach on the more remote eastern end of the island, we did leave for lunch one day in order to go to Hazel's, where Hazel Eugene, whose wanderings after she left St. Lucia included New Orleans, was said to serve what she sometimes called Caribbean Creole cooking. Hazel's turned out to be on the ground floor of a sort of aqua house that had goats wandering around the back and a neighbor who seemed to be the island's leading collector of auto bodies. Its signs identified it as SEABREEZE: GROCERY, RESTAURANT, BAR, and while we were there Hazel would occasionally leave the kitchen to pour a couple of shots or to fill a shopping list that might consist of a box of

Kraft Macaroni & Cheese dinner, a bottle of rum, and a beer for the ride home. She also waited on tables, and in that role she began a lot of sentences with "I could do you . . ." as in "I could do you some of my fried chicken with cottage fries" or "I could do you some codfish fritters and some of my special pumpkin soup to start." Hazel did us all of that, plus some blackened shark and some seafood creole and some puffed shrimp and some chicken curry and a plate of assorted root vegetables that tasted an awful lot better than they sounded or looked. When it was over, I was just about ready to admit that I might have sold St. John short.

I don't mean I regretted bringing along the extra suitcase. Hazel's was too far to drive at night. Places to eat dinner were limited, although at least one restaurant in Cruz Bay, the Lime Inn, had fish from the Caribbean, of all places, and served it grilled, without even a dash of sunblock on the side. And, of course, we had one dress-up evening in the main dining room at Caneel Bay. What was being sold there, I realized, was simulation of membership in the most prominent country club in town—at a cost that might seem considerable but is, I assume, nothing compared to the kick of the real club's annual dues. The food is of the sort that is described by the most enthusiastic members as "not highly seasoned," and the waiters, playing the role of old club retainers, serve it in a manner so true to the rituals of the upper-middle-class past that you even get a little tray of olives and carrot sticks to nibble on while you're waiting for your shrimp cocktail. The night we were there, the menu offered a marinated conch appetizer as the single reminder that we were on an island rather than in one of the better suburbs, and it listed some California wines as the single reminder that we hadn't found ourselves, willy-nilly, in 1954.

All of which means that we often ate dinner at the place with a one-and-a-sliver-bay view—grilled tuna with some pasta on the side, a great meal of spaghetti with garlic and oil and sun-dried tomatoes, and, finally, the fruits of Alice's risotto kit. It occurred to me, as we ate the risotto and talked about risotto in Milan, that behind our shopping there may have been an unconscious desire to create the Italian West Indies. In fact, I informed those at the table, it hadn't been a bad try—although it might have been improved by bringing along a little more focaccia for the picnics.

Back home, we decided that surviving on St. John had been easy enough to merit a return engagement. A few months later we heard that Hazel had closed her restaurant and taken her talent for Caribbean Creole cooking elsewhere. It was a blow, but not a blow severe enough to change our minds about going back. After all, we still had the country ham.

3

Diving an Snorkeling in the Virgin Islands

Introduction

By Marcia
Andrews

Updated by
Gary
Goodlander

Sliding down beside the anchor line, we could see the shape of the wreck. The *Rhone*'s bow was dark against white sand, even in 80 feet of water. We leveled off at the midsection, taking in the scene; the stern, its big propellers dug into rocks and coral, was uphill in a distant gloom. As we neared the bottom, a small striped fish nosed my buddy's elbow, like a puppy. There were several of them, hand-size sergeant major fish, objecting to us larger creatures invading their territory; then they darted off. Bigger fish were milling about below, parading through the ship's hatches and broken hull, showing silvers and blues—about the only colors visible at this depth. We were looking for the big barracuda that like to hang around and watch divers. "They're curious," say the dive guides. "Just don't wear anything shiny. If you don't look like a lure, you're okay."

Sure.

Our guide, an instructor from a Tortola dive shop, tapped a section of the ship's hull, drawing our attention to a hole. When the resident spotted moray eel poked out six inches of ugly head, all five divers danced back in a startled chorus line. The guide slipped the Central Casting eel something from her pocket, then continued the tour. She led the way to an opening in the ship's side and, grinning—as well as a person can through a mouthpiece and mask—she urged us to follow her into the ship. Instead, my dive buddy and I, by mutual hand-signal agreement, hovered over the deck, watching the others enter the hulk, then reemerge, swimming across a patch of purple fan coral.

The wreck of the H.M.S. *Rhone*, just off the western tip of Salt Island in the British Virgin Islands, is the region's star dive attraction. Not only is it old (sunk in 1867 in sheltered water), large (a more-than-600-foot, 2,434-ton steamer), and accessible (a short trip from Road Harbour, Tortola), but it was made famous in an '80s wet-T-shirt movie called *The Deep.* For nearby dive shops, it's a bonanza, the perfect place to launch student divers in open-water diving. Once they've seen the *Rhone* and a nearby reef covered with coral, sponges, and fish, most new divers are very enthusiastic about the sport.

There's a lot of dive excitement in both the British and United States Virgin Islands. The waters are ideal for discovering marine life—whether you snorkel (swim with mask, snorkel, and fins on the surface) or are trained to dive and explore reefs close-up with scuba gear and air tanks. Though seasoned divers may pursue wilder dive sites in the lower Caribbean, the Virgin Islands have variety—caves, walls, wrecks, lush reefs, pinnacles—and more than their share of practical advantages:

- Access is easy. Most anchorages are close to live reefs. Whether they're charted dive sites or not, nearby coral heads are mini-ecosystems, home to the region's rich mix of fish and coral. (Waterproof booklets on flora and fauna are widely available.)

- Dive shops are generally well equipped and operate with high standards, thanks, in part, to strong competition in the area, and to a high volume of experienced divers who would know a second-rate dive shop when they saw one.

- Great beginner-level diving conditions include warm, calm seas (80° at the surface and waves seldom more than 3 feet); excellent visibility, up to 120 feet (especially late spring through summer); and shallow coral reefs full of life. Experienced divers will find dramatic drop-offs, caves, and canyons.

- Full-service dive operations are on all major islands, with experienced guides to spot tidal current and sea conditions, then lead you to any of 100 dive sites. Guided dives are the norm here—"because we get so many novices," say dive professionals.

- Attractions for nondivers make this a more versatile place than the "divers' camps" on islands with few beaches, resorts, or historic sites.

In all but a few remote backwaters, scuba divers are required to show certification of training—a C-card—from an internationally recognized program in order to obtain the essential air tanks. If you already have the C-card, you can rent equipment and get air fills, and join others on guided dives virtually anywhere in the world. If you're an old hand, then diving on your own—off your boat or from a beach—is just a matter of renting filled air tanks. No one flies their own tanks from home to well-supplied resort areas, but don't forget your C-card. Most divers, however, especially on their first Virgin Islands visit, do hire dive guides, if only for their knowledge of local attractions and the convenience of well-equipped dive boats.

If you don't have a C-card, it is possible to accomplish the entire 32- to 40-hour scuba open-water certification course in as few as four days of vacation, but it's hard work. Professionals suggest new divers take a two-part approach: Do the classroom study and pool exercises (basic swimming and equipment skills) through a dive school or a YMCA program at home, or even with mail-order materials and an 800-number for a certified instructor. National Association of Underwater Instructors (NAUI) and the Professional Association of Diving Instructors (PADI) both provide reputable toll-free and mail-order services, which allow you to study independently before taking your tests. But keep in mind that it's better to do all this in advance. No one wants to spend romantic tropical evenings doing scuba homework. With a transfer from your home instructor, Virgin Islands dive instructors trained and certified by one of the U.S. organizations will lead you through four open-water dives and check your qualifications for a C-card.

If you are thinking about taking up scuba, the Virgin Islands are ideal for trying it out at a resort course. Typically such a course lasts from 2 PM to 4 PM and starts on a beach or at poolside with a lecture about the equipment and the basics of diving. Students put on the equipment and use part of a tank of air, or the first of two tanks, to try breathing underwater. After a pause to regroup or to move to a dive site, divers explore a reef, usually at 30- to 40-foot depths. A single-tank resort course costs from $55 to $70. Also, this is just a sample dive and doesn't count toward certification—that requires classroom work. Many hotels promote a package deal or a direct line to a nearby dive shop. But, be aware that the experience could be discouraging if you find a bored instructor handing out ill-fitting equipment and sloppy advice. Given the time and opportunity, you should try to observe a resort class in progress, or even talk to the instructors about their courses. With so many fine diving professionals around, you can avoid the ones who'd obviously rather be leading a wreck dive at 90 feet—and don't hide their impatience.

The minimum age for PADI scuba instruction is 12, and that's for temporary certification. The young diver must upgrade his or her training at age 15 in a brief course with an instructor. Dive-boat operators usually require that children younger than 12 remain in their parents' charge while on the boat or snorkeling. Some shops do have real (not toy) fins, masks, and snorkels to fit children age two and up. To encourage young people, **"Discover Scuba"** programs developed by PADI allow 12-year-old children to try on equipment and breathe underwater in a swimming pool. Ask your local dive shop about similar opportunities.

Part of any scuba-training program is a review of the sea life and how to respect the new world you're exploring, but awareness is even keener these days. Dive professionals recognize the value of protecting fragile reefs and ecosystems in tropical waters. The result is instructors who emphasize look-don't-touch diving (the unofficial motto is: Take only pictures, leave only bubbles), and increasing government control and protection of dive sites, especially in such heavily used areas as the Virgin Islands. Both the British and U.S. territories have active park departments with programs to place moorings in some of the most popular anchorages and dive locations (the objective is to keep too many anchors from tearing up the coral).

Park services in both territories are working with local charter companies, divers, and fishermen to protect the area and inform visitors. The placement of moorings, regulations for their use, and fees are published in pamphlets found at customs offices, dive operations, and park-service offices: B.V.I. National Parks Trust (Box 860, Road Town, Tortola, BVI, tel. 809/494–3904) and Virgin Islands National Parks (6310 Estate Nazareth, St. Thomas, USVI 00802, tel. 809/775–6238).

Most dive operations are connected to retail/rental shops and are affiliated with NAUI or PADI. The latter is most evident in the Virgin Islands.

The YMCA, too, trains and certifies divers in the United States but isn't involved in resorts and shops. All three training groups give internationally recognized certification courses, and NAUI or PADI shops in resort areas will take you open-water diving to complete classroom and pool instruction begun by another group in the states. (You bring a letter or form from your hometown instructor. The local instructor notes your skills and signs your diving log.) Though each has its own style, you don't have to match organizations.

For lists of hometown dive shops, as well as introductory and safety information, each scuba training group has a national office: PADI (1251 E. Dyer Rd., Suite 100, Santa Ana, CA 92705, tel. 800/729–7234), with the most instructors and training facilities; NAUI (Box 14650, Montclair, CA 91763–1150, tel. 714/621–5801); and the **National YMCA SCUBA Program** (Oakbrook Sq., 6083–A Oakbrook Pkwy., Norcross, GA 30093, tel. 404/662–5172), which will locate the nearest YMCA instructor in your area. Other training groups who are not affiliated with dive shops include the **Association of Canadian Underwater Councils** and **Los Angeles County Underwater Unit.**

Everyone gets excited about the perils of diving: the bends and large killer fish. This is why all diving certification courses like PADI and NAUI stress accident prevention and diver safety so thoroughly. But the basic rules for safe diving are both simple and easily understood; fools ignore them at their own peril. Physical requirements for diving are general fitness and the ability to swim comfortably. Scuba is no longer some sort of macho giant-squid–wrestling club. Scuba training is widely available, thus resulting in hundreds of thousands of new American divers being certified annually. About a third of them are women.

On the most-feared list are sharks, barracuda, and moray eels. But it's the sea urchins and fire coral that cause pain—when you accidentally bump them. It's easier to remember to be cautious about the big or defensive fish, knowing not to attract them with shiny jewelry or taunt them by poking into crevices.

Since most sport diving occurs in shallow water, pressure-related diving accidents (the bends) are rare. However, they *do* still occur. If a scuba diver loses his air supply, panics, holds his breath, and swims rapidly to the surface, he can get "decompression sickness." This rapid decrease in atmospheric pressure can result in the release of nitrogen bubbles into his body tissues. These bubbles cut off the oxygen supply to the brain, and can rapidly cause nausea, severe pain in the joints and abdomen, and, in extreme cases, death.

Placing the patient in a recompression chamber as soon as possible, and then bringing him "back down" to the pressure where the accident occurred, allows for a gradual reduction of that pressure, and thus prevents the dangerous accumulation of nitrogen within the diver's body.

A word of caution: There was recently a small but vocal group of "deep dive" advocates in the region. It maintained that deep diving was not nearly as dangerous as it had been perceived to be. A number of these divers are no longer with us, having expired somewhere below the 400-foot mark. *Never* exceed the PADI or NAUI recreational "sport diving" depth limits.

For direct assistance in diving emergencies through medical professionals and information about scuba safety, you can contact **Divers Alert Network (DAN)** (Box 3823, Duke University Medical Center, Durham, NC 27710, tel. 919/684–2948 or 800/446–2671). In a dive emergency contact the **U.S. Coast Guard** (VHF Channel 16, or tel. 809/776–3497 on St. Thomas, 1/729–6800 in San Juan). There are 10 recompression chambers in the Caribbean. There's one on St. Thomas (tel. 809/776–2686, or call St. Thomas Hospital at 809/776–8311) and one in San Juan (tel. 1/865–2000, ext. 3462 or 4584). Ask your dive shop about their emergency plan and about nearby facilities.

Access to diving in the Virgin Islands is easy, and you can buy dive trips a day at a time or in packages. Vacationers with C-cards who prefer serendipity to schedules can walk into a dive shop at 8 AM and sign on for the next departure of a day-trip dive boat—or, if that's full, book the afternoon trip. The dive operator will discuss experience levels to make sure the planned dive suits you (for example, a dive with two tanks to an 80-foot-deep wreck and then a reef at 35 feet). They'll outfit you with needed gear (no vacationers lug their own tanks or weight belts), and point you to the pop machine for après-dive refreshment. That typical two-tank, two-location day trip takes about three hours and costs $60–$75. It's rare, but in high season you could wait several days for space on a boat. That's why, if diving is the focus of a trip, most people buy a dive package, either directly from a dive operator, through a travel agent, or through a specialist.

A few travel agents specialize in diving vacations. **Rascals in Paradise** (650 5th St., Suite 505, San Francisco, CA 94107, tel. 415/978–9800 or 800/872–7225) tracks resorts worldwide that specialize in family vacations for divers with children. **East Coast Divers** (280 Worcester

Rd., Framingham, MA 01701, tel. 508/620–1176 or 800/649–3483) is another that specializes in affordable dive packages.

To say prices vary is an understatement. Would you believe from $400 to $2,000? One of the least expensive packages we've noted was for hotel and diving, ". . . from $400, four nights/six dives." The other extreme is the ultimate scuba-training experience: private lessons, one-on-one, over five days for $750 plus accommodations. Since hotels, on Tortola for example, range from spartan to haute, Baskin-in-the-Sun quotes hotel-dive packages, such as seven nights/eight days, at prices ranging from $700 to $2,000 per week, per person.

Remove the hotel from the equation, and dive-package prices are influenced by whether or not you need instruction and whether you contract for a package or day-by-day diving. The most popular packages are for one week. A four-day certification course may cost from $350 to $425; sometimes it can be completed in as few as three days. If you've done your classroom and pool work you can schedule the required four open-water certification-completion dives in just two days, for as little as $250. Here's a representative day-trip dive package: six dives over several days, $200–$250, or an average $32–$38 per dive. That price buys you the dive leader's knowledge of the area, the boat ride, six full tanks, and use of any other equipment you need.

Rates for diving trips, equipment, and instruction don't vary from season to season—demand is evened by smart locals (summer means uncrowded dive boats and calmer, clearer waters) who dive until the northerners return in winter. Reduced rates for live-aboard dive boats and hotel/dive packages reflect low-season rates for living space, not diving guides and equipment.

Dive Operators

Dive-shop operators provide the visiting certified diver with knowledge of local conditions and guidance to dive sites, boats, rental equipment, and tanks and fills. Instruction and equipment are available from most shops, and many will arrange reduced-price hotel/dive packages.

The U.S. Virgin Islands
St. Thomas

Aqua Action Watersports (6501 Red Hook Plaza, Suite 15, Red Hook 00802, tel. 809/775–6285) is a full service, PADI shop with all levels of instruction. It also rents sea kayaks and Windsurfers.

Chris Sawyer Diving Center (6300 Estate Frydenhoj, Suite 29, Red Hook, St. Thomas, VI 00802-1411, tel. 809/775–7320 or 800/882–2965) has a custom 42-foot dive boat. It caters to small groups for daily one- and two-tank dives and night dives, and runs a weekly trip to the *Rhone*. It's also based at Stouffer Grand Beach Resort (tel. 809/775–1510, ext. 7850).

Dean Johnson's Caribbean Diving Institute. (Buccaneer Mall, Suite 106–208, St. Thomas, 00802, tel. 809/775–7610) was formerly the Joe Vogel Diving Company, the oldest certified dive operation in the U.S.V.I. It offers both PADI and NAUI instructors, and will dive even if only one person shows up.

Dive In (Sapphire Beach Resort and Marina, Box 8088, 00801, tel. 809/775–6100 or 800/524–2090) has a PADI dive center running beach or boat dives and night tours. It emphasizes beachfront suites and villas with complimentary water sports and tennis, and children ages 12 and under get free food and lodging.

Seahorse Dive Boats (Crown Bay Marina, Suite #505, 00802, tel. 809/

774–2001, fax 809/777–9600) is a PADI operation which runs both day and night dives at 58 different sites.

St. Thomas Diving Club (7147 Bolongo Bay, 00802, tel. 809/776–2381 or 800/538–7348) is a divers' resort at Bolongo Bay. It's a PADI five-star facility with sales, rentals, and introductory and certification courses. It welcomes people who have completed their dive certification classwork at home and wish to take their open water dives with them.

Underwater Safaris (Box 8469, 00801, tel. 809/774–1350) is conveniently located in Long Bay at the Ramada Yacht Haven Marina—which is also home to the U.S.V.I. charterboat fleet. It is a PADI five-star dive operation which specializes in Buck Island dives to the wreck of the WWI cargo ship *Cartenser Sr.* The vessel rests in 50 feet of clear water, and is St. Thomas's most popular wreck dive. It offers both morning and afternoon dives seven days a week, and a popular "resort dive" (which doesn't include certification) off Buck Island for only $59 per person.

St. Croix **Anchor Dive** (Box 5588, Salt River Marina, Sunny Isle 00823, tel. 809/778–1522) offers both wall and boat dives. It's a five-star PADI Instructor Development Center with a strong background in resort and certification instruction.

Cane Bay Dive Shop (Box 4510, Kingshill 00851, tel. 809/773–9913) is a PADI operation on the north shore.

Cruzan Divers (12 Strand St., Frederiksted 00840, tel. 809/772–3701 or 800/352–0107) serves divers on the West End. It's a PADI operation, and has both 40- and 20-foot dive boats.

Dive Experience, Inc. (Box 4254, Strand St., Christiansted 00822–4254, tel. 809/773–3307 or 800/235–9047) is a PADI five-star training facility providing the range from certification to introductory dives. It specializes in groups of two to 12 and offers regularly scheduled morning, afternoon, and night dives.

Dive St. Croix (59 King's Wharf, Box 3045, Christiansted 00820, tel. 809/773–3434 or 800/523–3483; fax 809/773–9411), takes divers to walls and wrecks—over 50 sites—and offers introductory, certification, and PADI, NAUI, and SSI C-card completion courses. Dive St. Croix is the only dive operation on the island allowed to run dives to Buck Island. It has custom packages with five hotels. It's also members of the International Association of Nitrox Divers (nitrox diving allows highly experienced divers to dive longer and deeper than usual).

V.I. Divers, Ltd. (Pan Am Pavilion, Christiansted 00820, tel. 809/773–6045 or 800/544–5911) is a PADI five-star training facility with a 35-foot dive boat and hotel packages. It has operated on St. Croix since 1971.

St. John **Coral Bay Watersports** (10–19 Estate Carolina, Coral Bay, St. John, VI, 00830, tel. 809/776–6850) is on the eastern tip of the island, close to many of the lesser visited dive sights off the island. It offers both PADI and NAUI certifications and conducts daily dive trips in season.

Cruz Bay Watersports Co., Inc. (Box 252, 00830, tel. 809/776–6234 or 800/835–7730, fax 809/693–8720) is a PADI and NAUI five-star dive center with three locations. Owner-operators Patty and Marcus Johnston offer reef, wreck, and night dives aboard four custom dive vessels. Dive packages include cozy villas, luxury condos, and private homes. Certifications and group rates are available. Daily dive trips leave from both Cruz Bay and the Hyatt Regency in Great Cruz Bay.

Low Key Water Sports (Box 716, 00831, tel. 809/693–8999, or 800/835–7718), at the Wharfside Village, offers PADI certification and resort courses, one- and two-tank dives, wreck dives, and specialty courses.

St. John Watersports (Box 70, 00830, tel. 809/776–6256) is a PADI center located in the Mongoose Junction shopping mall. It does a number of different reef and wreck dives around St. John, and is owned by Caribbean chartering pioneer Stu Brown of Proper Yacht Charters.

The British Virgin Islands
Tortola

Baskin-in-the-Sun (Box 108, Road Harbour, tel. 809/494–2858 or 800/233–7938), run by Alan Jardine, is Tortola's only five-star PADI dive center. It has three locations, three dive vessels, and links with four Tortola hotels. Specializing in package tours, it is the largest operation on the island. Its hotel/dive packages range from economical to sky's-the-limit.

Blue Water Divers (Box 846, Road Town, tel. 809/494–2847), at Nanny Cay, is operated by Mike and Keith Royle, both PADI instructors. Their services include dive tours, introductory courses, instructors' courses, air fills, and tank and equipment rentals. They'll meet an anchored sailboat and take divers to reefs or wrecks.

Underwater Safaris Ltd. (Box 139 Road Town, tel. 809/494–3235 or 800/537–7032) runs wreck-of-the-Rhone and reef dives daily and offers PADI training, equipment sales, and rentals. It will fashion sail-and-dive or hotel-dive packages for you. In the Mooring Yacht Charter Marina, it is associated with three hotels and has three dive boats of various sizes.

Virgin Gorda and Anegada

Dive BVI (VG Yacht Harbour, tel. 809/495–5513 or 800/848–7078) has locations at Virgin Gorda Yacht Harbour, Leverick Bay, and Peter Island. It provides tours, instruction, air fills, and equipment sales/rentals and will rendezvous with your boat.

Scuba Trips by The Kilbrides (North Sound, tel. 809/495–9638 or 800/932–4286), at Bitter End Yacht Club, is that resort's operator of daily dive and snorkel trips. Bert Kilbride, who is still the driving force behind this operation, is a living diving legend in Caribbean. He is also one of the most respected treasure hunters in the world—in addition to being a mesmerizing storyteller.

Dive-boat Trips

Live-aboard dive boats used to offer spartan bunks and gung-ho diving. Those below are full of other cruising amenities, so nondivers may happily come along. Since live-aboards are less popular in the Virgin Islands than in regions where dive sites are far-flung, some of the boats merely visit the B.V.I. on their way from other parts of the Caribbean. Other special operations include instruction in basic scuba and in photography.

Travel agents can direct you to the hotel that fits your vacation needs and has connections to a nearby dive operator. In the Virgin Islands no beachfront resort is more than a few minutes from a dive boat.

Trimarine (Box 3069, Road Town, Tortola, tel. 800/494–2490, fax 809/494–5774) operates a large, 105-by-44-foot trimaran, *Cuan Law*, based at Road Town, Tortola. It focuses on scuba but offers windsurfing, snorkeling, and shore trips. Basic scuba gear and tank fills are included; regulators and buoyancy jackets are rentable. Rates include food and beverages (yes, liquor), and prices are approximately $1,400 per person per week.

Club Med 1 (7975 N. Hayden Rd., Scottsdale, AZ 85258, tel. 800/258–2633 or 800/453–7447) is like a cruise ship for divers. Only certified divers have access to scuba gear and dive instructors, as well as lavish cruising quarters. The 191-cabin ship is unique for carrying five masts, electrically controlled sails, and a landing-craftlike stern deck that serves as a marina at any anchorage. Four large, inflatable boats transport as many as 40 people to dive sites. Weekly in-season cruises depart and return to Martinique and spend three days of the trip in waters off Virgin Gorda, Jost Van Dyke, and St. Thomas. Rates vary from $2,000 to $2,600, depending on the season, Christmas week costs about $3,000.

Rainbow Visions Photography (Box 680, Road Town, Tortola, tel. 809/494–2749) teaches underwater photography and provides video or still equipment for rental or sale, plus film processing.

Dive Sites

The U.S. Virgin Islands
St. Thomas
The north shore holds the most attractions, prompting several dive shops with stores in St. Thomas harbor to locate their boats in Red Hook Bay, close to **Thatch Cay** and **Hans Lollik Island.** Thatch Cay is famous for tunnels and arches that are full of light and sea life. Hans Lollik offers plenty of pinnacles and ledges.

When weather conditions favor the eastern and southern parts of the island, dive boats frequent **St. James Bay** and rocks called Cow and Calf. **French Cap,** south of St. Thomas, is another attractive pinnacle, standing in 80 to 100 feet of water. Sea and anchoring conditions here make it more suitable for experienced boat handlers.

Beach dives are rare on St. Thomas because run-off from land development has altered the sea life close to shore. One exception, **Coki Point,** across from Thatch Cay, is a 20- to 30-foot dive popular for resort courses.

The ***Rhone,*** in the B.V.I., exerts its pull in St. Thomas, and many dive operations plan weekly, all-day trips to the wreck, adding about $30 to the normal dive package and requiring a 7 AM departure for a 4:30 PM return.

St. Croix
Local divers have reported that the 1989 hurricane, Hugo, effectively cleaned the reefs around St. Croix, in some cases stirring the sand to unearth new anchors, cannons, and other relics. On shallow reefs damage was done, but broken coral has been swept away, leaving more fish and new growth.

From Christiansted, the dive sites are abundant, starting with the most popular beach dive and resort-course site, at **Cane Bay,** a 25-minute van ride away. From the beach, divers can swim or take a dinghy about 100 yards to a dramatic wall that's covered in a coral garden.

Salt River Bay, nearer Christiansted, is remarkable for its submarine canyon ending in a waterfall. The trench provides exciting walls, and there's a pinnacle in 90 feet of water.

St. Croix's East End is lined with reefs, and **Buck Island Reef National Monument,** operated by the park service, is a lush protected area with shallow, marked coral gardens, particularly attractive for snorkelers.

St. John
Since about two-thirds of St. John is part of the U.S. parks system, its beaches and rocky points are less changed than those of the developed islands. The points, outside anchorages all around the island, are attractive to snorkelers and divers. **Lind Point,** just north of Cruz Bay, was one of the first sites in the area that was provided with buoys for dive boats. For more information on anchorages and moorings, check the park's visitor center or customs offices, and

dive shops for the park's guide; or order the guide from the parks system office in St. Thomas.

If you're diving on your own along the rocks south of **Coral Harbour,** then **Coral Bay Watersports** (tel. 809/776–6850) can help arrange tank refills and dive trips. They also specialize in underwater videos. On the south-central shore, around **Lameshur Bay,** there's a Virgin Islands Ecological Research Station and a lot of pristine reefs to explore.

The British Virgin Islands **Tortola** The wreck of the **R.M.S. *Rhone*,** in depths ranging from 30 to 80 feet, is a major feature for Tortola dive shops. The beaches of Tortola itself are left largely to snorkelers in favor of dive sites on nearby **Norman, Peter, Salt, Cooper,** and **Ginger islands.** There are caves that are easily accessible along **Treasure Point** on Norman, and most of the yacht-threatening rocks are great places to explore coral gardens and canyons.

Virgin Gorda and Anegada **The Baths,** those large boulders that litter the western tip of Virgin Gorda, are attractive for snorkeling but too shallow for divers. Most of the diving is around **The Dogs,** west of Virgin Gorda, and at the reef along **Eustatia,** at the north end of the island.

Great Dog features a grotto, mostly in 45 feet of water and covered with hard and soft corals, schooling reef fish, and lobster. The south side of Great Dog is known for sightings of turtles and for its stands of magnificent elkhorn coral. Nearby **Cockroach Island** has a feature called **The Visibles,** a pinnacle in 80 feet of water that starts about 15 feet from the surface. Dive shops usually time this dive to minimize the effect of a fairly swift current when the tides change.

An important thing to remember when diving the reefs around private islands is that you are not invited to come on shore. **Necker Island**—one of the most private islets in the Caribbean—is popular with celebrities and royalty who pay a lot of money for seclusion. Sites surrounding Necker Island can be challenging because of their exposure to the Atlantic surge, but dive guides also know how to time the trips to such sites as **The Invisibles,** another spectacular pinnacle. The reefs behind **Eustatia Island** are especially interesting because their northern sides are open to deeper water, drawing larger fish specimens, including eagle rays.

Anegada's wreck-strewn waters (about 300 recorded mishaps) contain six divable wrecks. Most of the accidents were to wooden boats that sank in the 1700s and have disintegrated, leaving little to explore. One of the best, a 220-foot steel cargo ship, the *Rokus,* sank on New Year's Eve, 1929, and is largely intact. Beach diving around the island can be excellent, in and out of reef canyons and through coral tunnels, to see eagle rays, tarpon, and huge jewfish. The key to handling these reefs is to have a guide show you how to get back to the beach, since you can't swim over the top of the reefs to regain shore.

Jost Van Dyke The reefs most mentioned in the area by divers are the same ones that confound sailors entering **White Bay** on the south shore.

Snorkeling

The majority of today's sport divers spend more time with snorkels in their mouths than scuba regulators—for good reason. Snorkeling provides a maximum of enjoyment with a minimum of hassle. There is no heavy, expensive, complicated equipment involved; many divers enjoy the naturalness of being nearly naked underwater. Scuba diving always requires advance planning; snorkeling can be a far more casual affair. There is usually no need for a boat, since many of the finest snorkel sites are adjacent to a beach. Besides, most tropical marine life lives fairly near the water's surface. There is no link between the depth of a dive and the participant's enjoyment. Many avid water sports enthusiasts progress from swimming to snorkeling to scuba—and then gradually drift back to snorkeling. The Silent World is even quieter without the hiss of a two-stage regulator.

Few places on this planet are as convenient to snorkel as the Virgin Islands. The dangers are few and easily avoided. Don't step on sea urchins or stingrays. Don't touch red or reddish brown coral; for that matter, don't touch *any* coral. Don't put your hand into dark holes—unless you want to play "patty cake" with a defensive moray eel. If spear fishing, remove all wounded fish from the water immediately. Ignore sharks and barracudas unless they act particularly aggressive; if so, retreat calmly without excessive splashing. Never snorkel alone. Don't wear shiny jewelry. Avoid areas with heavy surf or strong currents.

The biggest danger to snorkelers today is being struck by a small powerboat or high-speed dinghy while resurfacing for air. To avoid this, snorkel as far away from boats as practical. Avoid busy harbors, dock areas, or navigational channels. Never snorkel at dusk or night. If you hear a motor vessel approaching, surface immediately, and clasp both hands together over your head. This makes you clearly visible, and means "Diver OK." (Waving your hands rapidly back and forth over your head means "Diver in Trouble. Need Help!") In addition, make sure you don't get hit by one boat while watching another. Sound direction can be confusing underwater. Finally, towing a floating dive flag is your best protection against getting run down.

There are literally hundreds of great snorkeling sites in the Virgins. It would take a large book to describe each in detail; and a dozen "experts" would give you a dozen different expert opinions on which was the best. Below are a few of these top-notch sites. Many of the dive operators listed above offer boat trips that include snorkeling at a number of these sites. Call individual operators for details.

Snorkeling Sites

The U.S. Virgin Islands **Magens Bay**—the largest, most breathtaking bay along St. Thomas's rugged north coast—has all the conveniences (parking, lifeguards, equipment rental, changing rooms, freshwater showers, restaurants, and bars) of civilization, and yet still offers excellent snorkeling within an easy walk. Ask a lifeguard where he recommends that day—certain areas in the bay are better than others if strong north winds are blowing.
St. Thomas

Farther east on St. Thomas's north shore is **Coki Point,** where famed Caribbean diver Joe Vogel has been diving for more than 20 years. "It's still one of the nicest beach dives in the Caribbean," he reports. "Plenty of reef; plenty of fish!" Check out the coral ledges close to the Coral World Underwater Tower.

Southeast from Coki is **Smith Bay.** Its windswept beach can be approached through the lovely Stouffer Grand Beach Resort.

Elsewhere on St. Thomas, **Hull Bay, Long Point,** and numerous other locations provide excellent areas for snorkeling, depending on sea and wind conditions. By boat, **Cow and Calf, Christmas Cove, The Brass Islands, Little St. James, Buck,** and **Hans Lollik** all have wonderful areas.

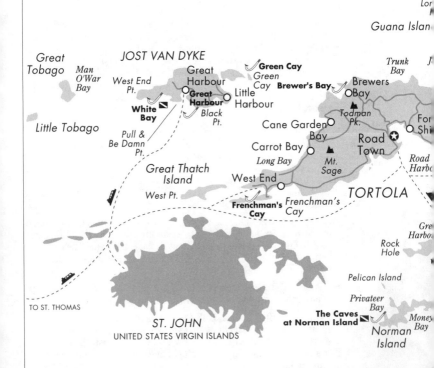

ATLANTIC

Lor

Guana Islan

*Great
Tobago*   *Man
O'War
Bay*

JOST VAN DYKE

*Great
Harbour*

*West End
Pt.*

**White
Bay**

**Great
Harbour**

*Little
Harbour*

*Black
Pt.*

Green Cay

*Green
Cay*

Brewer's Bay

*Trunk
Bay*

**Brewers
Bay**

J

Little Tobago

*Pull &
Be Damn
Pt.*

*Great Thatch
Island*

West Pt.

*Cane Garden
Bay*

Carrot Bay

Long Bay

West End

**Frenchman's
Cay**

*Frenchman's
Cay*

*Todman
Pk.*

*Mt.
Sage*

**Road
Town**

*Road
Harbo*

TORTOLA

*For
Shi*

*Gre
Harbo*

*Rock
Hole*

Pelican Island

*Privateer
Bay*

**The Caves
at Norman Island**

*Norman
Island*

*Money
Bay*

TO ST. THOMAS

ST. JOHN
UNITED STATES VIRGIN ISLANDS

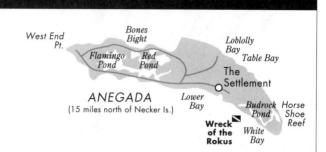

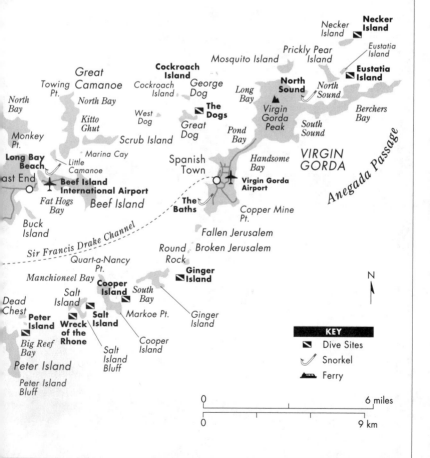

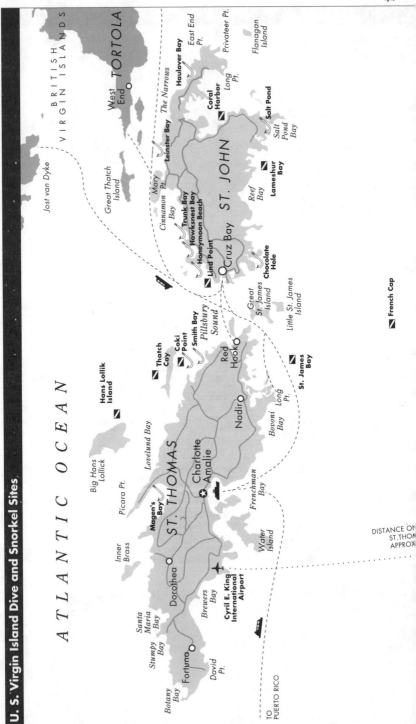

U. S. Virgin Island Dive and Snorkel Sites

ATLANTIC OCEAN

BRITISH VIRGIN ISLANDS

Jost van Dyke

TORTOLA

West End

Great Thatch Island

The Narrows

Haulover Bay

East End Pt.

Privateer Pt.

Long Pt.

Flanagan Island

Coral Harbor

Salt Pond

Leinster Bay

Salt Pond Bay

Mary Pt.

Cinnamon Bay

ST. JOHN

Reef Bay

Lameshur Bay

Trunk Bay

Hawksnest Bay

Honeymoon Beach

Lind Point

Cruz Bay

Chocolate Hole

Great St. James Island

Little St. James Island

Hans Lollik Island

Thatch Cay

Coki Point

Smith Bay

Pillsbury Sound

Big Hans Lollik

Red Hook

St. James Bay

Lovelund Bay

Picara Pt.

Long Pt.

Bovoni Bay

Nadir

Inner Brass

ST. THOMAS

Magen's Bay

Charlotte Amalie

Santa Maria Bay

Dorothea

Frenchman Bay

Stumpy Bay

Brewers Bay

Water Island

Botany Bay

Fortuna

David Pt.

Cyril E. King International Airport

French Cap

DISTANCE ON
ST. THOM
APPROX

TO
PUERTO RICO

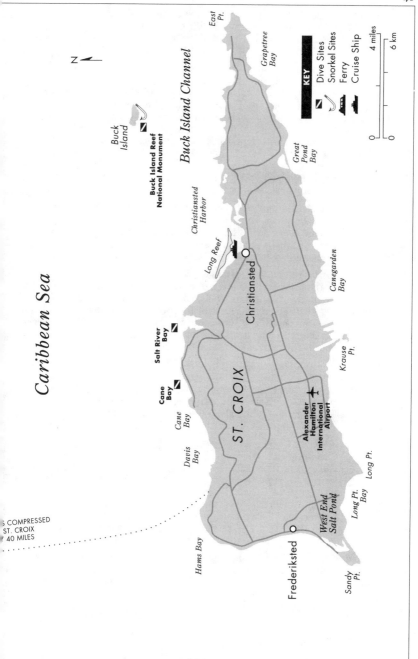

Caribbean Sea

Buck Island Channel

East Pt.

Grapetree Bay

Buck Island

Buck Island Reef National Monument

Great Pond Bay

Christiansted Harbor

Long Reef

Canegarden Bay

Salt River Bay

Christiansted

Cane Bay

Cane Bay

Krause Pt.

Davis Bay

ST. CROIX

Alexander Hamilton International Airport

Long Pt.

Hams Bay

Long Pt. Bay

Long Pt.

West End Salt Pond

Frederiksted

Sandy Pt.

COMPRESSED
ST. CROIX
40 MILES

N

KEY

Dive Sites
Snorkel Sites
Ferry
Cruise Ship

4 miles
6 km

0   0

St. John St. John offers more pristine dive and snorkel sites located closer together than any other of the Virgin Islands. The best are all located within the boundaries of the National Park.

Nearly everyone would agree that **Trunk Bay**'s Underwater Trail within the National Park on St. John is the best location on the island for beginning divers. There are changing rooms, freshwater showers, equipment rentals, a snack bar, plenty of off-street parking, and even a professional lifeguard on duty. St. John resident Cynthia Smith provides a basic equipment demonstration on the beach daily, and will help you adjust your mask and snorkel gear properly. The self-guided 225-yard-long trail itself has large underwater "road" signs which clearly identify nearby coral life and other areas of special interest. This is a perfect "first snorkel" for the whole family. The fact that it is located at one of the world's most beautiful beaches is an additional bonus.

Leinster Bay is a particularly interesting snorkel. The water is usually calm, clear, and uncrowded. Access is easy by land or sea. The shallow ocean floor offers a little bit of everything within easy view, and sea life is abundant. Caution: This area is a popular overnight anchorage, so be especially careful of approaching power craft.

Further to the east is **Haulover Bay.** This small bay—usually rougher than Leinster—is often deserted. The snorkeling here is highly dramatic, with ledges, walls, nooks, and sandy areas located close together. It's a favorite spot for snorkelers who live on St. John. West of Leinster is **Hawksnest Bay.** Usually calm except in large northerly swells, it offers some interesting reefs along the rocky shore which surrounds the sandy beach. Elsewhere on St. John, **Salt Pond, Chocolate Hole,** and **Honeymoon Beach** offer excellent snorkeling.

The National Park Service (tel. 809/776–6201) on St. John regularly offers a wide variety of park ranger-guided marine-related tours. Walking and wading along the coast is always an enjoyable interlude; accompanied by an expert, it can also be a highly educational experience.

St. Croix The premier snorkeling site here is the **Buck Island Reef National Monument.** This 850-acre island-and-reef system, 2 miles north of St. Croix, is particularly pristine, thanks to its protected status. The 2,000-yard eastern barrier reef is especially impressive, as is the entire north side of the island. An excellent snorkel for the beginner, Buck Island also provides nice drop-offs for the experienced diver. More than 250 species of fish have been recorded here, as well as a wide variety of sponges, corals, and crustaceans.

The British Virgin Islands Many tourists to the British Virgin Islands arrive by ferry at Soper's Hole, West End, Tortola, and there are a couple of dive sites *Tortola* within walking distance of the ferry terminal. The southwest side of the harbor (actually the western tip of **Frenchman's Cay**) has some interesting coral and sea life close to the shore. Caution: Keep a wary eye on fast yacht tenders and powercraft zipping too close to shore. Occasionally, a strong current in this area makes diving unadvisable.

Perhaps the best spot in good weather is **Brewer's Bay** on Tortola's north side. You can spend a few hours or a few days snorkeling here. The anchorage is seldom used, yet picture perfect. Just ashore is Mount Healthy, where the ruins of an old windmill makes for an interesting, if dry, excursion. Farther to the east is **Long Bay Beach** on Beef Island. Heading east toward the airport, take the first road on your left after the tiny bridge. This area is usually calm and un-crowded—only the sound of the planes taking off from the nearby airport occasionally mars its perfection.

Other Islands Elsewhere in the Virgin Islands, countless dive sites are still almost untouched. The most popular snorkeling and swimming area in Virgin Gorda is **The Baths.** Swimming from the bright blue ocean through dark underwater openings, and then quietly surfacing into the dimly lit caves is a thrill never to be forgotten. The **North Sound** area of the island has dozens of good spots.

On Jost Van Dyke, **White Bay, Great Harbour,** and, just offshore, **Green Cay,** are all excellent snorkeling sites, as are **The Caves** on **Norman Island.** The islands of Salt, Peter, Ginger, Cooper, and Anegada all combine to present a lifetime of snorkeling possibilities.

Further Reading

To identify specimens you discover underwater or to read about diving in general, here's a basic library.

Guide to Coral and Fishes of Florida, the Bahamas and the Caribbean, by Idaz and Jerry Greenberg (Seahawk Press), uses more than 200 color illustrations of coral and fish with brief, understandable text. Saltwater-reef fish are vibrantly painted as they appear in shallow water and sunlight. The book is soft-bound and waterproof.

Fishwatchers Guide to West Atlantic Coral Reefs, by Charles C. G. Chaplin and Peter Scott (Harrowood Books), shows 184 species of fish, drawn in detail and color as they appear through a face mask—including head-on and top-down views. The text is concise and offers tips on how to spot elusive varieties. The softbound book is printed on plastic.

Skin Diver Magazine (8490 Sunset Blvd., Los Angeles, CA 90069) is a thick (average 180 pages) monthly with regular features on dive locations, equipment, photography, and safety issues. Its advertisements for dive locations and packages are helpful. It is available at newsstands; truly the dive traveler's guide.

Scuba Times (Box 365, Mt. Morris, IL 61054) is a bimonthly magazine that concentrates on active divers' pursuits, leading occasional expeditions to challenging dive sites. The slim magazine features remarkable photography and personal accounts of experiences, along with dive-resort and package listings. It is available at newsstands.

Diving and Snorkeling in the BVI, by Jeff Williams (DIVEntures Publishing, Box 115, Hopkinton, MA 01748) is an excellent diving guide written by an experienced local diver.

4 Sailing in the Virgin Islands

Introduction

By Marcia
Andrews

Updated by
Gary
Goodlander

Within a few hours after you alight in St. Thomas and unload the taxi at Red Hook Bay, you can sail across Pillsbury Sound, anchor in St. John's Caneel Bay, have dinner on deck, watch the sun set behind an age-softened, jungle-covered volcano, and simply forget whatever plagued you that morning. It sounds like a lot to accomplish in one day, but you wouldn't be rushed. On a chartered boat, you can set your own pace, including fast access to the most beautiful locations in the islands.

For instance, Caneel Bay is a quiet, natural area, little more than an hour's sail from Red Hook's busy harbor. Viewed from a moonlit deck, the bay is a Gauguin scene in silhouette. A few sailboats float in the foreground, their masts tracing slow S-curves in the sky. Beyond the ghostly white hulls, a crescent of white sand is fringed with palm trees. The lights of the Caneel Bay Plantation resort sprinkle the hillside and faint arpeggios of a steel band ride the offshore breeze.

When a bright moon illuminated the packed white sand under our anchored boat, it was amazing what we could see through the still, gin-clear water. There were starfish and sea slugs and schools of minnows darting in and out of the boat's shadow. One shape sliding from under our boat was huge, and scenes from *Jaws* came to mind as we watched the fish glide out to sea. It was no shark, only a prowling, curious barracuda, and much smaller than the 6-foot a maxispecimens that can hover around nearby reefs. But, water magnifies things. So does the spell of your first night on a boat in the tropics.

With a sailing fleet of several hundred boats, based mostly in harbors on St. Thomas, Tortola, and Virgin Gorda, access to the island attractions is remarkably easy, year-round from all directions. There's no prescribed itinerary, and no best boat to charter. You can sail aboard a "fully crewed" boat with an experienced captain and cook, or sail independently on a "bare-boat" charter. The selection of high-quality, professionally run operations competing for your business in the Virgin Islands is unrivaled.

The Virgin Islands can match every cruising sailor's wish list:

- Sunny days, in the 70- to 80-degree range

- Steady trade winds, usually 12–25 knots from the east-northeast in winter, 10–15 knots from the southeast in summer

- Varied, exotic scenery, from the Danish-built harbor towns of Charlotte Amalie, Road Town, or Christiansted, to small, remote beaches along jungle shores, to the boulder-strewn moonscapes of Virgin Gorda

- Protected anchorages that are free; slips to rent for about $1 per foot of boat; moorings, about $15 per night

- Tides of less than 2 feet; generally predictable currents

- Short passages between islands. The archipelago—except for St. Croix and Anegada—is about 40 miles long, crow-flying style, and could be circumnavigated in two days of serious sailing.

- Easy access to onshore attractions, most of which cluster around harbor towns

If reliable winds, lower prices (as much as 50% off), and uncrowded anchorages were the only drawing points, summer chartering would be more popular. Thanks to trade winds, summer temperatures in the islands are usually below those in the United States. But since everyone wants to escape northern snows, high season persists, December through April. If you chartered in September and October (hurricane season), you'd be nearly alone—and nervous.

Though all of the islands are your cruising playground, crewed-charter operations are concentrated in the American territory and bareboat charters dominate in the British islands. In fact, the B.V.I. reportedly are home to more boat bunks than hotel beds. The British half also boasts an amazing array of anchorages, with one impressive statistic to make the point: There are 16 good anchorages within one hour's sail of Tortola's Road Harbour, home base for the Moorings, the Caribbean's biggest bare-boat fleet.

The more developed U.S. ports, full of duty-free treasures, cruise-ship crowds, and tourist-worthy night spots, provide contrast with the quieter British islands. The B.V.I.'s lower population density means quieter anchorages, smaller towns, and easygoing people. Avid cruisers set out to sample both man-made and natural attractions on all the islands. They sail across borders, taking in stride immigration and customs rules as well as the British visitor's tax—an effort to make up for their lack of hotel-room income. Some U.S. sailors are reluctant to cross territories because of the customs formalities, which is a shame, considering that doing so costs so little in time and money, and pays off so many times over in experiencing the diversity of this intriguing area.

Whatever type of vessel you charter, make sure that it is allowed to go where you want it to. The U.S.V.I. and the B.V.I. are separate countries with distinctly different marine regulations. Not all charter vessels in the B.V.I. are legally allowed to visit the U.S.V.I. Some B.V.I. bare-boat companies actively discourage their customers from entering U.S.V.I. waters. Check in advance.

To visit the British Islands, a passport is highly recommended. Although a U.S. voter's registration card often suffices, its acceptance seems to depend upon the mood of the immigration official. Also, American citizens often have numerous problems with clearing back into the United States with only a voter's registration card as identification. U.S. boats entering British territory usually are allowed to check in and out simultaneously. You'll find the office at one of the ports listed below and will meet for a few minutes with officials to complete forms. The skipper must show officials the crews' identification (passports) and the boat's papers and must pay a visitors' tax of $4 per person per day and $10–$15 per visit for the boat. British-registered boats pay $2 per person per day visitors' tax in high season and 75¢ per person per day, May 1 through November 30. If the vessel you've chartered has not paid its annual Commercial Recreational Cruising Permit fee, you'll have to pay an additional $25–$45 charge (depending on length of vessel) per charter.

British customs/immigration offices operate 8:30–3:30 weekdays; 8:30–12:30 Saturday. Holiday clearances cost more for overtime—and that's if you can reach anyone. It's best to plan your arrival and departure to avoid overtime charges. Always ask for a receipt. Avoid attempting to clear within an hour of opening or closing. Governmental offices in the Caribbean tend to open slowly and close quickly. Impatience can be misconstrued as rudeness here. Instead, begin all conversations with a warm smile, a friendly greeting, and a brief chat. Proper dress is required: No bare feet or bare chests. Offices are on Tortola (Road Town, West End ferry dock), Jost Van Dyke (Great Harbour), and Virgin Gorda (VG Yacht Harbour).

British-registered boats entering U.S. waters pay no fees, but the skipper must visit the customs/immigration office and present the crew and boat papers to clear in and out. U.S. customs-office hours are Monday–Saturday 8–5. The easiest clearance is through Cruz Bay on St. John, where officers are on the waterfront. St. Thomas harbor offices are wharfside, but formal customs must be completed at the Federal building on Veterans Drive. St. Croix clearance is at wharfside, Gallows Bay, but you call customs (tel. 809/773–1011) for directions and notify immigration (tel. 809/778–1419) to have an inspector come over from the airport. This is one reason that so few cruising yachts bother with St. Croix.

Just outside any of the charter harbors lies the world's most popular cruising playground, with six large islands and dozens of smaller cays (miniislands). The Virgin Islands are a cluster of old volcanoes. They're distinct and visible on every horizon and perfect for line-of-sight navigation. As one charter outfit puts it, the United States and British Virgin Islands combined—excluding St. Croix and Anegada—could be transplanted into the waters of New York's Long Island Sound. Good visualization, bad idea.

Why exclude St. Croix? Although its shoreline might be great fun to explore, the island sits alone, about 35 miles south of the group. Plus, the prevailing winds from the east make it more work to visit than most vacationers will bother with. Hence, St. Croix offers a fleet of smaller day-sail boats but few live-aboard charters. Anegada is counted out because it is some 15 miles north of the group, and surrounded by reefs, coral heads, and unpredictable currents. Most bare-boat charter contracts specify Anegada as off-limits, but its reefs and wrecks make it a prime attraction for dive boats looking for spectacular scuba and snorkeling opportunities.

Winnowing your cruising options in the Virgin Islands starts with deciding between a crewed or a bare-boat charter. Crewed charters can be for everyone, even old salts who sometimes choose to sail with a captain or with a captain and a cook, to guarantee a relaxed vacation. Though cruising unassisted is reserved for people with at least basic sailing skills, it's not cut and dried. If you've mastered the basics of sailing a dinghy, you and your party can take a learn-to-cruise vacation, to train with internationally recognized instructors at the Offshore Sailing School (tel. 800/221–4326), located in Tortola's Road Harbour, or Annapolis Sailing Schools (tel. 800/638–9192), in St. Croix. You'll live on a cruising boat and, with some courses, graduate by sending the instructor to shore for the last days of your vacation.

Crewed Charters

The captain and mate of our chartered 54-foot ketch knew how to cast the island spell immediately. They met us on the docks at Piccola Marina Bar, on St. Thomas, double-checked our special provisioning orders (nouvelle and local cuisine, French wines and diet soda), then began a gentle patter about the quirks of living aboard their classic mahogany boat: "Stow anything that might roll off the bunks and break, wear soft-sole shoes, if any." While we surveyed the boat's three private cabins, poked into lockers, checked the plumbing and the stereo system, they eased us away from the mooring and into the island tempo—no hurry.

Crewed sailboats are run by an intriguing international subculture of old salts and young adventurers. Our captain and his wife—both Canadians—sail around the Caribbean on a boat that represents their net worth, and are available for the Virgin Islands charter season through a U.S. broker. Like most cruising matchmakers, the broker had auditioned this crew and boat at a gathering of local skippers a couple of years before. Since we six were sharing about 600 square feet of space for 10 days, matching us for group chemistry was important.

Starting months in advance, with a list of options and a questionnaire, the broker probed our wishes (white-knuckle sailing? raucous parties? marine biology? quiet therapy?). Based on our reaction to size and price, the broker furnished brochures showing boats, cabin layouts, and crew resumes. We asked for a fast boat with moderate amenities. As soon as we met at the marina, our crew sensed what we needed. They sailed us to their favorite spot for a swim and a quiet evening.

The transition to cruising was easy: Out of city clothes; into bathing suits and deck shoes. With T-shirts and shorts for shore cover, that's about all you'll need except for casual dining-out clothes and a windbreaker in case the evening is cool. Men won't need a blazer unless you plan to visit the most formal resort dining room. For women a skirt or easy dress is optional—you're going to be climbing ladders in and out of the boat's dinghy to get to restaurants that cater mostly to "yachties" whose uniform is knit shirts and khaki shorts. Even in some of the most luxurious surroundings, dress is casual—maybe *upscale* casual, but casual.

Since we four were a mix of sailors and potential sailors, the crewed charter was ideal: The captain's local knowledge meant we didn't have to worry about where the underwater rocks were hiding or whether the anchorage would be comfortable. But our captain never shooed anyone away from the wheel or discouraged us from turning a winch or hauling on a jib sheet. The mate's skill as sail handler, cook, and concierge guaranteed that we could play all day—sail a few hours to the next anchorage, survey sea life with snorkeling gear, embarrass ourselves on their sailboard, join a scuba trip on a boat from a shore-based dive shop, take the dinghy ashore to beachcomb . . . or simply decorate the deck of our own boat. Sure, there was time for activities in whatever town we were near, but the main attraction was the boat.

Crewed-charter costs vary greatly. A relatively modest boat with a small crew can be quite affordable; however, the Caribbean boasts a number of palatial vessels which charter for more than $20,000 a week.

The average cost for comparison purposes—based upon a charter party of six and a typical fully crewed charter boat of around 50 feet—is from $1,200 to $1,800 per person per week, with all food, beverages, water-sports equipment, and port fees included. A tip of between 10% and 15% is appreciated for captain and crew.

A couple can expect to pay between $1,600 and $2,300 each for a top-of-the-line 41-foot boat—not bad considering they are getting the most private, most exclusive "catered" vacation in the world.

Another option is to hire a bare boat, and then allow the company to recommend an experienced skipper. In this case, you pay for all provisions, do all the cooking and cleaning, and the captain is your guest for all dinners ashore. This can save money, but bear in mind you are only hiring a "navigational" captain, and thus will not be enjoying the same level of personalized service most fully crewed charter boats offer. While this option can be a good choice for the experienced charterer, it has all the disadvantages of both fully crewed chartering and bare boating while offering few of the advantages of either. Usually the money saved isn't worth it.

Remember: A bare boat is totally under the charterers' command— they (temporarily) have all the rights and responsibilities of a yacht owner. However, a boat with a licensed captain is under that *captain's* command. Of course, that captain will usually attempt to accommodate the charterers' wishes in every way—but the final decision on all matters rests with the captain.

When you sign a crewed-charter contract, there will be language about the company's insurance liability and yours. If you hire a captain and a boat, the owner's insurance covers his actions, not yours (if you fall overboard, for instance, only your personal insurance applies).

Bare-boat Charters

A sailboat, with or without crew, is the individualist's choice. It assumes you'll set your own pace and enjoy sailing, even tacking half a day on a zigzag course to a beach you could see with binoculars from the start.

Bare-boat charters, designed for people who'd rather plan, sail, and explore on their own, have steadily increased in the Virgin Islands since the early '60s, when the first boat owner handed over the keys, untied dock lines, and waved bon voyage to a visiting sailor. The charter business has become very sophisticated, with formalized applications from sailors, including a sailing-experience resume and references. There are competitive offerings from charter companies, such as rate reductions, extra amenities to boost low-season summer business, and everything's signed and sealed with a deposit of up to 50% of the charter cost, months in advance.

Not for beginning sailors, bare boating is an excellent way to graduate from sailing a boat of twentysomething feet at home to spending two weeks on a 32-foot cruiser. Many sailors quickly move up to the most popular cruising setup—a 42-foot boat, with six people sharing the cost, the work, and the fun. The usual stay is two weeks, considering that the airfare is a major part of your vacation budget.

The boats aren't exotic. Bare-boat fleets are fairly homogenous, with low-maintenance fiberglass boats predominating. Some companies specialize in ultraluxury bare boats, in case you want to try out your dream boat. Standard cruising equipment includes a furling headsail that rolls up on a cable at the front of the boat (so you never have to drag a sail to and from the bow). Everyone tows a dinghy or carries it on the boat—you may not ever take the big boat to a dock, unless you require water or fuel. Many boats also have a windlass to lift the anchor mechanically, and all have swim ladders, off-the-stern charcoal grills, and the standard two-burner, one-oven marine stoves below. On larger boats, you may find air-conditioning and a refrigeration unit, as well as the ice-cooled chest for food storage, but many people decide it's too annoying to run the boat's engine the required number of hours to power all that refrigeration.

Though the Virgin Islands are famous for making navigation easy, every bare-boat charter party needs willing, able sailors and at least one member whose boat handling and anchoring experience meets the charter company's minimum standards. (They're adept at spotting pretenders.) For your own enjoyment of the adventure, someone in your party must have the expertise to read charts and avoid obstructions, anchor the boat securely, and confidently operate such boat systems as the VHF radio and diesel engine. If such a person is not aboard then you will not have an enjoyable vacation. Damaging the vessel—and possibly injuring yourself at the same time—can turn even the nicest vacation into a salt-stained nightmare.

Many companies or brokers will arrange airline bookings, suggest itineraries, and stock the boat with food, drink, supplies, and optional toys. After that, you're on your own. The charter base may ask that you check with them daily by radio for messages or call if you need advice or assistance. But remember that the primary job of a bare-boat company is to provide you with a well-functioning seaworthy boat—not to instruct you daily on basic seamanship via radio. Some charter companies have chase boats; any will arrange to send another boat to you in a pinch (no one wants to declare an emergency). If you're unsure of your skills, most companies can assign a captain to spend a day or two aboard your boat (for $100–$150 per day) to show you the ropes.

Bare-boat chartering is often a congenial gathering of four to six people who enjoy sailing and each other—as well as dividing the costs of a 30- to 50-foot boat. Researching and planning together adds to the fun. Most sailors select a boat and make reservations at least six months in advance for high-season charters, or earlier to guarantee holiday dates. Our ritual is to book a boat, then call a planning meeting to discuss the optional activities (fishing, shopping, diving), a rough itinerary, and the food and drink. We prefer to buy partial provisioning (about half the dinners for the trip and most of the breakfasts and lunches) or less (a starter kit to get us through the first day) for highly personal reasons:

- Many charter companies still load the boat with canned foods, processed meats, frozen beef, and other items no longer on our diet.

- There are restaurants at or behind every marina, no kidding, and we enjoy sampling island food.

- Local markets, within walking distance of many marinas, can yield great fruit, seafood, and local specialties. We like to explore the communities and replenish our supply of fresh foods.

Provisioning costs about $18–$26 per person per day if you let the charter company supply every meal. Beverages are extra. Partial provisioning, for about $16, assumes you'll have three of seven dinners ashore.

Bare-boat cruising in style costs about the same as staying in a midrange resort—and with less opportunity to run amok in bars or duty-free shops. The bare boat costs from $50 to $100 per person, per day, assuming you fill every bunk—and some people prefer the luxury of a foursome on a five-bunk boat. However, it is still possible to rent a cramped, hard-used 30-foot sloop for $1,200. The price range reflects such things as the optional equipment (refrigeration) and the age or reputation of the boat: It's prudent to ask for a boat in charter service under five years.

When you charter a bare boat, be aware that the boat-owner's liability insurance doesn't cover your errors, just the owner's. In bare-boat contracts, there is usually a security deposit against property damage, from $500 to half the charter cost. To avoid problems, don't anchor too close to other vessels; topside damage is the primary reason most bare-boat charterers lose their deposits. Always put down two anchors, and "set" them carefully with a seven-to-one scope (seven times as much line as the depth of water you're in) so there is no possibility of dragging. Keep a sharp eye on your vessel's dinghy, or your security deposit will disappear along with it.

Sailing with Children

You've seen the ads showing only romantic young couples and no children. They're missing a major point. If you cruise with children at home, you'll love doing it in the tropics: steady sailing breezes, relaxed beach time, colorful towns, and accessible snorkeling can make this a rich and memorable family vacation. The transition to Caribbean sailing will be easiest if you charter a boat like the one you sail at home. Bring your children's safety gear, too: the harness and tether to keep them inside the lifelines, the comfortable life jackets they'll wear constantly.

If family cruising is an experiment you'd like to try on vacation, start with a crewed charter and a boat the broker believes will foster safety for children and relaxed sailing for you. For example, a cockpit with an open stern (rare, anyway) would pose an absurd risk for a toddler. You will still need to bring safety gear for your child. Captains can usually round up small-size snorkeling gear. Though you may have to challenge a broker or two to arrange a toddler-friendly charter, there are crews that are especially good with youngsters. Note that the crews may insist, up front, that they haven't the time or skills to be baby-sitters. If a crew seems even mildly resistant to the idea of children on board, select another.

On land, casual open-air restaurants, shops, and entertainment allow parents who want to bring children along to not feel trapped when a child grows restless.

Selecting a Charter

Boats and captains operating in the U.S.V.I. (or picking up passengers from U.S. ports) must be U.S. Coast Guard–licensed. Crewed charters in the B.V.I. are operated by people with British Yacht Masters' Tickets, a system comparable to Coast Guard licensing.

In either case, besides confirming the boat's and crew's status with a broker, you can verify their good standing by contacting voluntary associations in both U.S. and British territories. Yearning for repeat customers, these groups discourage contact with sloppy operators who could ruin your vacation. The U.S. fleet belongs to **Virgin Islands Charteryacht League** (Flagship-Anchor Way, St. Thomas, USVI 00802, tel. 800/524–2061, fax 809/776–4468). The British fleet works with **Charter Yacht Society of the B.V.I.** (Box 3069, Road Town, BVI, tel. and fax 809/494–6017).

Most sailboats in the Virgin Islands are 42 feet long and chartered to bare-boat sailors, but the companies will find a captain for any boat. There are smaller boats, too. On Virgin Gorda, Bitter End Yacht Club has 30-foot boats (great for two or four people). Crewed boats are often 50 feet or longer.

With so many high-profile charter companies around, few private boats are offered for bare-boat charter in the Virgin Islands. If you decide to check the sailing-magazine classified ads hoping for a bargain in a freelance, transient boat you should focus on getting a strict contract and references. We rented a private boat out of Palm

Beach to sail to the Bahamas with good results. But that gamble didn't risk the disappointment of finding an unworthy boat in a foreign port after a long flight. Occasionally these can be great deals. But, far too often the hassles endured are not worth the money saved.

All else being okay, ask private-boat owners for names of several recent customers, and check with them for their experiences. In more than 16 years of chartering we've relied on personal recommendations but have never been asked to give a reference.

Brokers

Brokers are extremely important when it comes to selecting a fully crewed vessel. There are about 200 *independent* brokers worldwide, and all have access to the same fleet of 300 boats operating in the Caribbean. The differences among them are in personal experience and up-to-the-minute information. The single most important decision a charterer in search of an enjoyable crewed charter can make is selecting a reputable broker.

How? Make sure your broker regularly attends the annual Caribbean charter yacht "viewing" shows on Tortola and St. Thomas—and has actually been aboard the vessels he represents. The best brokers are on a first-name basis with their captains. If this is not the case with your broker, find another. Reputable brokers never offer "additional" discounts on fully crewed charter vessels—charter fees are a matter of public record and nonnegotiable. Good brokers are interested in making sure you have ". . . the sailing vacation of a lifetime!" so you'll rebook with them next year; bad brokers are interested primarily in "selling" you on any boat—so they can collect their commission.

A broker's general services:

- An interview at the time of your initial inquiry to determine your vacation expectations, budget, and other pertinent information.

- A timely response with specific brochures on recommended boats.

- A timely follow-up to narrow the selection and to make knowledgeable suggestions based on customer input.

- Matches crew "personalities" with the broker's professional (yet subjective) assessment of the potential charterers' needs.

- Gives advice and help with island travel arrangements, including air and hotel.

- Coordinates with the crew all details in regard to the actual charter contract: special food and beverage preferences, any special occasions to be celebrated during the voyage, etc.

Blue Water Cruises (Box 292, Islisboro, ME 04848, tel. 800/524–2020, fax 207/734–8847) has an excellent worldwide reputation; owner Nancy Stout has lived on St. Thomas for over 20 years. She knows the industry inside and out and provides an extensive information packet on request.

Ed Hamilton & Co (Box 430, N. Whitefield, ME 04353, tel. 800/621–7855, fax 207/549–7822) books both bare and crewed boats, and has since 1972. This knowledgeable company books flights without charge, and offers a free informational packet.

Lynhollen Yacht Charters (601 University Ave. #150, Sacramento, CA 95825, tel. 800/821–1186) is one of the top west coast brokers.

Lynn Jachney (Box 302, Marblehead, MA 01945, tel. 800/223–2050, fax 617/639–0216) is widely experienced and has been booking quality charters for 23 years. Her husband, Dick Jachney, owns Caribbean Yacht Charters (CYC), which is the largest bare-boat company on St. Thomas. She has extensive contacts throughout most of the Caribbean, and is very up-to-the-minute on boats and crews; she is consistently one of the top three brokers in the world.

Regency Yacht Vacations (Long Bay Rd., St. Thomas, USVI 00802, tel. 800/524–7676, fax 809/776–7631) in St. Thomas is located on the Yacht Haven docks. This brokerage team, headed up by Kathy Mullen, has an excellent reputation for keeping close tabs on its boats. It is among the top three brokers in the world.

Russell Yacht Charters (404 Hulls Hwy., Suite 27, Southport, CT 06490, tel. 800/635–8895, fax 203/255–3426), established nearly 20 years ago, has a solid reputation.

Ann-Wallis White (Box 4100, Horn Point Harbor, Annapolis, MD 21403, tel. 800/732–3861) is hardworking and ultraselective with her boats and crews—very knowledgeable about the global chartering industry.

Virgin Island Sailing (Mill Mall, Tortola. Write: Box 11156, St. Thomas, USVI 00801, tel. 800/233–7936 or 800/272–4566, fax 809/494–6774), based in the B.V.I., is one of the top brokerage houses in the Caribbean.

Yacht Vacations (Box 11179, St. Thomas 00801, tel. 800/524–5008, fax 813/637–5994), with offices in Long Bay, Charlotte Amalie, is in daily contact with its captains.

Charter Companies

Bare-boat charter companies own and operate fleets of boats in the Virgin Islands, maintaining local facilities and services for customers. Many have offices in the United States or Canada, as well as at their island fleet locations. They're all quick to respond with brochures, boat layouts, questionnaires, and price sheets. Although you can still rent a small, basic bare boat for less than $1,000 a week, most bare boats in the Virgins cost $2,000–$4,000 a week. Generally speaking, bigger boats with more "toys" are more expensive. Many bare-boat companies offer extraordinary discounts (up to 50%) during the slowest summer months.

The U.S. Virgin Islands
St. Thomas

Avery's Boathouse, Inc. (Box 5248, St. Thomas Harbour 00803, tel. 809/776–0113), was the first charter business in the Virgin Islands. Its boats are near the heart of the waterfront action—a great way to enjoy Charlotte Amalie as you begin or end your trip. Its fleet of economical 30- to 40-foot Pearsons offers some of the best value around.
Caribbean Adventures (51 Long Bay Rd., St. Thomas 00802, tel. 800/626–4517, fax 809/774–2283), Yacht Haven Marina, has a good starting location near the attractions of town. Its seven-boat fleet ranges from 35 to 65 feet.
Caribbean Sailing Charters Inc. (tel. 800/824–1331, fax 404/992–0276), at Yacht Haven Marina in St. Thomas Harbour, has a 23-boat fleet, including Beneteau, Morgan, and Catalina yachts. Boats are all relatively new and range in size from 35 to 50 feet.
Caribbean Yacht Charters (Box 583, Marblehead, MA 01945, tel. 800/225–2520, fax 617/639–0216), Compass Point, East End, has a fleet of 40 yachts, including a Sabre 36 and a Frers 51. It is currently the largest bare-boat operation on St. Thomas, and 50% of its fleet is less than 18 months old.

Caribbean Yacht Owners Association (Box 9997, St. Thomas 00801, tel. 800/944–2962, fax 809/774–6910), in Yacht Haven Marina, offers some of the lowest prices in the area for a generally well-tended fleet. Ask the boat's age: under five years is preferred.

Island Yachts (18B Smith Bay, Red Hook, St. Thomas 00802, tel. 800/524–2019, fax 809/779–8557), based in Red Hook, is a midsize operator with a diverse fleet of 15 boats, ranging from a 30-foot S2 to a Beneteau 51 and an Albin 43 Trawler.

Ocean Incentives (American Yacht Harbor, Red Hook, St. Thomas 00802, tel. 800/344–5762, fax 809/775–6712) is a newer operation with a 16-boat fleet ranging from 28 to 51 feet. It just added an O/Day 34 and a Gulfstar 44.

VIP Yacht Charter (Box 6760, St. Thomas 00804, tel. 800/524–2015, fax 809/776–3801), at Saga Haven Marina, has power boats in the 37- to 53-foot range, with skippers or instruction available. Boats are loaded with amenities, such as microwave ovens, cellular phones, and TV. Prices are generally 20% higher than sailboats of comparable size.

St. Croix   **Annapolis Sailing School** (Box 3334, 601 6th St., Annapolis, MD 21403, tel. 800/638–9192, fax 410/267–7205), Christiansted, offers one-week live-aboard cruising courses, including a sail from St. Croix to the B.V.I.

St. John   **Proper Yacht Charters** (Box 70, Cruz Bay, St. John 00830, tel. 809/776–6256, fax 809/693–9841), Caneel Bay, is a small operation on the quiet island, specializing in the finely made, luxuriously finished 40- to 51-foot Hinkleys many sailors covet. Few Hinkleys are available for bare-boat charters—so book early.

The British Virgin Islands   **Catamaran Charters** (1650 S.E. 17th St., Suite 207, Ft. Lauderdale, FL 33316, tel. 800/262–0308, fax 305/462–6104) rents catamaran sailboats. Its 39- to 50-foot Privilege cats have four double cabins, numerous heads, and double showers. Sunning mattresses and trampolines between hulls make the most of the deck.

Tortola

Conch Charters, Ltd. (19 Donegani Ave., Suite 207, Pt. Claire, Québec, Can. H9R 2V6, tel. 800/521–8939, fax 809/494–5793) has boats of 31–51 feet berthed in Road Town. Most are high-performance C&Cs and Beneteaus.

The Moorings (19345 U.S. 19 N, Suite 402, Clearwater, FL 34624, tel. 800/535–7289, fax 813/530–9747), based in Road Town, is the largest operator in the islands, with a generally new, well-maintained fleet of 150 cruise-design boats. It has the most high-performance Beneteau yachts backed by an excellent location and staff. This company is generally considered to be the best managed bare-boat operation in the world.

North South (655 Dixon Rd., Suite 18, Toronto, Ontario, Can. M9W 1J4, tel. 800/387–4964, fax 416/242–8122) has 27 boats in its fleet; it's based out of Nanny Cay.

Sunsail (2 Prospect Park, 3347 NW 55th St., Ft. Lauderdale, FL 33309, tel. 305/484–5246 or 800/327–2276, fax 305/485–5072), at West End, has more than 50 well maintained boats ranging from 30 to 55 feet.

Tortola Marine Management Ltd. (Box 3042, Road Town, tel. 203/854–5131 (CT) or 800/633–0155, fax 809/494–2751), at Road Reef Marina, has an unusual selection of boats. Besides 33- to 51-foot monohulls, TMM's 22-boat fleet includes Lagoon 47s and Privilege 39s, shallow-draft catamarans that allow exploration of bays deeper hulls can't reach.

Tropic Island Yacht Management Ltd. (Box 532, Maya Cove, tel. 800/356–8938, fax 809/495–2155) has an interesting range of boats, from a 37-foot catamaran to a Beneteau 51. The cats are lower priced, but ask for the newest boats in the fleet of 30.

Virgin Gorda **Bitter End Yacht Club** (875 N. Michigan Ave., Suite 3707, Chicago, IL 60611, tel. 800/872–2392, fax 312/944–2860), North Sound, is a 90-room resort with 11 charter boats and over 100 day-sailers and sailing dinghies available at no extra charge to resort guests. Charter boats include Freedom 30s, which are very-easy-to-handle boats. Charter rates are average, but these include provisioning. Check land-and-water-combination vacation deals.

Misty Isle Yacht Charters (Box 1118, Virgin Gorda, BVI, tel. 809/ 495–5643, fax 809/495–5300), at Virgin Gorda Yacht Harbour, has a fleet of 10 boats, including a 30-foot C&C, a 37-foot powerboat, and an Erwin 38.

Small Powerboat Rentals

Another interesting way to see the islands is by small rental powerboat. This can be a surprisingly affordable option. A 40-hp, outboard-driven, open 18-footer rents for less than $150 a day, while a twin-engine, mega-muscle powerboat is correspondingly higher. Most companies (but not all) require you to top off the fuel tanks at the end of the day—remember marina fuel is very expensive here. Slower boats are safer and more economical, but generally considered not as much fun.

The Virgin Islands have numerous regattas, yacht races, fishing contests, board sailing events, and organized "booze cruises" which can only be enjoyed via watercraft. The New Year's Eve bash on Jost Van Dyke is world renowned for its wildness. These small rental boats can provide an ideal way both to join the party, or to get away from it all—depending on whim. A small deposit is usually required, as is a major credit card. Some companies are restricting rentals to persons 25 and older.

A couple of safety rules to remember: Don't ever "beach" the boat even momentarily, since sand and sandpaper are ideal mediums to scratch fiberglass. All boats come with good anchoring gear, as well as all USCG-required safety equipment. In shallow water, be especially careful not to nick the prop. Watch your engine gauges, as well as the color of the water ahead.

The U.S. On St. Thomas most of the rental companies are within a few steps of **Virgin Islands** each other in Red Hook harbor. Comparison shopping is easy. Advance reservations are a good idea, as the cheaper boats tend to rent first. However, there is now usually enough competition to assure someone a decent boat at a good price even on the spur of the moment.

Club Nautico (American Yacht Harbor, 00802, tel. 809/779–2555) has a wide selection of large and faster boats. Their 22-foot Makos with 185-hp Johnson outboards go for as low as $175 a day, while their 32-foot Scarab (which includes a USCG licensed captain and an awesome 400 horsepower) goes for $450. A major credit card is required, and you must have prior boating experience.

Nauti Nymph (American Yacht Harbor, 00802, tel. 809/775–5066) has 12 boats ranging from 20-foot, 150-hp craft to 27-foot, 300-hp speedsters. They range in price from $205 to $285, and include snorkel gear.

See and Ski (American Yacht Harbor, 00802, tel. 809/775–6265) specializes in 21-foot Makos with 150-hp outboards and 32-foot Scarabs (with captain). These range from $205 to $450.

St. John **Ocean Runner** (Cruz Bay, Box 141, St. John 00831, tel. 809/693–8809) has a well-maintained fleet of 20- to 25-foot open powercraft, which range in price from $195 to $285 per day. It's conveniently located on the downtown beach right next to the ferry dock. A deposit of $500 or a major credit card is required.

The British On Tortola, **Offshore Sail & Motor** (Box 281, Road Town, tel. 809/
Virgin Islands 494–4726 or 800/582–0175) rents small powercraft for between $125 and $275 per day. It has a dozen boats ranging from 14 to 25 feet, and is centrally located at Nanny Cay Marina.

On Virgin Gorda, **Euphoric Cruises** (Box 55, Virgin Gorda Yacht Harbor, tel. 809/495–5542) has small Boston Whalers and other craft available by the hour, day, or week.

Daysail Boats

Dozens of daysail boats operate out of the Virgins, varying from large multi-passenger "cattle-marans" with live music, swinging dance floors, and crowded cockpit bars, to quiet couple-only charters on small sailing vessels gently anchored in pristine, lonely coves. Take your pick.

Daysail Boats The following vessels have been day chartering in the Virgins for many years, and have a reputation for excellence.

On St. Thomas, the *Kon Tiki* (tel. 809/775–5055) is the wildest multi-passenger "booze cruise" in the Caribbean. Be ready to bop till you drop, and watch out for those blender drinks!

In the Red Hook area on the east end of St. Thomas, Neil Lewis's island-built wooden schooner *Alexander Hamilton* (tel. 809/775–6500) is a favorite with local sailors. Neil will enchant you with his colorful stories of 25 years of chartering, and even sing you a tune accompanied by his battered guitar.

On St. John, Cruz Bay has been "snug harbor" for Bob Nose (tel. 809/776-6922) and his 32-foot double-ender *Alcyone* for many years. He's a fountain of island lore; ask him about diving for lobsters for Jimmy Carter.

Another popular St. John daysailor is the 50-foot wide-deck, multi-passenger catamaran *Stampede* (tel. 809/693–8000, ext. 1756) of Great Cruz Bay.

On St. Croix, don't miss an exciting daysail to Buck Island on one of the fast trimarans, for which St. Croix is famous. The wonderful, skilled West Indian sailors known locally as the "Buck Island Captains" gather daily on the seawall by the Chart House restaurant.

Daysail Of course, daysail charter boat companies tend to come and go with
Charter the tradewinds. The best way to select one that fits your needs is to
Companies visit a large resort's activities desk or an independent booking agent.

The following businesses can effortlessly book you on a submarine ride, a parasail boat, a kayak trip, a jet ski ride, a Hobie Cat sail, or a half-day, inshore, light-tackle fishing excursion. They get customer feedback on a daily basis, and know exactly what type of boats and crew they are booking. They will be happy to answer your questions.

On St. Thomas, call the **Red Hook Charter office** (Box 57, 00802, tel. 809/775–9333). **Coconut Charters** (6501 Red Hook Plaza, Suite 201, 00802, tel. 809/775–5959) usually has a number of multi-hull vessels doing daysails. **The Charter Boat Center** (tel. 809/775–7990 or 800/866–5714) at Red Hook books a number of local daysail boats, as well as bare-boat and crewed-charter vessels.

On St. Croix, try one of the many tours run by **Mile-Mark Charters** (Box 3045, 59 King's Wharf, Christiansted 00822, tel. 809/773–2628 or 800/524–2012; fax 809/773–9411). **Big Beard's Adventure Tours** (Box 4534, Pan Am Pavilion, Christiansted 00822, tel. 809/773–4482) runs trips to Buck Island and beach barbecues using both a catamaran and a glass-bottom boat called *Sea Spy*. Captain Heinz's trimaran, the *Tetoro II* (Box 25273, Christiansted 00824, tel. 809/773–3161) departs for full- or half-day Buck Island trips from Cay Marina.

On St. John, **Connections** (Box 37, 00831, tel. 809/776–6922, fax 809/776–6902) represents a dozen of the finest local boats; many of their employees have actually worked on the boats they book.

Tortola daysail boats generally work out of **Village Cay Hotel and Marina** (Box 145, Road Town, tel. 809/494–2771). Or call **Caribbean Connections** (Box 3069, Road Town, tel. 809/494–3623) to see who currently is offering the best daysails at reasonable rates.

Practical Information for Sailors

Important VHF marine radio is standard equipment on all charter boats and
VHF channels many local shore operations. It's an ideal way to keep in touch with other vessels, the international marine operator, your charter company, or to make dinner reservations. However, please remember that a marine radio is also an important safety communication device, and there are strict international rules governing its operation. Channel 16 is for calling and distress ONLY. Immediately switch to another channel after making contact with your party. Always use your vessel's official radio call sign and name at the beginning and end of each contact. The U.S. Coast Guard and various other government agencies are monitoring Channel 16 (and 22A) at all times. Chatting on Channel 16 is simply not allowed.

Other important radio services include:

- Weather reports, Channel 28

- Port operators and harbor masters, Channel 12

- Ship to ship or to marinas/restaurants/dive shops, Channel 68

- Private ship to ship, Channel 70

- Ship to ship for safety only, Channel 6

- B.V.I. Tortola Radio (tel. 809/494–3425) and U.S. Virgin Islands Radio (WAH) (tel. 809/776–8282) on St. Thomas will place collect long distance calls for you via your VHF marine radio. Contact them on Channel 16, and they will assign you a working channel to switch to. Your vessel can be reached by calling one of the above numbers—but only for a hefty charge. The traffic list is usually read hourly, and announced on Channel 16. Private cellular phones can be rented through many charter companies, or directly from **VITEL Cellular** (tel. 809/776–8588) or **Cellular One** (tel. 809/777–7777).

Important Declaring an emergency at sea (on VHF Ch. 16) is a drastic move,
Phone reserved for boats in imminent danger—after asking help from the
Numbers charter company's chase boat, nearby marinas, or other boats. The
same restraint applies to calling out rescuers or reporting problems
sighted from land. However, should you require emergency outside
assistance because either human life or substantial property loss is
involved, turn on your VHF radio to Channel 16, and while depress-
ing the microphone switch on the side of the microphone, clearly repeat the words "MAYDAY! MAYDAY! MAYDAY!" and then your
vessel's name and location. Then release the microphone switch, and
listen carefully. If possible, have someone monitor the radio
throughout the emergency. Make sure when the emergency is over
to repeatedly announce on Channel 16 that you no longer require
assistance. Following are onshore contacts: **U.S. Coast Guard Marine Safety Division,** St. Thomas, tel. 809/776–3497; **Virgin Islands
Search and Rescue Ltd.,** Tortola, tel. 809/494–4357, fax 809/494–
5166. VISAR can usually be reached directly on Channel 16, or via
Tortola Radio, which also monitors Channel 16.

Emergency In the United States Virgin Islands: **Ambulance/Emergency,** dial
Medical 922; **St. Thomas Hospital** (Charlotte Amalie), tel. 809/776–8311; **St.
Services** **John Clinic** (Cruz Bay), tel. 809/776–6400; **St. Croix Hospital**
(Christiansted), tel. 809/778–6311.

In the British Virgin Islands: **Emergencies** (Tortola), dial tel. 999 to
reach **Tortola Hospital** (Road Town, tel. 809/494–3497). There are
two **clinics** on Virgin Gorda: Valley, tel. 809/495–5337; Gorda Sound,
tel. 809/495–7310.

Marinas and Anchorages

Charter companies provide navigational charts and begin your vacation with a discussion of current weather conditions and favored
anchorages. As you navigate between islands, clusters of masts will
confirm you've found popular spots: You can join in—or avoid them
and study the charts for more secluded spots. Some of the pertinent
harbors for supplies and entertainment are listed below.

Islands with northern shores exposed to the Atlantic swell protect
the rest of the islands from pounding surf, but they're not popular as
anchorages. A few north-facing bays are interesting lunch stops or
good for an overnight stay in rare summer periods when weather
and surge are mild.

The U.S. **St. Thomas Harbor at Charlotte Amalie** is a bustling port, busiest in
Virgin Islands the islands, that should be visited for its color and excitement. Char-
St. Thomas's lotte Amalie can be toured, on foot, in half a day. You can shop
Southern Shore town for duty-free goodies or gather supplies, wines, and fresh produce at Market Square at the end of Main Street. Or check out open-
air stands at the docks for island fruits and vegetables brought to
town by boat.

There's no quiet hideout for a boat close to town. The passage of
large cruise ships, island ferries, and commercial traffic adds constant boat wake to the natural surge that reaches into the harbor.
That surge makes anchoring stern-to at the waterfront pretty
bumpy, even dangerous. For comfort, your best bet is to find
anchoring space close to Yacht Haven Marina on the west side of the
inner harbor. Or call ahead to rent a slip with such services as water,
ice, fuel, and showers, plus cable TV and phone hookups.

Red Hook Bay is usually a good, if busy, anchorage. There are numerous marinas to the west of the anchorage, and an array of restau-

rants behind each dock. Red Hook is a convenient stop for eastbound boats heading for St. John or Tortola, but it's a busy, crowded harbor. **Christmas Cove** on nearby Great St. James Island, and nearby **Cowpet Bay** on St. Thomas can be pleasant anchorages, but a southern slant to the trade winds can make both somewhat rolly.

The north side of St. Thomas is seldom traveled, and most of its harbors are not recommended for overnight anchoring. **Magens Bay,** however, is home to dozens of permanently moored boats, and many locals use it as an overnight anchorage in settled weather.

St. John's The island is about 66% U.S. preserve, with most of the 20 beaches
Halo of protected by the National Park Service, for all the ecology-sensitive
Harbors reasons. That makes them very clean and attractive to most cruising sailors. Among the favored places to anchor overnight, several have restricted beach access noted in cruising guides, if not on your charts: **Caneel, Hawksnest, Maho, Francis, Leinster,** and **Haulover bays** provide plenty of protection while you explore the parklike island.

The southeastern hook of St. John forms **Coral Harbour** and its several inner harbors, **Round Bay, Hurricane Hole,** and **Coral Bay,** the cultural center of the island. The attractions here are people, artisans, and historical sites, not commerce.

The south coast of St. John may be your best chance to have a solo anchorage and a private piece of beach. But isolation means you should also lock the boat against the '90s brand of pilfering pirate. The cruiser-tested anchorages are **Salt Pond Bay; Lameshur bays,** both Great and Little; **Chocolate Hole;** and **Great Cruz Bay,** where you'll rejoin the crowd.

The British **Cane Garden Bay** is really on the northwest shore, but is mentioned
Virgin Islands here because its northern end is an interesting overnight anchorage
Tortola's in the summer when there's no swell, or you may pick up a mooring
Western and in front of Rhymer's beach hotel. Why bother? It's a beautiful tropi-
Southern cal setting, and the beach often becomes a carnival scene, with bars,
Shores, Jost restaurants, and steel-band-centered parties.
Van Dyke
Sopers Hole is deep, with a limited anchoring space near the East End and numerous marina slips (radio ahead for space) or moorings for rent. Though shops and services are growing, sailors still taxi to nearby resorts or to Road Town (about 15 miles) for entertainment. Customs and immigration are near the north shore.

Jost Van Dyke is the logical overnight anchorage after you've explored Tortola's northwest shore. There are five good overnight spots, though **Little Harbour** is so popular it fills up early (4 PM is considered quitting time for cruisers who want the best overnight anchorages). There's always plenty of anchoring room in **Great Harbour,** but be sure to anchor well off the beach, as the water rapidly becomes shallow here. Farther south, **White Bay** is a lovely spot in settled weather, but only enter in good light: The entrance through the small barrier reef can be tricky.

Road Harbour is protected from the swell, but holding ground in the anchorage close to town is imperfect, and a south wind makes it worse. Anchor in **Baughers Bay** and take a dinghy to town, or radio ahead for dock space at marinas along the outer or inner harbor. Road Town, capital of the B.V.I., is historic, pretty, gently British, and worth a day's tour, whether you need the customs office, supplies, or a shore dinner.

A T L A N T I C

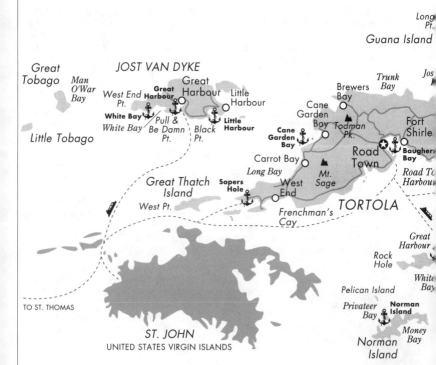

Long Pt.

Guana Island

Great Tobago

Man O'War Bay

JOST VAN DYKE

Great Harbour

Trunk Bay

Brewers Bay

Jos

West End Pt.

Great Harbour

Little Harbour

Cane Garden Bay

Fort Shirle

White Bay

White Bay

Pull & Be Damn Pt.

Black Pt.

Little Harbour

Cane Garden Bay

Todman Pk.

Baugher Bay

Little Tobago

Carrot Bay

Long Bay

Mt. Sage

Road Town

Road Ta Harbour

Great Thatch Island

Sopers Hole

West End

Frenchman's Cay

TORTOLA

West Pt.

Great Harbour

Rock Hole

White Bay

Pelican Island

Privateer Bay

Norman Island

TO ST. THOMAS

Money Bay

ST. JOHN
UNITED STATES VIRGIN ISLANDS

Norman Island

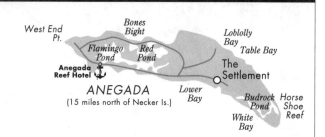

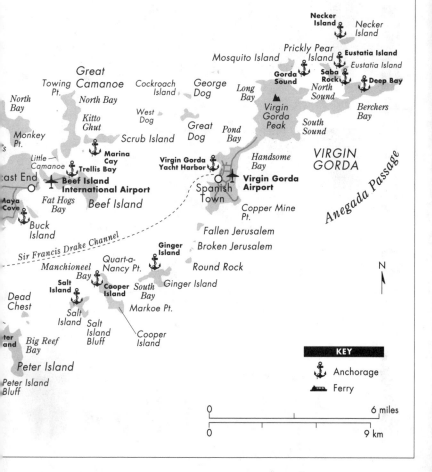

64

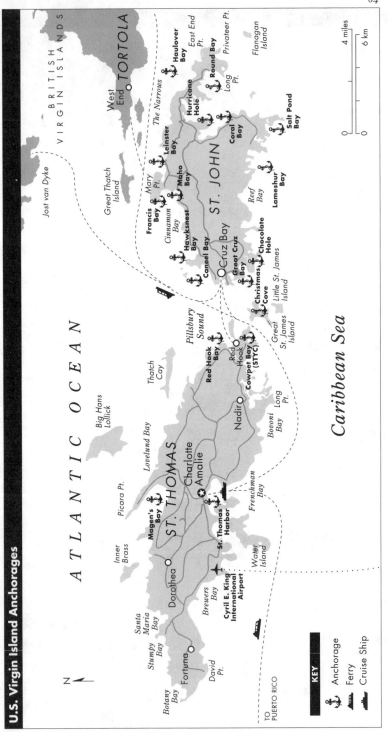

Tortola's Eastern Shores and Small Islands

From **Maya Cove** north and east to **Marina Cay** (both with good anchorages) are the dramatic cruising grounds that draw sailors to the area. Besides numerous fair-weather anchorages, **Trellis Bay** provides shelter in most blows. On shore, check out local artisans' works, quirky entertainment at "The Last Resort," and reportedly excellent West Indian food at Conch Shell Point. Proximity to the airport makes it an unromantic anchorage, however.

Islands across Sir Francis Drake Channel

Five smaller islands (**Norman, Peter, Salt, Cooper,** and **Ginger**) form the southern boundary of the cruising area and anchored sailboats cluster in their harbors like sea urchins. Check the charts carefully since some likely looking spots (**Salt Island Bay** and **Lee Bay**) aren't suitable for overnight stays because of poor holding ground, or because the coves are too deep.

Virgin Gorda's Western Shores

Everyone visits the Baths on Virgin Gorda's southern tip, where volcanic debris has been eroded into a tumble of gargantuan boulders. The boulders are prized for the pools and grottoes they form, but the beach is unsheltered and hard to approach by dinghy (you WILL get wet). Anchoring nearby is challenging in too-deep, rock-filled water. Since the docks at **Virgin Gorda Yacht Harbour** (room for 120 boats) are a good spot to take on fuel, ice, and supplies, many skippers park the boat there and take a taxi to the Baths or to explore the island.

From Virgin Gorda Yacht Harbour to **Gorda Sound** there are several day anchorages, but no solid overnight havens. The sound, though, is totally accommodating, with sheltered anchorages in every direction and a wealth of shoreside attractions. Just east of Gorda Sound, anchorages on **Necker Island, Eustatia Island** (days only), and **Saba Rock** put you close to snorkeler's heaven. Those same reefs complicate reaching **Deep Bay,** around the corner from Saba Rock, but it's a fine summer anchorage.

The anchorage off the **Anegada Reef Hotel** is a good one but can be tricky to enter in poor light. Call Lowell Wheatley on VHF Channel 16 for help in guiding you in. The holding ground is excellent, but two anchors are recommended—the wind often picks up at night. NOTE: This area is off-limits to many bare boats. Exercise caution at all times; many of the coral heads in this area are uncharted.

Further Reading

Cruising World magazine (Box 3400, Newport, RI 02840–0992, tel. 401/847–1588); *Sail* magazine (275 Washington St., Newton, MA 02158–1630, tel. 800/745–7245); **Yachtsman's Guide to the Virgin Islands** (Box 610938, North Miami, FL 33261–0938, tel. 305/893–4277); and **Cruising Guide to the Virgin Islands** (Cruising Guide Publications, Inc. Box 1017, Dunedin, FL 34697–1017, tel. 813/733–5322) are good, reliable publications that include useful information about boat chartering and navigation.

5 The United States Virgin Islands

Introduction

By Tricia Cambron

Updated by Pamela Acheson and Jordan Simon

At first glance, a typical Monday morning at the Squirrel Cage coffee shop on St. Thomas in the United States Virgin Islands might not seem much different than what you'd find back home in St. Paul, or Atlanta, or Steamboat Springs. A traffic cop strolls in to joke with the waitress and collect his first cup of coffee; a high-heeled secretary runs in from across the street for the morning paper and some toast; a store clerk lingers over a cup of tea to discuss the latest political controversy with the cook.

But is the coffee shop back home nestled in a bright pink hole-in-the-wall of a 19th-century building, only steps away from a park abloom with frangipani—in January? Are bush tea and johnnycake on the morning menu along with oatmeal and omelets?

Probably not.

It is the combination of the familiar and the exotic found in the U.S.V.I. that defines this "American Paradise," and explains much of its appeal. The effort to be all things to all people—while remaining true to the best of itself—has created a sometimes paradoxical blend of island serenity and American practicality in this U.S. territory 1,000 miles from the southern tip of the U.S. mainland.

The postcard images you'd expect from a tropical paradise are here: Stretches of beach arc into the distance, and white sails skim across water so blue and clear it stuns the senses; red-roof houses add their spot of color to the green hillsides' mosaic, along with the orange of the flamboyant tree, the red of the hibiscus, the magenta of the bougainvillea, and the blue stone ruins of old sugar mills; and towns of pastel-tone European-style villas, decorated by filigree wrought-iron terraces line narrow streets climbing up from a harbor. Amid all the images can be found moments—sometimes whole days—of exquisite tranquility: an egret standing in a pond at dawn, palm trees backlit by a full moon, sunrises and sunsets that can send your spirit soaring with the frigate bird flying overhead.

The other part of the equation are all those things that make it so easy and appealing to visit this cluster of islands. The official language is English, the money is the dollar, and the U.S. government runs things. There's cable TV, Pizza Hut, and McDonald's. There's unfettered immigration to and from the mainland and investments are protected by the American flag. The American way has found success here—islanders have embraced American-style marketing and fast food, making the U.S.V.I.'s Radio Shack, Wendy's, and Kentucky Fried Chicken sales leaders for their franchises. Visitors to the U.S.V.I. have the opportunity to delve into a "foreign" culture, while anchored by familiar language and landmarks. Surely not everything will suit your fancy, but chances are that among the three islands—St. Thomas, St. Croix, and St. John—you'll find your own idea of paradise. Park yourself on a bench under a bay rum tree and munch on a crispy, conch-filled pastry while observing the social scene. Rent a jeep, stop for a bucket of take-out fried chicken, and head for the beach. Check into a beachfront condo on the East End of St. Thomas, eat burgers, and watch football at a beachfront bar and grill. Or check into an 18th-century plantation great house on St. Croix, dine on Danish delicacies, and go horseback riding at sunrise. Pitch a camp in the pristine national park of St. John, take a hike, read a book, or just listen to the sounds of the jungle at night. Dance the night away on St. Thomas, watch turtles nest on St. Croix, kayak off the coast of St. John, or dive deep into "island time"

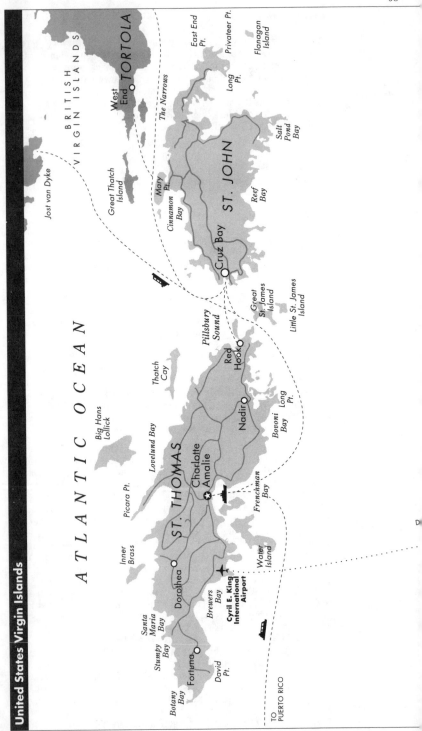

United States Virgin Islands

ATLANTIC OCEAN

BRITISH VIRGIN ISLANDS

Jost van Dyke

Great Thatch Island

West End

TORTOLA

The Narrows

Mary Pt.

East End Pt.

Privateer Pt.

Flanagan Island

Long Pt.

Salt Pond Bay

Cinnamon Bay

ST. JOHN

Reef Bay

Cruz Bay

Great St. James Island

Little St. James Island

Pillsbury Sound

Thatch Cay

Red Hook

Big Hans Lollick

Lovelund Bay

Nadir

Bovoni Bay

Long Pt.

Picara Pt.

Charlotte Amalie

ST. THOMAS

Frenchman Bay

Inner Brass

Dorothea

Water Island

Santa Maria Bay

Brewers Bay

Cyril E. King International Airport

Stumpy Bay

Fortuna

Botany Bay

David Pt.

TO PUERTO RICO

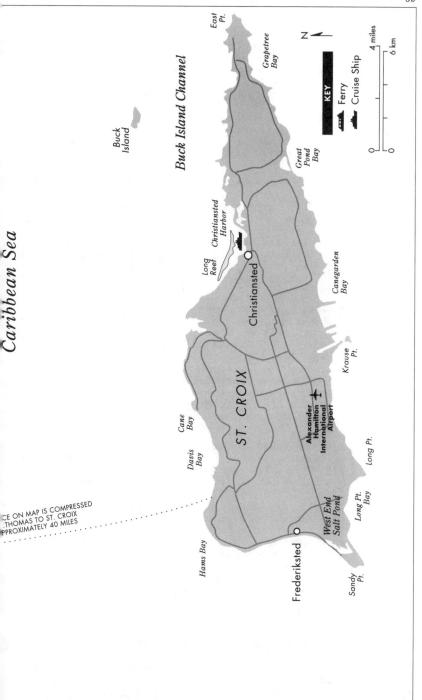

Caribbean Sea

Buck Island Channel

East Pt.

Grapetree Bay

Buck Island

Great Pond Bay

Long Reef

Christiansted Harbor

Canegarden Bay

Christiansted

Krause Pt.

ST. CROIX

Cane Bay

Davis Bay

Alexander Hamilton International Airport

Long Pt.

Long Pt. Bay

Hams Bay

West End Salt Pond

Frederiksted

Sandy Pt.

CE ON MAP IS COMPRESSED
THOMAS TO ST. CROIX
PPROXIMATELY 40 MILES

N

KEY
Ferry
Cruise Ship

4 miles
6 km
0
0

and learn the art of "limin'" (hanging out, Caribbean-style) on all three.

Still, these idyllic bits of volcanic rock in the middle of the Caribbean Sea have not escaped the modern-day worries of overdevelopment, trash, crime, and traffic. The isolation and limited space of the islands have, in fact, even accentuated these problems. What, for example, do you do with 76 million cans and bottles imported annually when the nearest recycling plant is across 1,000 miles of ocean? Despite dilemmas such as this, wildlife has found refuge here. The brown pelican is on the endangered list worldwide but is a common sight in the U.S.V.I. The endangered native tree boa is protected, as is the hawksbill turtle whose females lumber onto the beaches to lay their eggs.

Preserving its own culture while progressing as an Americanized tourist destination is another problem. The islands have been inhabited in turn by Arawak, Taino, and Carib Indians; Danish settlers and Spanish pirates; traders and invaders from all the European powers; Africans brought in as slaves; migrants from other Caribbean islands; and, finally, Americans, first as administrators, then as businesspeople and tourists. All of these influences are combining to create a more homogeneous culture, and with each passing year the U.S.V.I. loses more of its rich, predominantly black, spicy Caribbean personality.

Sailing into the Caribbean on his second voyage in 1493, Christopher Columbus came upon St. Croix before the group of islands including St. Thomas, St. John, and the British Virgin Islands. He named St. Croix "Santa Cruz" (called Ay Ay by the Carib Indians already living there) but moved on quickly after he encountered the fierce and inhospitable residents. As he approached St. Thomas and St. John he was impressed enough with the shapely silhouettes of the numerous islands and cays (including the B.V.I.) to name them after Ursula and her 11,000 virgins, but he found them barren and moved on to explore Puerto Rico.

Over the next century, as it became clear that Spain could not defend the entire Caribbean, other European powers began moving in and settling the islands. During the 1600s the French were joined by the Dutch and the English on St. Croix, and St. Thomas had a mixture of European residents in the early 1700s. By 1695 St. Croix was under the control of the French, but the colonists had moved on to what is today Haiti, and the island lay virtually dormant until 1733, when the Danish government bought it—along with St. Thomas and St. John—from the Danish West India Company. At that time settlers from St. Thomas and St. John moved to St. Croix to cultivate the island's gentler terrain. St. Croix grew into a plantation economy, but St. Thomas's soil and terrain were ill-suited for agriculture. There the island's harbor became an internationally known seaport because of its size and ease of entry; it's still hailed as one of the most beautiful harbors in the world.

Plantations depended on slave labor, of which there was a plentiful supply in the Danish West Indies. As early as 1665 agreements between Brandenburger Company (which needed a base in the West Indies from which to ship the slaves they'd imported from Africa) and the West India Company (which needed the kind of quick cash it could collect in duties, fees, and rents from the slave trade) established St. Thomas as a primary slave marketplace.

It is from the slaves who worked the plantations that the majority of Virgin Islanders find their ancestry. More than likely the sales clerk who sells you a watch or the waitress serving your rum punch trace their lineage back to ancestors captured in Africa some 300 years ago and brought to the West Indies, where they were sold on the block, priced according to their comeliness and strength. Most were captured along Africa's Gold Coast, from the tribes of Asante, Ibo, Mandika, Amina, and Woloff. They brought with them African rhythms in music and language, herbal medicine, and such crafts as basketry and wood carving. However, there is some evidence that the African influence began long before the Europeans traded slaves through the West Indies. Entries from Christopher Columbus's journal recount tales of island natives who told Columbus of black people who came from the south bearing a cargo of gold-tip metal spears. In any case, the West Indian/African culture comes to full bloom at Carnival time, when playing "mas" (with abandon) takes precedence over all else.

The Danes were among the first Europeans to settle in the Virgin Islands, and they ruled for nearly 200 years. Their influence is reflected in the language, architecture, religion, and the phone book: Common island family names, such as Petersen, Jeppesen and Lawetz, bear out the Danish influence, as do street names, such as Kongen's Gade (Queen Street), and Kronprindsen's Gade (Prince Street). The town of Charlotte Amalie was named after a Danish queen. The Lutheran Church is the state church of Denmark; the Frederick Lutheran Church in St. Thomas, the oldest predominantly black Lutheran congregation in the world, celebrated its 326th anniversary in 1992. Jews came to the territory as early as 1665, as shipowners, chandlers, and brokers in the slave trade. Today their descendants coexist with nearly 1,500 Arabs—95% of whom are Palestinian. East Indians are active members of the business community. Hispanics make up 50% of St. Croix's population.

St. Thomas, St. Croix, and St. John were known collectively as the Danish West Indies until the United States bought the territory in 1917, during World War I, prompted by fears that Germany would establish a U-boat base in the western hemisphere. The name was changed to the United States Virgin Islands, and, almost immediately thereafter, British-held Tortola and Virgin Gorda—previously known simply as the Virgin Islands—hastily inserted "British" on the front of their name.

In the 1960s Pineapple Beach Resort (today Stouffer Grand Beach Resort) was built on St. Thomas, Caneel Bay was built on St. John, direct flights from the U.S. mainland began, and the islands' tourism industry was born. In 1960 the total population of all three islands was 32,000. By 1970 the population had more than doubled, to 75,000, as workers from the B.V.I., Antigua, St. Kitts-Nevis, and other poorer countries down island immigrated to man the building boom. When the boom waned the down-islanders stayed, bringing additional diversity to the territory but also putting a tremendous burden on its infrastructure. Today there are an estimated 50,000 people living on the 36 square miles of St. Thomas (about the same size as Manhattan), 50,000 on the 84 square miles of pastoral St. Croix, and about 3,500 on 14-square-mile St. John, two-thirds of which is a national park. The per capita income in the U.S.V.I. is the highest in the West Indies. Just over one-quarter of the total labor force is employed by the government, and about 10% work in tourism or tourism-related jobs.

Agriculture has not been a major economic factor since the last sugarcane plantation on St. Croix ceased operating in the 1960s, but a few farmers—and hotels—on that rural island still produce some of the mangos, pineapples, and herbs you'll find on your plate. The cuisine of the islands reflects a dependency on a land that gives grudgingly of its bounty. Root vegetables such as sweet potato, hardy vegetables such as okra, and stick-to-your-ribs breads and stuffings were staples 200 years ago, and their influence is still evident in the fungi (cornmeal and okra), johnnycake (fried bread), and sweet-potato stuffings that are ever-present on menus today. The fruits are sweet (slaves drank a sugar water made from sugar apples for the energy to cut sugarcane). Beverages include not only rum, but coconut water, fruit juices, and maubey, made from tree bark and reputedly a virility enhancer.

The backbone of the V.I. economy is its $700 million tourism industry, but at the heart of the islands is an independent, separate being: a rollicking hodgepodge of West Indian culture with a sense of humor that puts sex and politics in almost every conversation. Lacking a major league sports team, Virgin Islanders follow the activities and antics of their 15 elected senators with the rabidity of Washingtonians following their Redskins. Loyalty to country and faith in God are the rule in the Virgin Islands, not the exception. Prayer is a way of life and ROTC is one of the most popular high-school extracurricular activities. In fact, in the first weeks of the Persian Gulf War more than 300 Virgin Islanders served on the front lines.

The struggle to preserve the predominantly black Caribbean-influenced culture is heating up in America's paradise. Recent elections put in a slate of senators whose slogan was "It's Our Turn Now," and native Virgin Islanders say they want access to more than just the beach when big money brings in big development. But the three islands are far from united as to exactly how they will balance continued economic growth and the protection of their number-one resource—scenic beauty. Many people on St. Thomas are ready for a moratorium on major developments, but the majority on St. Croix say a moratorium would drive the final nail into the coffin for the ailing economy that Hurricane Hugo began building. St. John, two-thirds of its land protected as a national park, just wants to be left alone.

The ongoing conflict between progress and preservation here is no mere philosophical exercise, and attempts at resolutions display yet another aspect of the islands' unique blend of character. In 1990 bulldozers clearing land on St. Thomas for a K Mart store uncovered the ruins of a 1,000-year-old Indian village. Soon a cooperative effort was underway between the developer, the local government, and the community to preserve the site without impeding business. The K Mart is now open and there will soon be an exhibit area with some of the artifacts found on the site.

Paradise, American style.

Essential Information

Government Tourist Offices

Information about the United States Virgin Islands is available through the following **U.S.V.I. Government Tourist Offices:** 225 Peachtree St., Suite 760, Atlanta, GA 30303, tel. 404/688–0906, fax 404/525–1102; 500 N. Michigan Ave., Suite 2030, Chicago, IL 60611, tel. 312/670–8784, fax 312/670–8789; 3460 Wilshire Blvd., Suite 412, Los Angeles, CA 90010, tel. 213/739–0138, fax 213/739–2005; 2655 Le Jeune Rd., Suite 907, Coral Gables, FL 33134, tel. 305/442–7200, fax 305/445–9044; 1270 Ave. of the Americas, Room 2108, New York, NY 10020, tel. 212/332–2222, fax 212/332–2223; 900 17th Ave. NW, Suite 500, Washington, DC 20006, tel. 202/293–3707, fax 202/785–2542; 1300 Ashford St., Condado, Santurce, Puerto Rico 00907, tel. 809/724–3816, fax 809/724–7223; and 2 Cinnamon Row, Plantation Wharf, York Place, London SW11 3TW, tel. 071/978–5262, telex 27231, fax 071/924–3171.

You can also call the Division of Tourism's toll-free number (tel. 800/USVI–INFO).

Arriving and Departing

From the U.S. by Plane
Airports and Airlines

One advantage of visiting the U.S.V.I. is the abundance of nonstop flights that can have you at the beach in a relatively short time, three to four hours from most East Coast departures. You may fly into the U.S.V.I. direct via **Continental** (tel. 800/231–0856) from Newark. You can also get there from Atlanta direct on **Delta** (tel. 800/221–1212) and from Baltimore and on **USAir** (tel. 800/428–4322). **American** (tel. 800/433–7300) flies direct from Miami, New York, Raleigh-Durham, and San Juan. Another option is to pick up a local flight from San Juan on **Sunaire Express** (tel. 809/778–9300).

Between the Airports and Hotels

Hotels on St. Thomas don't have airport shuttles, but taxi-vans at the airport are plentiful. Per person fees, set by the Virgin Island Taxi Commission, are from the airport to Marriott's Frenchman's Reef, $4.50; to Point Pleasant, $6; to Bluebeard's Castle, $3.50; and to Grand Palazzo, $6.50. During rush hour the trip to East End resorts can take up to 40 minutes, but half an hour is typical. Driving time from the airport to Charlotte Amalie is 15 minutes.

From the U.S. by Ship

Virtually every type of ship and major cruise line calls at St. Thomas; only a few call at St. Croix. One or both of these ports is usually included as part of a ship's eastern Caribbean itinerary. For a sailing aboard an ocean liner, contact **Cunard Line** (555 5th Ave., New York, NY 10017, tel. 800/528–6273), **Holland America Line** (300 Elliot Ave. W, Seattle, WA 98119, tel. 206/281–3535), **Princess Cruises** (10100 Santa Monica Blvd., Los Angeles, CA 90067, tel. 310/553–1770), **Regency Cruises** (260 Madison Ave., New York, NY 10016, tel. 212/972–4499), or **Royal Caribbean Cruise Line** (1050 Caribbean Way, Miami, FL 33132, tel. 305/539–6000). For a cruise aboard a luxury yacht, contact **Renaissance Cruises** (1800 Eller Dr., Suite 300, Box 350307, Fort Lauderdale, FL 33335, tel. 800/525–2450), **Royal Viking Line** (95 Merrick Way, Coral Gables, FL 33134, tel. 800/422–8000), or **Seabourn Cruise Line** (55 San Francisco St., San Francisco, CA 94133, tel. 800/351–9595). To travel aboard a real wind-powered sailing ship, contact **Star Clippers** (4101 Salzedo Ave., Coral Gables, FL 33146, tel. 800/442–0551), or **Windstar Cruises** (300 Elliot Ave. W, Seattle, WA 98119, tel. 800/258–7245). Itineraries and ship deployments change frequently, so contact your cruise line for the latest scheduled sailings.

For more information on cruising, *see* Fodor's *Cruises & Ports of Call 1995.*

Getting Around

By Plane

Sunaire Express (tel. 809/778–9300) has frequent jet-prop service daily between St. Thomas and St. Croix, between St. Thomas and San Juan, and between St. Croix and San Juan. **Leeward Islands Air Transport** (LIAT) (tel. 809/774–2313) has service from St. Thomas, St. Croix, and San Juan to Caribbean islands to the south. **American**

Eagle (800/433–7300) offers frequent flights daily between San Juan and St. Thomas, and between St. Thomas and St. Croix.

By Car   Any U.S. driver's license is good for 90 days here; the minimum age for drivers is 18, although many agencies won't rent to anyone under the age of 25.

Driving is on the left side of the road (although your steering wheel will be on the left side of the car). The law requires drivers and passengers to wear seat belts: Many of the roads are narrow and the islands are dotted with hills, so there is ample reason to drive carefully. Even at a sedate speed of 20 miles per hour, driving can be an adventure—for example, you may find yourself in a stick-shift jeep slogging behind a slow tourist-packed safari bus at a steep hairpin turn on St. John. Give a little beep at blind turns. Note that the general speed limit on these islands is only 25–35 mph, which will seem fast enough for you on most roads. Jeeps are particularly recommended on St. John, where dirt roads prevail.

By Taxi   Taxis of all shapes and sizes are available at various ferry, shopping, resort, and airport areas on St. Thomas and St. Croix, and respond quickly to a call. U.S.V.I. taxis do not have meters, but you need not worry about fare-gouging if you (1) check a list of standard rates to popular destinations, required by law to be carried by each driver, and often posted in hotel and airport lobbies and printed in free tourist periodicals, such as *St. Thomas This Week*, and (2) settle on the final bill before you start out. Fares are per person, not per destination, but drivers taking multiple fares (which often happens, especially coming in from the airport) will charge you a lower rate than if you're in the cab by yourself.

By Bus   Although public buses are not the quickest way to get around on the islands they are a fun and inexpensive mode of transportation to parts of St. Thomas. The island's 20 new deluxe mainland-size buses make public transportation a very reasonable and comfortable way to get from east and west to town and back (there is no service north, however). St. Croix and St. John have no public bus system, and residents rely on taxi vans and safari buses for mass transportation.

By Moped   It is not advised to rent mopeds on St. Thomas, where roads are steep, winding, and full of traffic. Mopeds are not rented on St. John, nor on St. Croix, where fast highway traffic would make the vehicles too dangerous.

By Ferry   Ferries are a great way to travel in the islands. There is ferry serice between St. Thomas and St. John and their neighbors, the B.V.I. (ferries do not go to St. Croix, which sits about 40 miles south of its nearest neighbor (St. Thomas) and is reachable by small plane or by seaplane.) There's something special about spending a day on St. John, and then joining your fellow passengers—a mix of fellow tourists, local families headed home after a day with relatives, and restaurant workers on the way to work—for a peaceful, sundown ride back to St. Thomas.

Ferries ply two routes between St. Thomas and St. John—either between the Charlotte Amalie waterfront and Cruz Bay or between Red Hook and Cruz Bay. The schedules: daily between Red Hook, St. Thomas, and Cruz Bay, St. John ferries leave Red Hook daily 6:30 and 7:30 AM and hourly 8 AM to midnight. They leave Cruz Bay for Red Hook hourly 6 AM to 10 PM and at 11:15 PM. The 15–20 minute ferry ride is $3 one way for adults, $1 for children under 12.

Between Charlotte Amalie Waterfront (near Coast Guard dock) and Cruz Bay, St. John, ferries leave Charlotte Amalie daily at 9 AM, 11, noon, 1, 3, 4, 5:30 and 7 PM. They leave Cruz Bay for Charlotte Amalie at 7:15 AM, 9:15, 10:45, 11:15, 1:15, 3:15, 3:45, and 5:15 PM. The fare for the 45-minute ride is $7 each way.

The *Reefer* (tel. 809/776–8500, ext. 445) is a brightly colored skiff that holds about 14 passengers and runs between the Charlotte Amalie waterfront and Marriott's Frenchman's Reef hotel every hour from 9 to 5, returning from the Reef from 8:30 until 4:30. It's a good way to beat the traffic (and is about the same price as a taxi) to Morningstar Beach, which adjoins the Reef. And you get a great view of the harbor as you bob along in the shadow of the giant cruise ships anchored in the harbor. The captain of the *Reefer* may also be persuaded to drop you at Yacht Haven, but check first. The fare is $3 one way and the trip takes about 15 minutes. There's no Sunday service.

Regular ferry service is also available between the U.S.V.I. and the B.V.I., making a day trip or an overnight trip an easy jaunt. It's a beautiful ride, especially if you arrive early enough to get to a top-side seat. Don't be surprised when seagulls ride along with you. You'll need to present proof of citizenship upon entering the B.V.I.; a passport is best, but a birth certificate or voter's registration card will suffice.

There's daily service between either Charlotte Amalie or Red Hook and West End or Road Town, Tortola, by either **Smiths Ferry** (tel. 809/775–7292) or **Native Son, Inc.** (tel. 809/774–8685), and to Virgin Gorda by Smiths Ferry. The times and days the ferries run change, so it's best to call for schedules once you're in the islands.

Fare is $18 one way or $35 round-trip, and the trip takes 45 minutes to an hour to West End, up to 1½ hours to Road Town; from Red Hook, the trip is only ½ hour.

There's also daily service between Cruz Bay, St. John and West End, Tortola, aboard the *Sundance* (tel. 809/776–6597). The ½-hour one-way trip is $18.

Telephones

The area code for all of the U.S.V.I. is 809, and there is direct dialing to the mainland. Local calls from a public phone cost 25¢ for each five minutes.

On St. John the place to go for any telephone or message needs is **Connections** (tel. 809/776–6922). Be aware that the telephone exchange throughout this island is in the process of being changed to **693**. At press time, however, the new number had not been fully integrated. When you dial the current listing a recording will redirect you if necessary. On St. Thomas, it's **Islander Services** (tel. 809/774–8128) on Store Tvaer Gade behind the Greenhouse Restaurant in Charlotte Amalie; or **East End Secretarial Services** (tel. 809/775–5262, fax 809/775–3590), upstairs at the Red Hook Plaza.

On St. Croix, visit the **Business Bureau** (42–43 Strand St., Christiansted, tel. 809/773–7601) or **St. Croix Communications Centre** (61 King St., Frederiksted, tel. 809/772–5800). The above businesses also provide copying and fax services, mail boxes, and long-distance dialing.

Mail

The main **U.S. Post Office** on St. Thomas is near the hospital, with branches in Charlotte Amalie and Frenchtown; there's a post office at Christiansted and Fredriksted on St. Croix, and at Cruz Bay on St. John. The **U.S. Postal Service** (St. Thomas, tel. 809/774–1950; St. Croix, tel. 809/773–1505; St. John, tel. 809/776–6871) offers **Express Mail**, one-day service to major cities if you mail before noon; outlying areas may take two days. Postal rates are the same as elsewhere in the United States: 29¢ for a letter, 19¢ for a postcard to anywhere in the United States, 45¢ for a ½-oz letter mailed to a foreign country. Bring stamps. Like everywhere, post office lines can be excruciatingly slow.

Got to get it there fast? **Federal Express** (tel. 809/774–3393) is alive and well, but get your package to the office in the **Windward Passage Hotel** (tel. 809/777–4140) on Veteran's Drive along the waterfront in Charlotte Amalie on St. Thomas, or to the St. Croix office in the **Villa La Reine Shopping Center** (tel. 809/778–8180) before 4 PM if you want overnight service.

Opening and Closing Times

Shops on Charlotte Amalie's Main Street on **St. Thomas** are open weekdays and Saturday 9–5. Havensight Mall shops (next to the cruise-ships dock) hours are the same, though some shops sometimes stay open until 9 on Friday, depending on how many cruise ships are staying late at the dock. You may also find some shops open on Sunday if a lot of cruise ships are in port.

Hotel shops, notably in the arcade at Frenchman's Reef, are usually open evenings, as well. **St. Croix** store hours are usually weekdays 9 to 5, but you will definitely find some shops in Christiansted open in the evening. Many stores close on Sundays.

On **St. John,** store hours are reliably similar to those on the other two islands, and Wharfside Village shops in Cruz Bay are often open into the evening.

Safety Precautions

Vacationers tend to assume that normal precautions aren't necessary in paradise. They are. Crime exists here, but not to the same degree that it does in larger cities on the U.S. mainland. Still, it's best to stick to well-lit streets at night and use the same kind of street sense (don't wander the back alleys of Charlotte Amalie after five rum punches, for example) that you would in any unfamiliar territory. If you plan on carrying things around, rent a car, not a jeep, and lock possessions in the trunk. Keep your rental car locked wherever you park. Don't leave cameras, purses, and other valuables lying on the beach while you snorkel for an hour (or even for a minute), regardless if you're on the deserted beaches of St. John or the more crowded Magens and Coki beaches on St. Thomas.

Dining

Just about every kind of cuisine you can imagine is available in the U.S.V.I. The beauty and freedom of the islands has attracted a cadre of professionally trained chefs who know their way around fresh fish and local fruits. And natives are beginning to realize how attractive their cuisine is to tourists. As a result you can dine on everything from terrific, cheap, native dishes such as goat water and johnnycakes, to imports such as hot pastrami sandwiches and raspberries in crème fraîche.

A word of warning about the cost of eating and drinking in the U.S.V.I.: If you are staying in a large hotel you will pay prices similar to those in New York City or Paris—in other words, dining out is usually expensive. Fancy restaurants may have a token chicken dish under $20, but, otherwise, main courses are in the high range. You can, however, find good inexpensive native restaurants, and the familiar fast-food franchises are plentiful on St. Thomas and St. Croix.

As for drinking, outside the hotels a beer in a bar will cost between $2 and $3 and a piña colada $4 or more.

St. Thomas is the most cosmopolitan of the islands and has the most visitors, so it is not surprising that the island also has the largest number and greatest variety of restaurants. St. Croix restaurants are both more relaxed, and, in some ways, more elegant. Dining on St. John is, in general, more casual; the emphasis is on simple food prepared to order in an informal setting at reasonable prices.

If you have a kitchen and plan to cook, you'll be able to find good variety in typical mainland-style supermarkets on both St. Thomas and St. Croix. St. John has several small markets scattered throughout the town of Cruz Bay, including the St. John Deli and Supermarket and Marina Market, but a recent happy addition is the expansion of Pine Peace minimart, which now has the largest selection and best prices on the island. Prices on all three islands are higher than on the mainland, but generally not outrageous.

Category*	Cost*
$$$$	over $35
$$$	$25–$35
$$	$15–$25
$	under $15

Average cost of a three-course dinner, per person, excluding drinks and service; there is no sales tax in the U.S.V.I.

Highly recommended restaurants are indicated by a star ★.

Lodging

The U.S.V.I. has a myriad of lodging options to suit any style, from luxury five-star resorts to casual condominiums and national campgrounds.

On all three islands you can choose a big luxury hotel, where you never need leave the premises. Instead, you may simply glide from air-conditioned splendor to hotel beach to windsurfing to pool bar to gourmet restaurant and end the night at the in-house disco. Advantages: They're opulent and obvious. Disadvantages: They are very expensive, and the value provided does not always coincide with the expense incurred.

On St. Thomas, guest houses and smaller hotels are not typically on the beach, but they offer pools and shuttle service to nearby beaches (St. Thomas is not a walking island)—and some have breathtaking views. A handful of historic hotels and inns above town offer a pleasing island ambience.

In keeping with its small-town atmosphere and more relaxed pace, St. Croix offers a good variety of more moderately priced small hotels and guest houses, which are either on the beach or in a rural setting where a walk to the beach is easy.

Accommodations on St. John defy easy categorization. People come here expressly to experience the unspoiled tropical setting, and the island's better-known lodging choices are keyed to this fact. The national-park campground offerings start with bare campsites (about as far back to nature as you could hope for, short of some deserted cay) and progress through standing tents, tent cabins, and small cottages. There is also a privately owned Swiss Family Robinson–style community of tent shelters on wood decks, connected by elevated boardwalks and separated by vegetation.

At the other end of the spectrum are luxury retreats of understated elegance that offer rest and relaxation of a high—and pricy—order, while taking care to fit into and not detract from their natural surroundings.

Between accommodations for the campers, the rich and powerful at rest, and environmentally conscious sybarites, there are moderately priced condominiums and inexpensive inns scattered throughout St. John—mostly in and around Cruz Bay—and plenty of private homes available for rent.

An especially appealing choice for the family or group of friends who wants an affordable casual beach vacation is to rent a condominium or private home. All three islands have good variety in style and price range. Most condos are on a beach or on a hillside with a spectacular view, and have fully equipped kitchens, laundry facilities, and swimming pools. Many have a restaurant and bar on the property and offer daily maid service (vital if you don't want to spend all your time washing beach towels).

The prices below reflect rates during high season, which generally runs from December 15 to April 15. Rates are from 25% to 50% lower the rest of the year.

Category	Cost*
$$$$	over $200
$$$	$150–$200
$$	$100–$150
$	under $100

All prices are for a standard double room, excluding 7.5% accommodations tax.

Highly recommended lodgings are indicated by a star ★.

St. Thomas

Introduction

The 36-square-mile island of St. Thomas is a juxtaposition of congested waterfront town—home to some of the best shopping in the Caribbean and the commercial center of the United States Virgin Islands—and white-sand beaches and green mountainsides whose picturesque loveliness can stand up against any in the Caribbean.

If you arrive by plane on St. Thomas, you'll land at the western end of the island; if by cruise ship, you'll come into one of the world's most beautiful harbors. Either way, one of your first sights of the island will be the town of Charlotte Amalie. From the harbor, you see an idyllic-looking village spreading up into the lower hills. Driving through town on the way to your hotel, you'll find yourself in the heart of a bustling seaport. If you were expecting a quiet village, its inhabitants hanging out under palm trees, you've missed that era by about 300 years. While its sister islands in both the British and United States Virgin Islands developed rural, plantation economies, St. Thomas cultivated its harbor and the island became a thriving commercial seaport very soon after it was settled by the Danes in the 1600s.

The success of the naturally perfect harbor was enhanced by the fact that the Danes—who ruled St. Thomas (with only a couple of short interruptions) from 1666 to 1917—managed to avoid getting involved in some 100 years' worth of European Wars. Denmark was the only European country with colonies in the Caribbean to stay neutral during the war of the Spanish succession in the early 1700s. Thus, products of the Dutch, English, and French islands—sugar, cotton, and indigo—were traded through Charlotte Amalie, along with the regular shipments of slaves. When the Spanish wars ended, trade fell off, but by the end of the 1700s, Europe was at war again, Denmark again remained neutral, and St. Thomas continued to prosper. Even into the 1800s, while the economies of St. Croix and St. John foundered as the cultivation of sugarcane moved on to more easily tilled fields elsewhere, St. Thomas's status remained strong. This prosperity led to the development of shipyards for repairing boats, a well-organized banking system, and a large merchant class. In 1845, Charlotte Amalie had 101 large importing houses owned by Englishmen, Frenchmen, Germans, Haitians, Spaniards, Americans, Sephardim, and Danes.

The Charlotte Amalie of today is still a harbor of superlatives, and you'll see a great variety of boats anchored in its blue waters, but today the trade is in tourists. Charlotte Amalie is one of the most active cruise-ship ports in the world. On almost any day of the year at least one, and sometimes as many as six, cruise ships are tied up to the dock or anchored outside the harbor. Gently rocking in the shadows of these giant floating hotels, you'll see just about every other kind of vessel imaginable: A big three-masted schooner that will take you on a sunset cruise complete with rum punch and a Jimmy Buffett soundtrack; and that yacht that looks like it could be straight out of a James Bond movie actually is—it starred in *Thunderball*. There are riverboat steamers, Polynesian-style thatch-roof rafts, and even a Chinese junk. Weaving around them all are ferries on their way to and from the B.V.I., and dinghies shuttling the boaties in to their landlubber jobs.

While the role of most of the above-mentioned boats is to re-create the romance of the tropics for the visitor, there are still working vessels to be found. Big container ships pull up in Sub Base, just west of the harbor, bringing in everything from cornflakes to tires, and anchored right along the waterfront are the picturesque down-island sloops like those that have plied the waters between the Leeward Islands for hundreds of years. They still deliver fruits and vegetables, but today they return down-island with modern-day necessities: refrigerators, VCRs, and carton after carton of disposable diapers.

The waterfront road through Charlotte Amalie was once part of the harbor. Before it was filled to build the highway, the beach came right up to the back door of the warehouses that now line the thoroughfare. Two hundred years ago, those warehouses contained indigo, tobacco, and cotton. Today the stone buildings house silk, crystal, linens, and Gucci leather. Exotic fragrances are still being traded, but by island beauty queens in air-conditioned perfume palaces instead of from open market stalls.

Pirates in the old days—the era of Blackbeard, Bluebeard, Captain Kidd, and any number of guys nicknamed "Peg Leg"—used St. Thomas as a base from which to raid merchant ships of any and every nation, though they were particularly fond of the gold- and silver-laden treasure ships heading from Mexico, Cuba, and Puerto Rico to Spain. There are still pirates around, but today's version use St. Thomas as a drop-off for their contraband: Illegal immigrants from neighboring Haiti and the Dominican Republic are smuggled in by boat to dark bays on the north side of the island, and planes drop waterproof bales of cocaine into Pillsbury Sound.

Out of Charlotte Amalie, you'll probably go east, if you're staying in a hotel. The western end of the island is the most undeveloped and, with the exception of some private homes, still relatively wild. If you're staying in the northside, you'll go up the mountain where the roads are lined with the dense greenery of giant ferns and philodendron, banana trees, and flamboyant trees that thrive in the cooler and wetter mountain climate. The quiet northside is where you get away from it all. The lush vegetation muffles the sound of all but the birds, and here you'll find many of the island's private villas for rent. In the drier areas to the south and to the east, the roads are lined with big cacti and succulents like giant aloes, punctuated with the bright colors of the hardy bougainvillea and hibiscus. The southeastern and far eastern ends of the island are flatter, and this is where you'll find the beachfront hotels and condominiums. At the eastern tip is Red Hook, a friendly little village anchored by the marine community nestled at Red Hook harbor.

Important Addresses and Numbers

Tourist Information The **U.S. Virgin Islands Division of Tourism** has an office in St. Thomas (Box 6400, Charlotte Amalie, USVI 00804, tel. 809/774–8784, fax 809/774–4390). There is a **visitor center** (tel. 809/776–9493) in Charlotte Amalie, across from Emancipation Square (next to Little Switzerland) and at Havensight Mall.

The **National Park Service** has a visitor center at the ferry area at Red Hook. There is an **American Express** office on St. Thomas (Guardian Bldg., across from Havensight Mall, tel. 809/774–1855).

Emergencies
Police To reach the police dial 915.

Hospitals The emergency room of **St. Thomas Hospital** (tel. 809/776–8311) in Sugar Estate, Charlotte Amalie is open 24 hours a day.

Air Ambulance **Bohlke International Airways** (tel. 809/778–9177) operates out of the airport in St. Croix. **Air Medical Services** (tel. 800/443–0013) and **Air Ambulance Network** (tel. 800/327–1966) also service the area from Florida.

Coast Guard For emergencies call the **Marine Safety Detachment** (tel. 809/776–3497) from 7 to 3:30 weekdays. If there is no answer, call the **Rescue**

Coordination Center (tel. 809/722–2943) in San Juan, open 24 hours a day.

Pharmacies **Sunrise Pharmacy** has two branches on St. Thomas: one at Wheatley Center (tel. 809/774–5333) and another in Red Hook (tel. 809/775–6600). **Drug Farm Pharmacy**'s main store (tel. 809/776–7098) is located across from the General Post Office; another branch (tel. 809/776–1880) is located next to St. Thomas Hospital.

Getting Around

By Car Some words of warning about driving in St. Thomas: Driving is on the left side of the road, and everybody here is in a hurry—though it's hard to imagine what the big rush is. Just drive defensively and don't let the person on your tail bother you.

Traffic can get pretty bad, but it needn't get in your way. Avoid driving in town at rush hour (7 AM–9 AM and 4:30 PM–6 PM), and don't drive along the waterfront any more than you have to, because it is frequently bumper-to-bumper. Instead, find the routes (starting from the East End, Route 38 to 42 to 40 to 33) that go up and over the mountain and then drop you back onto the Veteran's Highway.

If you are going to drive, be sure to get one of the new maps that include both the route number and the name of the road that is used by locals. The standard U.S.V.I. map does a pretty good job, but the "Island Map of St. Thomas" (Earle Publishing, Box 1859, St. Thomas 00801, tel. 809/775–4557) gives even more detailed names as well as landmarks. It's generally available anywhere you find tourist maps and guidebooks.

You can rent a car from **ABC Rentals** (tel. 809/776–1222 or 800/524–2080), **Anchorage E-Z Car** (tel. 809/775–6255), **Avis** (tel. 809/774–1468), **Budget** (tel. 809/778–9636), **Cowpet Rent-A-Car** (tel. 809/775–7376 or 800/524–2072), **Dependable Auto** (tel. 809/774–2253 or 800/522–3076), **Discount** (tel. 809/776–4858), **Hertz** (tel. 809/774–1879), **Sun Island** (tel. 809/774–3333), or **Thrifty** (tel. 809/776–7200).

By Taxi In town, taxi stands are located across from **Emancipation Gardens** (in front of Little Switzerland behind the post office) and along the waterfront. But you probably won't have to look for a stand, as taxis are plentiful and routinely cruise the streets. Walking down Main Street, you'll be asked "back to ship?" often enough to make you never want to carry another shopping bag.

Away from Charlotte Amalie, you'll find taxis available at all major hotels, and at such public beaches as Magens Bay and Coki Point. Calling taxis will work, too, but allow plenty of time.

Like cabbies the world over, St. Thomas drivers run the gamut from the friendly to the rude. Nine times out of 10 you'll be treated well, but if you are cheated or treated rudely, take the license number and report the driver to the **V.I. Taxi Commission** (tel. 809/776–8294).

By Bus In 1990 St. Thomas acquired 20 new, roomy air-conditioned buses, which made public transportation a viable alternative to taxis for the first time. Service runs from town to the eastern and western ends of the island. There is no service to the north. Buses run about every 20 minutes from clearly marked VITRAN bus stops. Fares are $1 between outlying areas and town and 75¢ in town. Ask the bus driver for a schedule.

Guided Tours

V.I. Taxi Association City-Island Tour (tel. 809/774–4550) gives a two-hour tour aimed at cruise-ship passengers that includes stops at Drake's Seat and Mountain Top. For just a bit more money (about $30 for two) you can hire a taxi and ask the driver to take the opposite route so you'll avoid the crowds. But do see Mountain Top: The view is wonderful.

Tropic Tours (tel. 809/774–1855) offers half-day shopping and sight-seeing tours of St. Thomas by bus on Monday, Wednesday, Friday, and Saturday ($18 per person). The full-day St. John tour ($40 per person) includes snorkeling and lunch, and is offered every day. They pick up at all the major hotels.

The *St. Thomas–St. John Vacation Handbook,* available free at hotels and the two tourist centers (*see* Tourist Information, *above*), has an excellent self-guided walking tour of Charlotte Amalie. Bird-watching, whale-watching, and a chance to wait hidden on a beach while the magnificent hawksbill turtles come ashore to lay their eggs, are all open to visitors. Write the **Virgin Islands Conservation Society** (Box 3839, St. Croix 00822, tel. 809/773–1989) for more information on hikes and special programs, or check the community calendar in the *Daily News* for up-to-date information.

Seaborne Seaplane Adventures (5305 Long Bay Rd., tel. 809/777–4491) offers narrated "flightseeing" tours of the U.S. and British Virgin Islands and day trips to St. Croix or St. John. Extra-large windows give exceptional views. The 40-minute tour is $78 per person, various day trips (golf, shopping, beaches, and more) range from $99 to $169 per person.

Atlantis **Submarine** (Havensight Mall, tel. 809/776–5650). Probably the only way any of us are going to go 150 feet under the sea, this submarine carries 46 passengers on a two-hour ride; it's air-conditioned, and there's a surface vessel that maintains constant radio contact. It's not cheap: $68 for an adult's day fare; $34 for youths 13–18; $25 children 4–12.

Kon Tiki (Yacht Haven Marina, tel. 809/775–5055). This party boat is a kick. Put your sophistication aside, climb on this big palm-thatch raft, and dip into bottomless barrels of rum punch along with a couple of hundred of your soon-to-be closest friends. Dance to the steel band, sun on the roof (watch out, you'll fry), and join the limbo dancing on the way home from an afternoon of swimming and beachcombing at Honeymoon Beach on Water Island. This popular three-hour afternoon excursion, with a mixture of cruise-ship passengers and hotel visitors, costs $29 for adults, $15 for children 12 and under (although few come on this party raft).

Exploring St. Thomas

St. Thomas is only 13 miles long and less than 4 miles wide, but it's an extremely hilly island, and even an 8- or 10-mile trip could take several hours. Don't let that discourage you, though, because the ridge of mountains that runs from east to west through the middle, and separates the Caribbean and Atlantic sides of the island, offers spectacular vistas and is a lot of fun to explore—especially in a jeep and with lots of time.

Numbers in the margin correspond to points of interest on the St. Thomas and Charlotte Amalie maps.

Charlotte Amalie This tour of historic (and sometimes hilly) Charlotte Amalie and environs is on foot, so wear comfortable shoes, start early, and stop often to refresh (there'll be plenty of opportunities). You may want to take your bathing suit, because there's a pool break about halfway through the tour.

A note about the street names: In deference to the island's heritage, the streets downtown are labeled by their Danish names. Locals will use both the Danish name and the English name (such as Dronnigen's Gade and Main Street), but most people refer to things by where they are located (a block toward the waterfront off Main Street, or next to the Little Switzerland Shop). It's best to ask for directions by shop names or landmarks.

❶ **Frenchtown,** where descendants of immigrants from St. Barthelemy (St. Barts), pull up their boats and display their catch of **❷** the day is about a half-mile southwest of **Charlotte Amalie.** Frenchtown's harbor has an abundance of yellowtail, parrot fish, and oldwife nearly as colorful as the fishermen's small boats. You may see a number of people cleaning fish on the jetty or bending elbows at the Maison Noel bar. If you want to get a feel for the residential district of Frenchtown take a moment to walk west to some of the town's winding streets, where the tiny wood houses have been passed down from generation to generation.

The island you see sitting about a quarter of a mile out to the west in Charlotte Amalie harbor is **Water Island.** It was once a peninsula of St. Thomas but a channel was cut through so U.S. submarines could get to their base in a bay just to the west, known today as Sub Base. Today, private residents live on the island.

East of Water Island is Hassel Island, a U.S.V.I. national park, with the ruins of the British military garrison (built during a brief British occupation of the U.S.V.I. during the 1800s) and the remains of a marine railway (where ships were hoisted onto land to the ship repair yard). Also on Hassel Island is the shell of the hotel that writer Herman Wouk's fictitious character, Norman Paperman, tried to turn into his own paradise in the book *Don't Stop the Carnival.* Presently there is no transportation to the island and nothing to service visitors once they arrive.

At the traffic signal (Frenchtown post office, on your right) turn right and walk east, back to Charlotte Amalie. You'll pass Tortola Wharf, where you can catch a ferry to the B.V.I. As you walk along Charlotte Amalie's harbor have your camera ready to capture the down-island merchant boats delivering bananas and pineapples from Antigua, Dominica, St. Kitts, and St. Lucia.

Cross the street at Windward Passage Hotel, and, just as it ends, turn into the Kronprindsens Alley. As you come through an archway at the end of the block you'll be facing the pale-pink Roman Catholic **❸** **Cathedral of St. Peter and St. Paul** consecrated as a parish church in 1848. The ceiling and walls of the church are covered in the soft tones of murals painted in 1899 by two Belgian artists, Father Leo Servais and Brother Ildephonsus. The San Juan–marble altar and side walls were added in the 1960s. *Tel. 809/774–0201. Open Mon.–Sat. 8–5.*

❹ Just to the east of the church is **75 Corner,** so named because under the old Danish numbering system the house on this corner was Number 75. (The corner in the opposite direction was once the end of the wharf (before the land was filled), where boats from Tortola brought cows for sale, and is known as Cow's Wharf Corner.

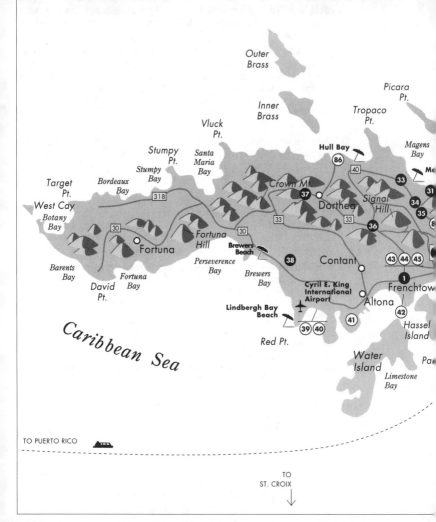

St. Thomas

Outer Brass

Inner Brass

Picara Pt.

Tropaco Pt.

Vluck Pt.

Magens Bay

Stumpy Pt.

Santa Maria Bay

Hull Bay
86

Stumpy Bay

40

33

Me

Target Pt.

Bordeaux Bay

Crown Mt.
37

Dorthea

Signal Hill

31

West Cay

318

33

34

Botany Bay

35

30

Fortuna Hill

30

33

36

8

Fortuna

Perseverance Bay

Brewers Beach

Contant

43 **44** **45**

Barents Bay

Fortuna Bay

Brewers Bay

38

1

Frenchtow

David Pt.

Cyril E. King International Airport

Altona

42

Caribbean Sea

Lindbergh Bay Beach

39 **40**

41

Hassel Island

Red Pt.

Water Island

Pa

Limestone Bay

TO PUERTO RICO

TO ST. CROIX

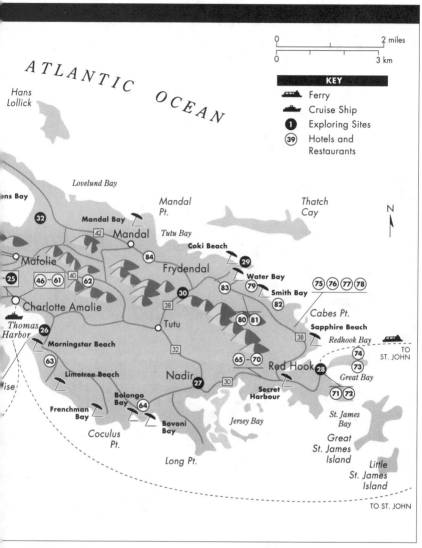

ATLANTIC OCEAN

Hans Lollick

Lovelund Bay

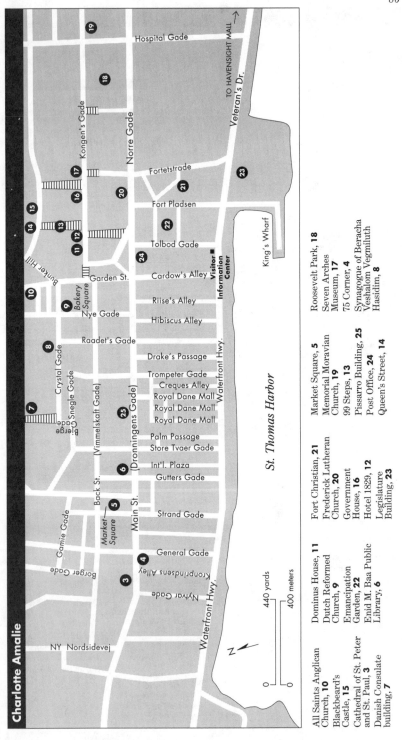

Charlotte Amalie

St. Thomas Harbor

Hospital Gade

TO HAVENSIGHT MALL →

Veteran's Dr.

Kongen's Gade

Norre Gade

Fortetstrade

Fort Pladsen

Tolbod Gade

Garden St.

Bunker Hill

Bakery Square

Nye Gade

Cardow's Alley

Riise's Alley

Hibiscus Alley

Raadet's Gade

Crystal Gade

Snegle Gade

Bjerge Gade

(Vimmelskaft Gade)

Drake's Passage

Trompeter Gade

Creques Alley

Royal Dane Mall

Royal Dane Mall

Royal Dane Mall

Palm Passage

Store Tvaer Gade

Int'l. Plaza

Gutters Gade

(Dronningens Gade)

Back St.

Market Square

Main St.

Strand Gade

Gamle Gade

General Gade

Kronprindsens Alley

Borger Gade

Nyvar Gade

NY Nordsidevej

Waterfront Hwy.

Waterfront Hwy.

King's Wharf

Visitor Information Center

440 yards

400 meters

N

All Saints Anglican Church, **10**
Blackbeard's Castle, **15**
Cathedral of St. Peter and St. Paul, **3**
Danish Consulate building, **7**

Dominus House, **11**
Dutch Reformed Church, **9**
Emancipation Garden, **22**
Enid M. Baa Public Library, **6**

Fort Christian, **21**
Frederick Lutheran Church, **20**
Government House, **16**
Hotel 1829, **12**
Legislature Building, **23**

Market Square, **5**
Memorial Moravian Church, **19**
99 Steps, **13**
Pissarro Building, **25**
Post Office, **24**
Queen's Street, **14**

Roosevelt Park, **18**
Seven Arches Museum, **17**
75 Corner, **4**
Synagogue of Beracha Veshalom Vegmiluth Hasidim, **8**

At 75 Corner take a left and continue on General Gade. You're entering the **Savan,** a neighborhood of small streets and small houses first laid out in the 1700s as the residential area for a growing class of "free coloreds," a middle class of artisans, clerks, and shopkeepers. You'll find a row of Rastafari shops along the first block.

Turn right at Strand Gade, toward the covered market, and you'll be at the beginning of the Charlotte Amalie shopping district.

❺ At **Market Square,** a cadre of old-timers sell papaya, taina roots, and herbs; and sidewalk vendors offer a variety of African fabrics and artifacts, tie-dye cotton clothes at good prices, and fresh-squeezed fruit juices.

East of Market Square about half a block is a large pink building typical of the 18th-century town houses common to the north side of the street. (The south side of the street is lined with the old warehouse that once reached to the water's edge). The merchants' homes were built across from the warehouses, with their stores downstairs and living quarters upstairs. The pink building was the home of St. Thomas merchant and landowner Baron von Bretton. It's the first ❻ recorded fireproof building. Today the building houses the **Enid M. Baa Public Library.** Its high-ceilinged, cool, stone-floor interior is perfect for an afternoon of browsing through the historic-papers collection or just sitting in the breeze by an open window reading the daily paper.

After a look at the library, walk to the end of the block and take a right on Store Tvaer Gade. Walk up the hill, across Back Street (Parrot Fish Records on your left), and turn right on Snegle Gade; walk a short block, and take a left on Bjerge Gade.

As you continue up a steep hill, the houses that you'll pass are the homes of many old St. Thomas families. The buildings' stucco walls drip bougainvillea, which hide most of the architectural detail. Stately dinner parties and sophisticated political soirées still dominate the social scene in these homes.

As you walk up Bjerge Gade you'll end up facing a weather-beaten but imposing two-story red house known as the **Crystal Palace,** so named because it was the first building on the island to have glass windows. The Crystal Palace anchors the corner of Bjerge Gade and Crystal Gade. Here the street becomes stairs, which you can climb ❼ to Denmark Hill and the old Greek Revival **Danish Consulate building** (1830), with its waving red-and-white flag.

Back at the corner of Bjerge Gade and Crystal Gade go east along Crystal Gade (you can't go west; the street begins here).

❽ At Number 15 Crystal Gade you'll come to the **Synagogue of Beracha Veshalom Vegmiluth Hasidim.** The synagogue's Hebrew name translates as the Congregation of Blessing, Peace, and Loving Deeds. Through the iron gates and green courtyard is the small synagogue. The building's white pillars contrast with rough stone walls, as does the rich mahogany of the pews and altar. The sand on the floor symbolizes the exodus from Egypt. Since the synagogue first opened its doors in 1833, it has held a weekly Sabbath service, making it the oldest synagogue building in continuous use under the American flag and the second oldest (after the one on Curaçao) in the Western Hemisphere. *15 Crystal Gade, tel. 809/774–4312. Open weekdays 9–4.*

One block east, down the hill, you'll come to the corner of Nye Gade. ❾ On the right corner is the St. Thomas **Dutch Reformed Church,** founded in 1744, burned in 1804, and rebuilt to its austere loveliness in 1844. The unembellished cream-color hall exudes peace—albeit monochromatically. The only touches of another color are the forest green shutters and carpet. *Tel. 809/776–8255. Open weekdays 9–5.*

Continue on Crystal Gade one block east and turn left (north) on Garden Street. You'll pass various small restaurants where blackboards hang on the door advertising bullfoot soup, goat water, and peas and rice. You'll find these dim shops cool, their proprietors friendly, and a stop at any one will reward you with a respite from the hills and the sun and provide a taste of authentic island cuisine. Continue north, veering left at the V in the road, about three blocks and you'll see the **All Saints Anglican Church** on your left. This church was built in 1848 from stone quarried on the island. Its thick, arched window frames are lined with the yellow brick that came to the islands as ballast aboard merchant ships. The merchants left the brick on the waterfront when they filled their boats with molasses, sugar, mahogany, and rum for the return voyage. The church was built in celebration of the end of slavery in the Virgin Islands in 1848. *Tel. 809/774–0214. Open Mon.–Sat. 6 AM–3 PM.*

Leaving All Saints church, turn right, and retrace your steps back into town again.

As you walk down Garden Street you'll pass a pink building with blue shutters on your left. Immediately past the building, which houses a shoe store and the Ralph Lauren factory outlet, are a set of steps going up to Government Hill. At the top of the steps is the **① Dominus House,** a yellow-brick building dating to 1854, typical of West Indian architecture of the 19th century. Today it houses Cafe S'Agapo, a Grecian oasis of blue-and-white stripe tablecloths and soft floral-print couches where you can rest over an espresso and pastry or a frozen yogurt. There's a full bar; and soups, salads, sandwiches, and freshly baked loaves of bread to take out are available (the olive bread is exceptional). Next door is the Fiddle Leaf (gourmet dining, open for dinner only), and beyond that is **Hotel 1829.** Its **②** bright coral walls accented with fancy black wrought iron, the Hotel 1829 has a darkly cool and romantic bar and a dining terrace where gourmet food is served, both with an exquisite harbor view framed by tangerine-color bougainvillea.

Keep walking up the hill to the east and you'll find yourself at the **③** foot of the **99 Steps,** a staircase "street" built by the Danes in the 1700s. (If you count the stairs as you go up you'll discover, like thousands before you, that there are more than 99.)

④ Up the steps you'll find another neighborhood, **Queen's Street,** which is even quieter and more removed than Government Hill. The homes are privately owned except for the **Mark St. Thomas Hotel and Res-** **⑤** **taurant** and Blackbeard's Castle. The tower of **Blackbeard's Castle** was built in 1679 and is believed to have been used by the notorious pirate Edward Teach.

Time Out   The castle is now the site of a charming guest house, a good restaurant, and a swimming pool open to lunch customers. Here you can lunch and sit by the pool, taking in the view from the terrace (one of the best spots in the neighborhood for sunset-watching, as well). If you linger here long you may well decide to finish the remainder of your tour another day.

⑥ Go down the steps and continue east to **Government House.** This elegant home was built in 1867 and is the official residence of the governor of the U.S.V.I. The first floor is open to the public. The stair-cases are of native mahogany, as are the plaques hand-lettered in gold with the names of the governors appointed and, since 1970, elected. (Brochures detailing the history of Government House are available, but you may have to search for them. Look behind or under the guest book to the left of the entrance.)

The three murals at the back of the lobby were painted by Pepino Mangravatti in the 1930s as part of the U.S. government's Works Projects Administration (WPA). The murals depict Columbus's landing on St. Croix during his second voyage in 1493; the transfer of the islands from Denmark to the United States in 1917, and a sugar plantation on St. John.

To tour the second floor you will have to be accompanied by the deputy administrator. You can call ahead (tel. 809/774–0001) to make an appointment for a tour, or you can take a chance that the officials will be in. It's worth the extra effort it takes to visit the second floor if for no reason other than the view you'll get from the terrace. Imagine the affairs of state of a colonial time being conducted in the hush of the high-ceiling, chandeliered ballroom. In the reception room are four small paintings by Camille Pissarro, but unfortunately they are hard to appreciate because they are enclosed in frosted-glass cases. More interesting, and visible, is the large painting by an unknown artist that was found in Denmark and depicts a romanticized version of St. Croix; the painting was purchased by former governor Ralph M. Paiewonsky, who then gave it to Government House.

After leaving Government House, head left to Charlotte Amalie's
⑰ newest historical attraction, the **Seven Arches Museum.** This restored West Indian home was built about 1800 and is still a private home. Ring the bell, and you'll be invited inside to see historic furnishings, cannon balls, and gas lamps. Behind the house is a quaint West Indian cottage. *Tel. 809/774–9295. Admission: $5. Open Tues.–Sun. 10–3 or by appointment.*

Head back down the hill past the lieutenant governor's house on
⑱ your left and the entrance to (Franklin D.) **Roosevelt Park.** The small monument on the south side of the park is dedicated to U.S.V.I. war veterans.

As you come out of the park on Norre Gade one block to your left is
⑲ the stone-and-brick **Memorial Moravian Church** built in 1884 and named to commemorate the 150th anniversary of the Moravian Church in the Virgin Islands. *Tel. 809/776–0066. Open weekdays 9–5.*

As you leave the church turn right (west) toward town. You're walking back toward Post Office Square on Norre Gade, which becomes Main Street. In the block before the post office you'll pass the
⑳ **Frederick Lutheran Church,** the second-oldest Lutheran church in the Western Hemisphere. The inside is highlighted by a massive mahogany altar. The pews, each with its own door, were once rented to families of the congregation. Lutheranism is the state religion of Denmark, and, when the territory was without a minister, the governor—who had his own elevated pew—would fill in. *Tel. 809/776–1315. Open Mon.–Sat. 9–4.*

Directly across from the Lutheran Church, through a small side
㉑ street, you'll see **Fort Christian,** St. Thomas's oldest standing structure, built 1672–87, and a U.S. national landmark. The clock tower was added in the 19th century. This remarkable redoubt has, over time, been used as a jail, governor's residence, town hall, court-

house, and church. Its dungeons now house a museum featuring artifacts of U.S.V.I. history. The building is currently undergoing renovation but some rooms are finished and open to the public. *Tel. 809/776–4566. Open weekdays 8:30–4:30; Sat. 9:30–4; Sun. noon–4.*

㉒ Across from the Fort is **Emancipation Garden,** which honors the freeing of slaves in 1848. Today the gazebo's smooth floor is used for official ceremonies, and is a preferred location for break-dancing youngsters.

On the other side of the garden and across the street is the **㉓** **legislature building,** its pastoral-looking lime green exterior concealing the vociferous political wrangling of the Virgin Islands Senate going on inside. Built originally by the Danish as a police barracks, the building was later used to billet U.S. Marines, and much later it housed a public school.

On the north side of the park is the 19th-century Grand Hotel building, which now houses offices and shops. In a large corner shop you'll find souvenirs ranging from seashells and Haitian wood carvings to T-shirts.

Across from the post office are memorials to three famous Virgin Islanders: educator Edith Williams, J. Antonio Jarvis (a founder of the V.I. *Daily News*), and educator and author Rothchild Francis, for whom Market Square is named.

㉔ Stop in the **post office** to contemplate the murals of waterfront scenes by *Saturday Evening Post* artist Stephen Dohanos. His art was commissioned as part of the WPA in the 1930s. Behind the post office, on the waterfront side of Little Switzerland, are the hospitality lounge and **V.I. Visitor's Information Center.**

The waterfront is lined with vendors, mostly selling cheap trinkets like those you'd find anywhere else in the world; but there is some local art outside of the galleries and shops in Palm Passage. Waterfront and Main streets are connected by cobblestone-paved alleys kept cool by overhanging green plants and the thick stone walls of the warehouses on either side. The alleys (particularly Royal Dane Mall and Palm Passage, Main Street between the post office and Market Square, and Bakery Square on Back Street) are where you'll find the unique and glamorous—and duty-free—shops for which Charlotte Amalie is famous (*see* Shopping, *below*).

As you head back along Main Street toward Market Square, you'll pass the Tropicana Perfume Shop, between Store Tvaer Gade and Trompeter Gade. The shop is housed in a building known as the **㉕** **Pissarro Building,** the birthplace of French Impressionist painter Camille Pissarro.

The South Shore and East End *Numbers in the margin correspond to points of interest on the St. Thomas map.*

The rest of our St. Thomas tour is by car. A quick count of cruise ships lined up along the Cruise Ship Dock and at anchor outside the harbor will give you some clue as to the probable traffic ahead—and how rapidly you'll be able to drive out of town. Leaving Charlotte Amalie take Veterans Drive (Route 30) east along the waterfront. You will pass Fort Christian, the legislature building, and other sites on your way out of town. Two points of reference are Bluebeard's Castle, the red-roof resort hotel in the hills, on your left; and, across the harbor on your right, the pink buildings of the Ramada Yacht Haven Hotel and Marina.

Bear to the right at **Nelson Mandela Circle** (Yacht Haven is on your right). You may want to stop at **Havensight Mall,** across from the dock. This shopping center is a less crowded (and less charming) version of the duty-free shopping district along Main Street in town. Havensight Mall is also where you'll find the offices for *Atlantis* Submarine, and the Dockside Book Shop, a bookstore where you'll get stateside prices instead of hotel markups. Or turn left across the street from the shopping center and head straight up the hill to **Paradise Point,** a scenic overlook with breathtaking views of Charlotte Amalie and the harbor; there's also a bar, a restaurant, and several shops.

Route 30 is narrow and winds up and down. It also changes names several times along the way; it is called Frenchman's Bay Road just outside town (sharp left turn at the top of the hill), then becomes Bovoni Road around Bolongo Bay. Whatever it is called, you will be treated to some southerly vistas of the Caribbean Sea (and, on clear days, St. Croix, 40 miles south) as you drive past Marriott's Frenchman's Reef Hotel and its luxurious companion, Marriott's Morningstar Beach Resort. Limetree Beach is next, with its nearly tame iguanas lumbering across the grounds of the Limetree Beach Resort, part of the Bolongo Everything Resort (offer them a hibiscus blossom; the iguanas are vegetarians and are attracted to the color red). Bolongo Beach Bay (more of the Bolongo Everything Resort) is around the next bend; the beach and tennis club are always bustling.

Resorts and restaurants are generally not on the main road but require taking turnoffs from the hillside down to beach level. Any one of them is a good rest stop.

27 A little farther on is **Clinton Phipps Racetrack** (tel. 809/775–4555), in Nadir (pronounced *Nah*dah). Races are held irregularly. Betting is conducted on the sidelines and is not a sanctioned activity—then, of course, neither is the pit-bull or cockfighting (but both are regular Sunday pastimes) held around the corner.

Continuing east (make a right turn at the Esso station), Route 30 becomes Route 32 and then is called Red Hook Road as it passes by **Benner Bay, East End Lagoon,** and **Compass Point.** A turn at the Compass Point sign brings you to For the Birds (Tex-Mex food on the beach), or to Windjammer and Raffles (for nautical ambience and seafood), and Dottie's Front Porch (for native food in a casual setting).

A right onto Route 322 will take you to the entrance to the **Virgin Islands National Park Headquarters.** This park consists of a dock, a small grassy area with picnic tables, and a visitors center in which maps and brochures are available. Just before the entrance to the park, the road branches to the right and heads past the Secret Harbor Beach Resort, the St. Thomas Yacht Club, the Bolongo Elysian Beach Resort, Cowpet Bay Condominiums, and the luxurious Grand Palazzo Hotel.

28 If you stay on Route 32 you'll come into **Red Hook,** where you can catch the ferry to St. John (parking available for $5 a day).

Red Hook has grown from a sleepy little town connected to the rest of the island only by dirt roads (or by boat) to an increasingly self-sustaining village. There's a new collection of small branches of about 20 Charlotte Amalie shops, including Java Wraps and Little Switzerland. There are also a few shops and a deli at American Yacht Harbor, and you can stop in at The Big Chill across the street for a frozen yogurt or croissant sandwich. Or walk along the docks and visit with sailors and fishermen and stop for a beer at Piccola Marina Cafe or the Warehouse bar.

Once you pass the ferry dock the main road swings toward the north shore and becomes Route 38, or Smith Bay Road, taking you past Sapphire Beach, a resort and restaurant with water-sports rentals and a popular snorkeling and windsurfing spot. **Smith Bay** is the next bay heading north and the site of the Sugar Bay Plantation Resort.

Next is the turnoff for Point Pleasant Resort, then you'll pass the lush green landscaping of Stouffer Grand Beach Resort, and finally you'll see a turnoff to the right for Coki Point Beach and Coral World.

The snorkeling is excellent at **Coki,** with reefs at its eastern and western ends. You may want to dash in for a swim or just do some people-watching while nibbling on a meat pâté snack (a fried meat- or conch-filled pie) that you can buy from one of the vendors. Don't leave valuables unattended in your car or on the beach at Coki Point. Instead, after a visit to Coral World next door, use their free lockers and changing rooms to store belongings. Patrons can use them for the day.

㉙ Just down from the beach is the entrance to **Coral World** (tel. 809/ 775–1555), with its three-level underwater observatory (call ahead for shark-feeding times), the world's largest reef tank, and an aquarium with more than 20 TV-size tanks providing capsulized views of life in the waters of the Virgin Islands and around the world. Coral World's staff will answer your questions about the turtles, iguanas, parrots, and flamingos that inhabit the park, and there's a restaurant, souvenir shop, and the world's only underwater mailbox, from which you can send postcards. Be sure to take a ride on the **Seaworld Explorer Semi-submarine,** a boat with underwater glass sides that visits nearby reefs. The 20-minute ($12) and 40-minute ($20) guided tours are a great underwater viewing option for those who tend to be claustrophobic. *Tel. 809/775–1555. Admission: $14 adults, $9 children. Open daily 9–6.*

㉚ Continue west on Route 38 and you'll come to **Tillet's Gardens,** where local artisans craft stained glass, pottery, gold jewelry, and ceramics. Tillet's paintings and silk-screened fabrics are also on display and for sale. The gardens encircle a shaded courtyard with fountains and an outdoor restaurant and espresso bar.

North Shore, Center Islands, and West The north shore is home to many inviting attractions, not to mention much lusher vegetation than is found on the rest of the island (this side of the island receives more rainfall than the Caribbean side). The most direct route from Charlotte Amalie is Mafolie Road (Route 35), which can be picked up east of Government Hill. But don't feel obligated to stay on this route. There are so many options through the mountains, and each unfolds different surprises. Therefore, on this tour we'll describe what there is to see and you can plot your own course.

㉛ In the heights above Charlotte Amalie is **Drake's Seat,** the mountain lookout from which Sir Francis Drake was supposed to have kept watch over his fleet and looked for enemy ships of the Spanish fleet. Magens Bay and Mahogany Run are to the north, with the B.V.I. and Drake's Passage to the east. Off to the left, or west, are Fairchild Park, Mountain Top, Hull Bay, and smaller islands such as the Inner and Outer Brass islands. The panoramic vista is especially breathtaking (and romantic) at dusk, and if you arrive late in the day you'll miss the hordes of day-trippers on taxi tours who stop at Drake's Seat to take a picture and buy a T-shirt from one of the many vendors. By afternoon the crowd thins and most of the vendors are gone.

Continuing east from Drake's Seat you'll come to an intersection, and if you proceed down the hill and follow Route 35 to the end you'll come to **Magens Bay Beach.** The most popular local beach on St. Thomas is often listed among the world's most beautiful beaches, and on weekends and holidays you'll find it hopping with groups partying under the sheds. There's also an outdoor bar, bathhouses, a nature trail, and a snack bar.

㉜ Another northside attraction is the **Mahogany Run Golf Course.** To get to Mahogany Run turn off Route 35 at the sign advertising Magens Point Hotel (Route 42) before you get to Magens Bay Beach. The road you'll be driving on was once bordered by a "run" of centuries-old mahogany trees (before they were cleared to build their namesake). The golf course was designed by Tom Fazio, and has been called one of the most spectacular in the world.

㉝ Heading west from Drake's Seat, stay on Route 40 to reach the **Estate St. Peter Greathouse Botanical Gardens.** Perched on a mountainside 1,000 feet above sea level, with views of more than 20 other islands and islets, is this unusual spot where you can wander through a gallery displaying local art, sip a complimentary rum or virgin punch while looking out at the view, or follow a nature trail that leads through nearly 200 varieties of tropical trees and plants, including an orchid jungle. *Rte. 40, St. Peter Mountain Rd., tel. 809/ 774–4999. Admission free. Open daily 9–5.*

㉞ From Route 40, head to Route 33 and **Mountain Top,** the location of the establishment that claims to have invented the banana daiquiri. Because you are more than 1,500 feet above sea level, there are some spectacular views from the observation deck. There are also a number of shops selling everything from Caribbean art to nautical antiques, ship models, and T-shirts.

㉟ Below Mountain Top is **Fairchild Park,** a gift to the people of the U.S.V.I. from the philanthropist Arthur Fairchild.

Along the road (Route 37) to **Hull Bay,** you may come across the fishing boats and homes of the descendants of settlers from the French West Indies who fled to St. Thomas more than 200 years ago. If you have the opportunity to engage them in conversation, you will hear speech patterns slightly different from those of other St. Thomians. Hull Bay, with its rougher Atlantic surf and relative isolation, is one of the best surfing spots on St. Thomas.

Time Out Follow Hull Bay Road to the beach, and you'll come to **Hull Bay Hideaway,** a rustic beach bar offering camping facilities, albeit severely primitive ones. (Bring lots of insect repellent.) Stop by on a Sunday afternoon and sip a beer while you listen to rock and roll played by the local dentist and his band.

If you head west from Mountain Top, on Crown Mountain Road **㊱** (Route 33) you'll come to **Four Corners.** Take the extreme right turn and drive along the northwestern ridge of the mountain through **Caret Bay, Sorgenfri,** and **Pearl.** There's not much here except peace and quiet, junglelike foliage, and breathtaking vistas. Near Bryan's **㊲** Plants you'll pass the **U.S. Department of Agriculture Inspection Station.** If you buy a plant, be sure to stop here to get the plant's roots sprayed for diseases and to get a certificate to present to U.S. customs when you leave the territory.

From Route 33, pick up Route 301 and then Route 30 and head south to **Brewer's Beach,** popular with the students at the nearby University of the Virgin Islands. Across from Brewer's is the entrance to the **Reichhold Center for the Arts** (tel. 809/774–8475), an amphitheater offering everything from Ray Charles, Robert Merrill, and the Puerto Rican Symphony Orchestra to local beauty pageants.

The road takes you through the university campus to Veterans Highway, which going west leads to the **Cyril E. King International Airport** and Lindbergh Bay Beach, and going east leads back to Frenchtown and Charlotte Amalie.

To wind down your tour, pull into Frenchtown and reward yourself for a long day's travels with a stop at **Epernay,** a Frenchtown wine bar tucked behind Alexander's Cafe. You'll find wines by the glass, hors d'oeuvres, and light meals to linger over while you contemplate life in the islands. *AE, MC, V. Open Mon.–Sat. 4:30 PM–1 AM (often until later Fri. and Sat.). Food served 5 PM–midnight.*

St. Thomas for Free

The views at **Drake's Seat, Paradise Point,** and **Mountain Top** are breathtaking and completely free.

Fort Christian, the 17th-century fort on the east end of Charlotte Amalie at the waterfront, is the oldest standing structure in the Virgin Islands.

What to See and Do With Children

Atlantis Submarine (*see* Guided Tours, *above*) gives children a chance to see dazzling tropical fish, fantastically shaped coral, and, if they're lucky, large sea turtles.

After a tour through **Coral World** (*see* Exploring St. Thomas, *above*), the youngsters will love snorkeling at Coki Beach next door.

If time is not limited, consider a day trip to the **St. John National Park** (*see* St. John, Guided Tours, *below*).

Off the Beaten Track

If you're on St. Thomas at full moon, grab the champagne (and the bug spray) and head for **Sapphire Beach** for the moonrise. The moon rises out of the sea, illuminating the beach in a most romantic light.

Shopping

St. Thomas has always been a commercial center, and the old stone buildings that once stored indigo, rum, and molasses bound for the European market now house perfumes from France, cameras from Japan, clothing from France and Italy, and silks and linens from China, bound to entice cruise-ship passengers on a shore-leave shopping spree.

Most people would agree that St. Thomas lives up to its self-described billing as a shopper's paradise. Even if shopping isn't your idea of paradise you still may want to slip in on a quiet day (check the cruise-ship listings—Monday and Saturday are usually the least crowded) to check out the prices. Among the best buys are liquor, linens, imported china, crystal (most stores ship), and jewelry. The sheer volume of jewelry available makes this one of the few items for which comparison shopping is worth the effort.

Most stores take major credit cards. There is no sales tax in the U.S.V.I., and shoppers can take advantage of the $1,200 duty-free allowance per family member and the additional 10% discount on the next $1,000 worth of goods, but remember to save your receipts.

Although you'll find the occasional salesclerk who'll make a deal, bartering is not the norm here, so don't go into a store expecting to haggle over prices.

★ *Shops listed below that reside in malls and shopping complexes that are off the map will not appear on the map legend with a corresponding bullet.*

Shopping Districts The prime shopping area in **Charlotte Amalie** is between Post Office and Market squares and consists of three parallel streets running east to west (Waterfront, Main Street, and Back Street) and the alleyways connecting them. Particularly attractive are **Royal Dane Mall** and **Palm Passage**, a quaint series of alleys between Main Street and the waterfront, and **Bakery Square** on Back Street.

Vendors Plaza, on the waterfront side of Emancipation Gardens, is a centralized location for outdoor vendors who sell handmade earrings, necklaces, and bracelets; straw baskets and handbags; T-shirts; fabrics; and hot sauces, spices, and local foods.

Havensight Mall, next to the cruise-ship dock, though not as charming as Charlotte Amalie, has parking and more than 50 shops, including an excellent bookstore, a bank, a pharmacy, and smaller branches of many Charlotte Amalie stores.

A Taste of Italy, on Back Street, includes several restaurants, shops, and an art gallery housed in a nicely restored historic building that wraps around a quiet courtyard.

West of town, the pink-stucco **Nisky Center** is more of a hometown shopping center than a tourist area, but there's a good bookstore (next to a bakery and yogurt shop), as well as a bank, gift shops, and clothing stores.

At long last, Red Hook now has a waterfront shopping area that includes smaller branches of a number of Charlotte Amalie stores. Art aficionados should plan their vacation around the annual Art Expo in December, a juried art show open to all Caribbean artists. For more information call Corinne Van Rensselar (tel. 809/775–4020, fax 809/775–2603).

Jim Tillet's Gardens (Estate Tutu, tel. 809/775–1405) is an oasis of artistic endeavor on the highway across from Four Winds Shopping Center. Jim and Rhoda Tillet have nurtured the arts in the Virgin Islands since 1959. Come here and watch craftsmen and artisans produce silk-screen fabrics, pottery, candles, watercolors, gold jewelry, stained glass, and other handcrafts. There's usually something special happening in the gardens, as well: There are art fairs three times a year and three series with evening programs once a month, "Cabaret in the Garden," "Fashion in the Garden," and the "Classics in the Garden" series, which brings classical musicians from around the world to play under the stars.

Don't forget **St. John** (*see* Shopping in St. John, *below*). A ferry ride (an hour from Charlotte Amalie or a half hour from Red Hook) will

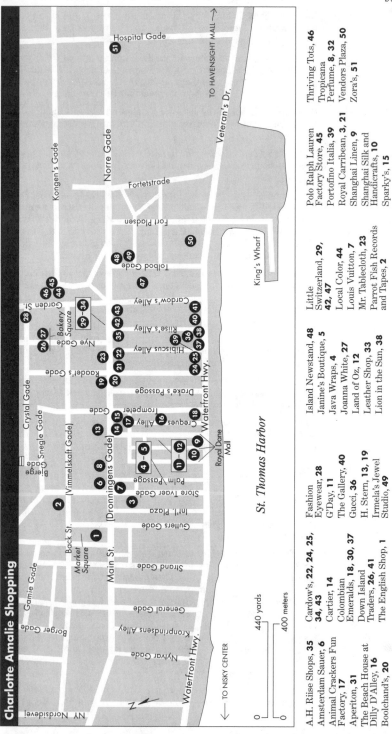

Charlotte Amalie Shopping

St. Thomas Harbor

A.H. Riise Shops, **35**
Amsterdam Sauer, **6**
Animal Crackers Fun Factory, **17**
Aperiton, **31**
The Beach House at Dilly D'Alley, **16**
Boolchand's, **20**

Cardow's, **22, 24, 25, 34, 43**
Cartier, **14**
Colombian Emeralds, **18, 30, 37**
Down Island Traders, **26, 41**
The English Shop, **1**

Fashion Eyewear, **28**
G'Day, **11**
The Gallery, **40**
Gucci, **36**
H. Stern, **13, 19**
Irmela's Jewel Studio, **49**

Island Newstand, **48**
Janine's Boutique, **5**
Java Wraps, **4**
Joanna White, **27**
Land of Oz, **12**
Leather Shop, **33**
Lion in the Sun, **38**

Little Switzerland, **29, 42, 47**
Local Color, **44**
Louis Vuitton, **7**
Mr. Tablecloth, **23**
Parrot Fish Records and Tapes, **2**

Polo Ralph Lauren Factory Store, **45**
Portofino Italia, **39**
Royal Carribean, **3, 21**
Shanghai Linen, **9**
Shanghai Silk and Handicrafts, **10**
Sparky's, **15**

Thriving Tots, **46**
Tropicana Perfume, **8, 32**
Vendors Plaza, **50**
Zora's, **51**

take you to the charming shops of **Mongoose Junction** and **Wharfside Village,** which specialize in unique, often island-made items.

Art Galleries **A.H. Riise Caribbean Print Gallery** (Riise's Alley off Main St., tel. 809/776–2303). Haitian and Virgin Islands art are displayed and sold here, along with art books and the exquisite botanical prints and note cards from Mapes de Monde.

The Gallery (Veteran's Dr., tel. 809/776–4641). Above the waterfront branch of Down Island Traders (and owned by the same people), The Gallery carries Haitian art, along with works by a number of Virgin Islands artists. Items on display include oil paintings, metal sculpture, wood carvings, painted screens and boxes, figures carved from stone, and oversize papier-mâché figures. Prices range from $50 to $5,000.

Joanna White (Palm Passage, tel. 809/774–3098). Ms. White, a popular local artist with an international reputation, has a working studio here. You'll see her distinctive etchings on handmade paper in both public and private establishments all around the island. Prices range from $90 to $900.

Mango Tango (Al Cohen Plaza at Raphune Hill, tel. 809/777–3995) represents a variety of U.S.V.I. artists and some from neighboring islands as well. A framing service is also available.

Books and **Dockside Bookshop** (Havensight Mall, Bldg. IV, tel. 809/774–4937).
Magazines This place is packed with books for children, travelers, cooks, and historians, as well as a good selection of paperback mysteries, bestsellers, art books, calendars, and art prints. There's a selection of books written in and about the Caribbean and the Virgin Islands, from literature to chartering guides to books on seashells and tropical flowers. There's no markup here.

Education Station Books (Nisky Center, tel. 809/776–3008). There is no markup at this full-service bookstore that concentrates on Caribbean literature and Black American and African history. There's also a large cookbook selection, a music section featuring jazz and "world beat" tapes from Africa, and prints by local artists. In addition, you can buy and sell used books of all types here.

Island Newsstand (Grand Hotel in Charlotte Amalie) and **Magazines** (Fort Mylner Shopping Center near Tillet Gardens). These two shops have the largest selection of magazines and newspapers on St. Thomas. Expect to pay about 20% above stateside prices.

Cameras and **Boolchand's** (31 Main St., tel. 809/776–0794; and Havensight Mall,
Electronics tel. 809/776–0302). A variety of brand-name cameras as well as audio and video equipment are featured here.

Royal Caribbean (two locations on Main St., tel. 809/776–4110; and Havensight Mall, tel. 809/776–8890). Shop here for cameras, camcorders, stereos, watches, and clocks.

China and **A.H. Riise Gift Shops** (Main St. and Riise's Alley and Havensight
Crystal Mall, tel. 809/776–2303). A.H. Riise carries Waterford, Wedgwood, Royal Crown, and Royal Doulton at good prices. A five-piece place setting of Royal Crown Derby's Old Imari goes for less than $350.

The English Shop (on the waterfront, tel. 809/776–5399 and Havensight Mall, tel. 809/776–3776). This store offers figurines, cutlery, and china and crystal from major European and Japanese manufacturers. Spode, Limoges, Royal Doulton, Royal Crafton, Royal Worcester, and Villeroy & Boch are featured. You can choose what you like from the catalogs here, and shopkeepers will order and factory ship it for you.

Little Switzerland (three locations on Main St. at Havensight Mall; tel. 809/776–2010). All of this establishment's shops carry crystal from Lalique, Baccarat, Waterford, Riedel, and Orrefors, and china from Villeroy & Boch and Wedgwood, among others. There is also an assortment of cut-crystal animals, china and porcelain figurines, and many other affordable collectibles.

Clothing
For Women **The Beach House at Dilly D'Alley** (Trompeter Gade, tel. 809/776–5006). Downstairs is the place for fancy T-shirts, sundresses, linen pants, and accessories; you'll find a giant selection of the latest swimwear.

G'Day (waterfront at Royal Dane Mall, tel. 809/774–8855). Everything in this tiny shop—from umbrellas to silk scarves to reasonably priced sportswear—is drenched in the bright colors of Australian artist Ken Done.

Janine's Boutique (8A–2 Palm Passage, tel. 809/774–8243). Here you'll find women's and men's dressy and casual apparel from European designers and manufacturers, including the Louis Feraud collection, and select finds from Valentino, Christian Dior, YSL, and Pierre Cardin. Luisa's features Italian designer fashions and leather accessories, including shoes. Luisa's is a favorite of locals and throws a sale every now and then that can garner you a once-in-a-lifetime buy.

Java Wraps (24 Palm Passage, tel. 809/774–3700). Indonesian batik creations are the specialty here—beach cover-ups, swimwear, and leisure wear for women, men, and children.

Lion in the Sun (Riise's Alley, tel. 809/776–4203). One of the best locations for Go Linen, Go Silk, Donna Karan, Sonya Rykiel, Giorgio Armani, and Hugo Boss, sportswear, suits, and dresses. There's a small men's collection. There's always a sales rack where some good deals can be found if you can't afford the rather lofty price tags on these gorgeous creations.

Local Color (Garden St., tel. 809/774–3727). St. Thomas artist Kerry Topper exhibits her colorful island designs on cool cotton T-shirts and casual clothing. Also for sale is wearable art by other local artists, unique jewelry, sundresses, shorts, and shirts in bright prints, and big-brim straw hats dipped in fuchsia, turquoise, and other tropical colors.

For Men **Polo Ralph Lauren Factory Store** (Garden St., tel. 809/774–3806). Selections change frequently here and it's worth checking back for amazing markdowns on men's suits, sportcoats, dress shirts, and more. There's also a women's section (one floor down), but the markdowns aren't usually as remarkable.

Portofino Italia (Hibiscus Alley, Waterfront, tel. 809/777–4020). This classy and extremely expensive store sells Italian clothing for men and women, featuring selections by Armani, Versace, Valentino, and Ferre.

For Children **Thriving Tots Boutique** (Garden St., tel. 809/776–0009). You'll find Caribbean clothing for children (infants to size 16), including locally made shorts sets, and sundresses.

Crafts and
Gifts **The Caribbean Marketplace** (Havensight Mall, Bldg. III, tel. 809/776–5400). This is the place to look for Caribbean handcrafts, including Caribelle batiks from St. Lucia; bikinis from the Cayman Is-

lands; and Sunny Caribee spices, soaps, teas, and coffees from Tortola. Visitors can make an appointment to tour the adjacent fragrance factory (tel. 809/774–2166).

The Cloth Horse (Fort Mylner Shopping Center, tel. 809/774–4761). Here you'll find signed pottery from the Dominican Republic; wicker and rattan furniture and household goods from the island of Hispaniola; and pottery, rugs, and bedspreads from all over the world.

Down Island Traders (Bakery Sq., Veteran's Dr., and Frenchman's Reef, tel. 809/774–3419). These traders deal in hand-painted calabash bowls ($10); finely printed Caribbean note cards; jams, jellies, spices, and herbs; herbal teas made of rum, passion fruit, and mango; high-mountain coffee from Jamaica; and a variety of handcrafts from throughout the Caribbean.

Shipwreckers/Lighthouse Marine (Mountaintop, tel. 809/774–4379). Marine antiquities and fascinating old bottles washed up by the sea are the main draw here.

Food **Gourmet Gallery,** with stores at the Sub Base and at Yacht Haven, has an excellent and reasonably priced wine selection, as well as condiments, cheeses, and specialty ingredients for everything from tacos to curries to chow mein. For fruits and vegetables, go to the **Fruit Bowl,** at Wheatley Center. **Pueblo Supermarket,** at various locations around St. Thomas, has virtually every item you might find in a stateside supermarket, but at higher prices because of the cost of shipping.

Jewelry **A.H. Riise Gift Shops** (Main St. and Riise's Alley and Havensight Mall; tel. 809/776–2303). St. Thomas's oldest and largest shop for luxury items, with jewelry, pearls, ceramics, china, crystal, flatwear, perfumes, and watches.

Amsterdam Sauer (14 Main St., tel. 809/774–2222). Many fine one-of-a-kind designs are displayed and available for sale here.

Aperiton (3A Main St., tel. 809/776–0780). A good spot for lovely jewelry made by Greek and Italian designers.

Cardow's (three stores on Main St., tel. 809/776–1140; two on the waterfront, one at Frenchman's Reef Hotel, three at Havensight, tel. 809/776–1140). Cardow's offers an enormous "chain bar" more than 100 feet long, where you're guaranteed 30%–50% savings off U.S. retail prices or your money will be refunded (within 30 days of purchase.)

Cartier (30 Trompeter Gade, tel. 809/774–1590). In addition to the fantastically beautiful and fantastically priced items, there are a surprising number of affordable ones as well, including Cartier silk scarves, which are cheaper than Hermés, and quite lush.

Colombian Emeralds (one on Main St., two on the waterfront, and one at Havensight Mall; tel. 809/774–0581). Well known in the Caribbean, this store offers set and unset gems of every description, including high-quality emeralds.

H. Stern (two on Main St., Havensight Mall, Frenchman's Reef, Stouffer Grand Beach Resort, and Bluebeard's; tel. 809/776–1939). One of the most respected names in gems.

Irmela's Jewel Studio (Tolbod Gade, tel. 809/774–5875). For 22 years Irmela has been offering some of the Caribbean's most exquisite jewelry designs inside the historic stone walls of the Grand Hotel.

She will design or create any custom piece of jewelry, and specializes in unusual gems and pearls.

Little Switzerland (three locations on Main St. and at Havensight Mall; tel. 809/776–2010). The sole U.S.V.I. distributor for Rolex watches, the store also does a booming mail-order business; ask for a catalogue.

Leather Goods   **Gucci** (Riise's Alley off Main St., tel. 809/774–7841 and at Havensight Mall, tel. 809/774–4090). Traditional Gucci-insignia designs for men and women are offered here: wallets, bags, briefcases, totes, walking shoes, and loafers.

The Leather Shop (Main St., tel. 809/776–3995; and Havensight Mall, Bldg. II, tel. 809/776–0040). You'll find mostly big names at big prices here (Fendi and Bottega Veneta are prevalent), but there are also some reasonably priced, high quality purses, wallets, and briefcases.

Louis Vuitton (24 Main St. at Palm Passage, tel. 809/774–3633). Here is an example of St. Thomas shopping at its most elegant. From scarves and umbrellas to briefcases and steamer trunks, all Vuitton workmanship is the finest.

Traveler's Haven (Havensight Mall, tel. 809/775–1798). This store features leather bags, backpacks, vests, and money belts.

Zora's (Norre Gade across from Roosevelt Park, tel. 809/774–2559). Fine leather sandals made to order are the specialty here, as well as a selection of made-only-in-the-Virgin-Islands backpacks, briefcases, and "fish" purses in durable, brightly colored canvas.

Linens   **Mr. Tablecloth** (Main St., tel. 809/774–4343). The friendly staff here will help you choose from their floor-to-ceiling array of linens, from Tuscany lace tablecloths to Irish linen pillowcases. You'll be pleasantly amazed at the prices.

Shanghai Silk and Handicrafts (Royal Dane Mall, tel. 809/776–8118) and **Shanghai Linen** (Waterfront, tel. 809/776–2828). These two stores do a brisk trade in linens and silks. The silk scarves, less than $15, make distinctive, packable gifts.

Liquor and Wine   **A.H. Riise Liquors** (Main St. and Riise's Alley and Havensight Mall; tel. 809/774–6900). This Riise venture offers a large selection of liquors, cordials, wines, and tobacco, including rare vintage cognacs, Armagnacs, ports, and Madeiras. They also stock imported cigars, fruits in brandy, and barware from England.

Al Cohen's Discount Liquor (across from Havensight Mall, Long Bay Rd., tel. 809/774–3690). A warehouse-style store with a large wine department.

Gourmet Gallery (Crown Bay Marina, tel. 809/776–8555; Yacht Haven Marina, tel. 809/774–5555). This aromatic grocery store (there's a bakery in the back) caters to the yachting crowd by offering one of the best wine selections on St. Thomas.

Music   **Modern Music** (across from Havensight Mall, tel. 809/774–3100). This place has the latest stateside and Caribbean CD and cassette releases, plus oldies, classical, and New Age music.

Parrot Fish Records and Tapes (Back St., tel. 809/776–4514). A stock of standard stateside tapes and compact discs, plus a good selection of Caribbean artists, including local groups can be found here. For a catalogue of calypso, soca, steel band, and reggae music, write to Parrot Fish, Box 9206, St. Thomas 00801.

Perfumes Where you buy perfume hardly matters, because prices are about the same in all stores.

Sparky's (Main St., tel. 809/776–7510). Recently spiffed up to match its neighbor, Cartier, Sparky's now has a wide range of perfumes and cosmetics. The impeccably turned-out salesclerks can also give you a facial and makeup lesson.

Tropicana Perfume Shoppes (2 Main St., tel. 809/774–0010; and 14 Main St., tel. 809/774–1834). Tropicana has the largest selection of fragrances for men and women in all of the Virgin Islands.

Sunglasses **Fashion Eyewear** (Garden St., tel. 809/776–9075). Tucked into a tiny building is this even tinier shop that sells sunglasses ranging from $40 to $450.

Toys **Animal Crackers Fun Factory** (Inside Sparky's, off Royal Dane Mall, tel. 809/774–4939). This place is a must-visit, whether the children are with you or back home anticipating their gifts. It's a playland jungle aswarm with parrots and pirates, teddy bears and penguins, and they all seem to be doing something—whistling, singing, talking, or walking.

Land of Oz (Royal Dane Mall, tel. 809/776–7888). This Oz has a huge selection of toys fashioned by European craftsmen that includes Royal Doulton collector dolls, Brio wood trains, German nutcrackers, and English wood sailboats.

Sports and Outdoor Activities

Fishing In the past quarter-century, some 20 world records, many for blue marlin, have been set in the waters surrounding the Virgin Islands, most notably at St. Thomas's famed North Drop. To book a boat, call **St. Thomas Sportfishing Center** (tel. 809/775–7990) or **American Yacht Harbor** (tel. 809/775–6454), or to find a trip that will best suit you, walk down the docks at either Red Hook marina and chat with the captains as they come in from fishing.

Golf Scenic **Mahogany Run** (tel. 809/775–5000), with a par-70, 18-hole course and a view of the B.V.I., lies to the north of Charlotte Amalie and has the especially tricky "Devil's Triangle" trio of holes.

Hiking **Point Pleasant Resort** (tel. 809/775–7200) offers a free self-guided nature walk. Stop by the front desk for the map and brochure. There's an ecowalk at **Magens Bay.**

Parasailing Parasailers sit in a harness attached to a parachute that lifts off from the boat deck until they're sailing high in the air. **Caribbean Watersports** (tel. 809/775–4206) operates out of five locations.

Sailing *See* Sailing in the Virgin Islands, Chapter 4.

Snorkeling/ See Diving and Snorkeling in the Virgin Islands, Chapter 3, for in-
Diving formation.

Tennis Just because you're staying in a guest house without courts doesn't mean you can't indulge in a set or two. Most hotels rent time to nonguests. For reservations call **Bluebeard's Castle Hotel** (tel. 809/774–1600, ext. 195 or 196), **Bolongo Bay** (tel. 809/775–1800, ext. 486), **Grand Palazzo** (tel. 809/775–3333), **Limetree Tennis Center** (tel. 809/774–8990), **Mahogany Run Tennis Club** (tel. 809/775–5000), **Sapphire Beach Resort** (tel. 809/775–6100), **Stouffer Grand Beach Resort** (tel. 809/775–1510), or **Sugar Bay** (tel. 809/777–7200). All of the above courts have lights and are open into the evening. **Frenchman's Reef Tennis Courts** (tel. 809/776–8500) has four courts for the use of guests only. There are two public courts at **Sub Base** (next to the Water and Power Authority), open on a first-come, first-served basis. The lights are on here until 8 PM.

Beaches

All beaches on St. Thomas are open to the public, but often you will have to walk through a resort to reach them. You'll find that resort guests will often have access to lounge chairs and floats that are off limits to nonguests; for this reason, you may feel more comfortable at one of the beaches not associated with a resort, such as Magens or Coki. Whichever one you choose, remember to remove your valuables from the car.

Coki Beach, next to Coral World, is a popular snorkeling spot for cruise ship passengers; it's common to find a group of them among the reefs on the east and west ends of the beach. If you are visiting Coral World you can use the lockers and changing rooms.

Magens Bay is usually lively because of its spectacular loop of white sand, more than a half-mile long, and its calm waters that are protected by two peninsulas. The bottom is flat and sandy, so this is a place for sunning and swimming rather than snorkeling. Food, changing facilities, and rest rooms are available.

The condo resort at **Secret Harbour** doesn't at all detract from the attractiveness of this covelike East End beach. Not only is it pretty, it is also superb for snorkeling—go out to the left, near the rocks.

At **Morningstar Beach,** close to Charlotte Amalie, many young residents show up for body surfing or volleyball. The pretty curve of beach fronts the Morningstar section of Marriott's Frenchman's Reef Hotel. Snorkeling is good near the rocks when the current doesn't affect visibility.

From **Sapphire Beach** there is a fine view of St. John and other islands. Snorkeling is excellent at the reef to the right or east, near Pettyklip Point. All kinds of water-sports gear are for rent from Sapphire Beach Resort.

The beach at **Hull Bay,** on the north shore, faces Inner and Outer Brass cays and attracts fishermen and beachcombers. It's open to rough Atlantic waves, making it the only place to surf on the island.

Dining

Dining on St. Thomas is relaxed and informal. Very few restaurants on the island demand a jacket and tie. Still, at dinner in the snazzier restaurants, shorts and T-shirts are highly inappropriate, and you would do well to wear slacks and a shirt with buttons. Dress codes on St. Thomas almost never call for women to wear skirts. The fancier restaurants on St. Thomas advise or require that you make reservations; at the restaurants reviewed below, reservations are not necessary unless otherwise mentioned.

If you're craving fries and a shake, you won't have to search too long or hard. **Arby's** on the waterfront has a new twist—a bar with a harbor view. **Burger King** and **Kentucky Fried Chicken** (one of four on St. Thomas) are also on the waterfront. There's a **McDonald's** at Wheatley Center, and **Pizza Huts,** on the waterfront, at Wheatley Center, and at Four Winds Plaza.

In addition to the restaurants reviewed below, hotel restaurants are mentioned in Lodging, *below.*

Charlotte **Blackbeard's Castle.** This romantic hillside restaurant is one of St.
Amalie Thomas's best. Enjoy a spectacular view of Charlotte Amalie and
★ the harbor as you dine alfresco on such gourmet delights as veal
chops stuffed with fresh vegetables, black forest ham, and mozzarella; grilled swordfish with tropical salsa; or fettuccine with grilled
chicken, sun-dried tomatoes, and feta cheese. Lunch offerings include excellent soups, sandwiches, and several pasta dishes. The à la
carte Sunday brunch is immensely popular. *Blackbeard's Castle,
tel. 809/776–1234. Reservations required. AE, MC, V. $$$$*

Entre Nous. The view here, from the terrace of Bluebeard's Castle
high over Charlotte Amalie's harbor, is as exhilarating as the dining
is elegant. While deciding between such main dinner courses as rack
of lamb, Caribbean lobster, veal, and chateaubriand you can watch
the light-bedecked cruise ships pull slowly out of the harbor.
*Bluebeard's Castle, tel. 809/776–4050. Reservations required. AE,
MC, V. No lunch. $$$$*

Fiddle Leaf. This longtime favorite on Government Hill has tables
open to the breezes and the sparkling lights of St. Thomas at night.
Specialties include sautéed shrimp West Indian style, grilled yellowfin tuna on a garlicky bed of spinach and roasted sweet peppers,
and rack of lamb roasted with a pecan crust. *Government Hill, near
Main St., tel. 809/775–2810. Reservations advised. AE, MC, V. No
lunch. Closed Sun. $$$$*

★ **Hotel 1829.** You'll dine by candlelight flickering over stone walls and
pink table linens at this restaurant on the terrace of the hotel. The
menu and wine list are extensive, from Caribbean rock lobster to
rack of lamb. Many items, including a warm spinach salad, are prepared tableside; and the restaurant is justly famous for its dessert
soufflés, made of chocolate, Grand Marnier, raspberry, or coconut,
to name a few. *Government Hill, near Main St., tel. 809/776–1829.
Reservations required. AE, MC, V. No lunch. $$$$*

Il Cardinale. Tucked into the second floor of a restored historic
building, this fine, candlelit Italian restaurant serves such specialties as eggplant wrapped around pine nuts, ricotta, and raisins;
penne with radicchio in a brandy, cream, and parmesan sauce; and
veal in a tomato, caper, and oregano sauce. The menu also offers a
wide choice of pastas as well as chicken and steak dishes, and the
wine list is extensive. *Taste Of Italy, 4–5 Back St., tel. 809/775–
1090. Reservations advised. AE, MC, V. $$$$*

★ **Virgilio's.** For the best northern Italian cuisine on the island, don't
miss this intimate, elegant hideaway. Eclectic art covers the two-
story-high brick walls. Come here for superb minestrone, perfectly
cooked capellini with fresh tomatoes and garlic, Spaghetti Peasant
Style (a rich tomato sauce with mushrooms and prosciutto), exquisite fresh fish, veal, and chicken dishes, and a host of daily specials.
Maître d' Alfredo is on hand day and night, welcoming customers
and helping the gracious staff. Don't leave without having a
Virgilio's cappuccino, a chocolate-and-coffee drink so rich it's dessert. *Back St., tel. 809/776–4920. Reservations advised. AE, MC,
V. Closed Sun. $$$$*

★ **Cafe Amici.** Striped umbrellas and a marble bar set the mood at this
outdoor café under the palms in Riise's Alley. You pay a premium for
the lunch served here, but the combination of the surroundings and
the food (fresh-baked bread, homemade cannelloni, hearty sandwiches, and a selection of salads) make it a good value. *Riise's Alley,
tel. 809/774–3719. AE, MC, V. No dinner. $$–$$$*

The Greenhouse Bar and Restaurant. Watch the waterfront wake up
at this large and bustling open-air restaurant, whose wait staff looks
like a bunch of all-American college kids on spring break. Breakfast
and lunch (good burgers, salads, and sandwiches) are good values,

and there are dinner specials (lobster, prime rib) nightly. You can work it all off dancing to the band that plays until the crowd clears. *Waterfront, tel. 809/774–7998. AE, DC, MC, V. $$–$$$*

★ **Little Bopeep.** Inside this unpretentious restaurant tucked behind the shops of Main Street is some of the best West Indian food on the island. Try the curried chicken, conch in Creole sauce, sweet potato stuffing, and fried plantains. *Back St., tel. 809/776–9292. AE, MC, V. $$*

Zorba's Cafe. Tired of shopping? Summon up one last ounce of energy and head up Government Hill to Zorba's. Sit and have a cold, cold beer or bracing iced tea in the 19th-century stone-paved courtyard surrounded by banana trees. Greek salads and appetizers, moussaka, and an excellent vegetarian plate top the menu. *Government Hill, tel. 809/776–0444. AE, MC, V. $$*

Hard Rock Café. A hot spot from the day it opened, this waterfront restaurant is pretty much like its namesakes around the world. Rock and roll memorabilia abounds, and the menu offers hamburgers, sandwiches, salads, and great desserts. Doors are open from 11 AM until 2 AM; there's always a wait for a table during prime meal times. *International Plaza on the Waterfront, tel. 809/775–5555. AE, MC, V. $–$$*

I Cappuccini. In the lower courtyard of A Taste of Italy shopping area, this quiet indoor-outdoor café serves a variety of sandwiches (including an excellent Italian ham sandwich) and pasta dishes. *A Taste of Italy. 4–5 Back St., tel. 809/775–1090. AE, MC, V. No dinner. $–$$*

Gladys' Cafe. Even if the food and prices didn't make this a recommended café, it would be worth going to for Gladys' smile. Try the Caribbean lobster roll. *Main St., tel. 809/774–6604. AE. No dinner. $*

East End **Romanos.** Inside this huge old stucco house in Smith Bay is a de-
★ lightful surprise: a spare, elegant setting and superb northern Italian cuisine. Owner Tony hasn't advertised since the restaurant opened five years ago, and it is always packed. Try the pastas, either with a classic sauce or one of Tony's unique creations, such as a cream sauce with mushrooms, prosciutto, pine nuts, and Parmesan. *97 Smith Bay, tel. 809/775–0045. Reservations advised. AE, MC, V. Closed Sun. $$$$*

Agave Terrace. Seafood is the specialty at this dimly lit, open-air pavilion restaurant; the catch of the day is listed on the blackboard nightly. Come early and have a drink at the Lookout Lounge, which has breathtaking views of the British Virgins; bartender Desmond has been here for 10 years. Its food enjoys almost as good a reputation as its view. The catch of the day prepared in half a dozen styles is the specialty. *Point Pleasant Resort at Smith Bay, tel. 809/775–4142. Reservations advised. AE, MC, V. Dinner only. $$$–$$$$*

Raffles. The ambience at this old-time local favorite serving Continental cuisine is exactly what you'd expect from a tropical island watering hole. Its rattan-and-dark-wood interior is elegant but not stuffy. *Compass Point, tel. 809/775–6004. Reservations advised. AE, MC, V. No lunch. $$$–$$$$*

Seagrape. This hotel-restaurant has an all-star location right on Sapphire Beach. The ocean laps gently at the shore, not far from your table. The menu is basically American, with a variety of steak and chicken dishes and fresh local fish. The food is well prepared, the setting is lovely, and staff is attentive and friendly. Some nights a band plays at the adjoining outdoor cocktail lounge. *Sapphire Beach Resort and Marina, tel. 809/775–6100. Reservations advised. AE, MC, V. $$$–$$$$*

Piccola Marina Cafe. Dockside dining at its friendliest is the trademark of this open-air restaurant close to the St. John ferry dock at Red Hook. The clientele is a mix of sailors and fishermen who work on the docks, and fresh fish and homemade pastas are presented as the specialties. The food is so-so, but the atmosphere delightful. New this year is a wood-burning oven that turns out pizzas that are nice and crispy. *Red Hook, tel. 809/775–6350. Reservations advised. AE, MC, V. $$$*

★ **East Coast Bar and Grill.** Three San Francisco boys came to the islands on vacation 10 years ago, bought a bar in Frenchtown, and now in their second location are on their way to becoming something of a restaurant legend. The menu is consistently good, and features fresh fish, burgers, chicken wings, and prime rib. You'll even enjoy the pace and being part of the hustle and bustle that keeps this place hopping seven nights a week. Reservations are not accepted, so you can expect a wait at the friendly bar. *Red Hook, tel. 809/775–1919. No reservations. AE, MC, V. No lunch. $$–$$$*

For the Birds. About a half dozen feet from the surf, this mostly Mexican restaurant serves up sizzling fajitas, barbecued baby-back ribs, seafood, and steak in a casual atmosphere. About 10:30 the fun shifts to the bar, pool tables, and disco floor. *Scott Beach, near Compass Point, tel. 809/775–6431. Reservations required for 6 or more. AE, MC, V. $$–$$$*

Eunice's Terrace. This excellent West Indian cook is justly famous. Her roomy, two-story restaurant has a bar and a menu of native dishes, including callaloo (a West Indian soup), conch fritters, fried fish, local sweet potato, fungi, and green banana. *Rte. 38, near Stouffer's Grand Beach Resort and Coral World, Smith Bay, tel. 809/775–3975. AE, MC, V. $–$$*

Frenchtown **Sugar Reef Cafe.** This café at the water's edge is the brainchild of three chefs who got their training at the elegant Hotel 1829 in Charlotte Amalie. The menu is eclectic/American, with seafood, soufflés, and homemade ice cream among the specialties. The blue-and-white-striped ceiling and vibrant, tropical fabrics contribute to the cheerful dining experience. *Sub Base, tel. 809/776–4466. Reservations advised. AE, MC, V. No lunch weekends. $$$*

★ **Alexander's Cafe.** This charming restaurant is a favorite with the people in the restaurant business on St. Thomas—always a sign of quality. Local media types, wine aficionados (the always-changing wine list offers the best value on the island), and people just out to relax pack this place seven nights a week. Alexander is Austrian, and the schnitzels are delicious and reasonably priced; pasta specials are fresh and tasty. Save room for strudel. Next door is **Alexander's Bar & Grill,** serving food from the same kitchen but in a more casual setting (and at slightly lower prices). *24A Honduras, tel. 809/ 776–4211. Reservations advised. AE, MC, V. $$–$$$*

The Chart House. In an old great house on the tip of the Frenchtown peninsula, this restaurant offers superb views and kebab and teriyaki dishes, lobster, Hawaiian chicken, and a large salad bar. *Villa Olga, Frenchtown, tel. 809/774–4262. Reservations accepted for 10 or more. AE, DC, MC, V. $$–$$$*

Victor's New Hide-Out. This landmark restaurant is a little hard to find, but the search is worth it. Native food—steamed fish, marinated pork chops, and local lobster—and native music are offered in a casual, friendly, West Indian atmosphere. *Sub Base, tel. 809/776– 9379. No credit cards. $–$$*

Northside **Ferrari's.** St. Thomas residents have consistently voted this the ★ "best value" restaurant in the *U.S.V.I. Daily News* poll. The menu features such traditional Italian staples as antipasto, clams oreganato, lasagna, manicotti, pizzas, and garlic bread. Pizzas, sandwiches, and salads are served at the bar from 4:30 until 11. *Crown Mountain Rd., tel. 809/774–6800. Reservations advised. AE, MC, V. No lunch. $$–$$$*

Bryan's Bar and Restaurant. High on the cool north side of the island, overlooking Hull Bay, this surfer's bar offers grilled fish, steaks, and a great teriyaki-chicken sandwich. A local hangout complete with pool table, it's casual and cheap. *Hull Bay, tel. 809/774–3522. No credit cards. $–$$$*

Sib's Mountain Bar and Restaurant. Here you'll find country music, football, burgers, barbecued ribs and chicken, and beers. This friendly two-fisted drinking bar, with a restaurant on the back porch, is a good place for a casual dinner after a day at the beach. *Mafolie Hill, tel. 809/774–8967. AE, MC, V. $–$$*

Lodging

St. Thomas has the most rooms and the widest variety of accommodations in the U.S.V.I. You'll find everything here, from the most spartan motel room to lavish resorts that cater to your every need. In between there are hotels and inns to match just about every taste and price range.

If your visit to St. Thomas is a special occasion, or you've got money to burn, there are world-class luxury resorts that will pamper you, albeit at a price of $300 to $500 a night, not including meals.

Those guests with more modest means will still find a tremendous variety from which to choose. Quite a number of fine hotels (many with rooms that feature kitchens and a living room area) are scattered around the island in lovely settings, and there are several charming guest houses and inns providing great views (if not always a beach at your door) and great service at about half the cost of the super-luxe beachfront pleasure palaces. A good number of the inns and guest houses are in the hills above the historic district of Charlotte Amalie and are a good choice if you like to get out and mingle in the local scene.

There are also inexpensive lodgings, if you're here on the cheap and just want a clean room to come back to after a day of exploring or beach-bumming. Most of the less expensive accommodations are right in town.

Families often choose to stay at one of the East End's condominium complexes which offer full kitchens but have daily maid service, on-site restaurants, and many resort amenities. The East End area is convenient to St. John, is home to the boating crowd, and has a fair number of fine restaurants within easy walking distance. Most of the condo complexes have swimming pools and tennis courts.

Although the condos are pricey (winter rates average $240 per night for a two-bedroom condominium, which will usually sleep six), so is the price of restaurant dining on St. Thomas, so you may come out about even if you cook your own meals. If you're staying in a condominium and plan to cook, you may consider bringing some nonperishable foodstuffs with you. Because of shipping costs (virtually everything is imported), U.S.V.I. food prices are usually as high or higher than those in the most expensive mainland U.S. cities.

Hotels and Inns
Charlotte Amalie
Emerald Beach Resort. Edged up next to the Island Beachcomber Hotel on Lindbergh Beach just across from the airport, this mini-resort has the feel of its much larger cousins on the East End. Each air-conditioned room in the two pink-stucco, three-story buildings

has its own terrace or balcony, palms, and colorful flowers that frame a view of the ocean. The rooms are decorated in modern tropical prints and rattan. A plus: The resort is popular with businesspeople so the pool and beach are rarely crowded. A minus: the noise from nearby jets taking off and landing, intermittently over a three-hour period each afternoon. *Box 340, 00804, tel. 809/777–8800 or 800/233–4936, fax 809/776–3426. 90 rooms. Facilities: pool, beach, restaurant, water sports. AE, D, MC, V. $$$$*

★ **Blackbeard's Castle.** This small and very popular hillside inn is laid out around a tower from which, it's said, Blackbeard kept watch for invaders on the horizon. It's an elegantly informal kind of place, where guests while away Sunday morning with the *New York Times*. Stunning views (especially at sunset) of the harbor and Charlotte Amalie can be had from the gourmet restaurant (*see* Dining, *above*), the large freshwater pool, and the outdoor terrace, where locals come for cocktails. Charlotte Amalie is a short walk down the hill and beaches are a short taxi ride away. Rates include complimentary continental breakfast. *Box 6041, 00801, tel. 809/776–1234, fax 809/776–4321. 20 rooms. Facilities: restaurant, bar, freshwater pool. AE, DC, MC, V. $$$*

Bluebeard's Castle. Though not exactly a castle, this large red-roof complex offers kingly modern comforts on a steep hill overlooking the town, which from Bluebeard's glistens at night like a Christmas tree. All rooms are air-conditioned and all have terraces. The hotel is a short taxi ride away from the shops of Charlotte Amalie and Havensight Mall. The hotel offers free transportation to Magens Bay Beach. *Box 7480, 00801, tel. 809/774–1600 or 800/524–6599, fax 809/774–5134. 170 rooms. Facilities: 2 restaurants, bar, pool, 2 tennis courts. AE, DC, MC, V. $$$*

Island Beachcomber Hotel. This hotel is near the airport (just east of the Emerald Beach Resort) but is enclosed by a fence and landscaping so that, once inside, you are not aware of the airport—until a plane takes off. However, the hotel is also right on Lindbergh Beach, and the low rates reflect its otherwise less-than-ideal location. *Box 2579, 00803, tel. 809/774–5250 or 800/982–9898, fax 809/774–5616. 48 rooms. Facilities: restaurant, beach, water sports. AE, DC, MC, V. $$–$$$*

Ramada Yacht Haven Hotel & Marina. This pink St. Thomas landmark anchoring the outer edge of Charlotte Amalie is part of sprawling Yacht Haven Marina. It is a lively spot, with a variety of shops and several restaurants and bars. Rooms are so-so (many need refurbishing), but those facing the water in the high-rise building overlook the ever-changing vista of marina, cruise ship dock, and harbor. *4 Lions Bay Rd., 00802, tel. 809/774–9700 or 800/228–9898, fax 809/776–3410. 151 rooms. Facilities: 2 restaurants, 1 bar, 2 freshwater pools. AE, DC, MC, V. $$–$$$*

Villa Blanca Hotel. Above Charlotte Amalie on Raphune Hill, is this hotel, surrounded by an attractive garden and with modern, balconied rooms with rattan furniture, kitchenettes, cable TVs, and ceiling fans. The eastern rooms face the Charlotte Amalie harbor; the western ones look out on rolling hills and a partial view of Drake's Channel and the B.V.I. *Box 7505, 00801, tel. 809/776–0749 or 800/231–0034, fax 809/779–2661. 12 rooms. Facilities: pool. AE, MC, V. $$–$$$*

Heritage Manor. The four rooms in the main structure of this vintage 1830s European-style guest house have gleaming tiles, brass beds, and 12-foot ceilings with expansive windows. These rooms, along with the other four that cluster around a tiny gem of a pool and a courtyard, are all decorated with city-theme prints (the "Tokyo Room" is coziness incarnate). Suites have refrigerators, and two rooms have kitchens. Although the hotel itself is lovely, guests should be cautious about wandering around the area after dark. At night, always take a taxi to and from the hotel. This is a place for those as interested in history as in the beach. Continental breakfast is complimentary during the winter season. *1A Snegle Gade, Box 90, 00804, tel. 809/774–3003 or 800/828–0757. 8 air-conditioned rooms, 4 with bath (another 4 rooms share 2 baths). Facilities: pool. AE, MC, V. $–$$*

★ **Hotel 1829.** This historic Spanish-style inn is popular with visiting government officials and people with business at Government House down the street. It's on Government Hill just at the edge of Charlotte Amalie's shopping area. Rooms, on several levels (no stairs), range from elegant and roomy to quite small but are priced accordingly, so there's one for every budget. It is said author Graham Greene stayed here, and it's easy to imagine him musing over a drink in the small, dark bar. The gourmet terrace restaurant (*see* Dining, *above*) is a romantic spot for dinner. The rooms have a wet bar, TV, and air-conditioning. There's a tiny, tiny pool for cooling off. *Box 1567, 00801, tel. 809/776–1828 or 800/524–2002, fax 809/776–4313. 15 rooms. Facilities: restaurant, pool. AE, DC, MC, V. $–$$*

Island View Guest House. This clean, simply furnished guest house rests amid tropical foliage on the south face of 1,500-foot Crown Mountain, the highest point on St. Thomas. As a result it has one of the most sweeping views of Charlotte Amalie harbor available from its pool and shaded terrace, where complimentary breakfast is served. All rooms have some view, but on the balconies of the six newer rooms (all with air-conditioning and a ceiling fan), perched on the very edge of the hill, you feel suspended in midair. *Box 1903, 00801, tel. 809/774–4270 or 800/524–2023, fax 809/774–6167. 14 rooms, 12 with private bath; 2 with shared bath; 3 have kitchenettes. Facilities: pool. AE, MC, V. $*

East End **Bolongo Elysian Beach Resort.** At this East End property, coral-color villas are stepped down the hillside to the edge of Cowpet Bay. Rooms are decorated in muted tropical floral prints. Activity is centered on a kidney-shape pool complete with waterfall and thatched-roof pool bar. The Palm Court restaurant has gained a strong local following, a sure sign of success. All rooms have air-conditioning, terraces, ceiling fans, cable TV, telephone, and honor bar, and some have kitchenettes. There's shuttle service to Bolongo Club Everything. *Box 51, Red Hook, 00802, tel. 809/775–1000 or 800/343–4079, fax 809/779–2400. 175 rooms. Facilities: 3 restaurants, 2 bars, freshwater pool, lighted tennis court. AE, MC, V. $$$$*

★ **Grand Palazzo.** The main building of this premier luxury resort resembles a villa in Venice and offers stunning ocean views through the lobby's French doors. Guest rooms, in six buildings that fan out from the main villa, are spacious and luxuriously furnished with European fabrics—they just might tempt you to stay inside. When you do venture out, you'll find elegance everywhere, from the beautiful pool to the gourmet restaurant and the casual alfresco lunch area. A multilingual staff, classical music, and 24-hour room service enhance the sophisticated atmosphere. Although a European tone of reserve and elegance abides in this resort, the accompanying superb service is still developing. *Great Bay, 00802, tel. 809/775–3333 or 800/283–8666, fax 809/775–4444. 150 rooms. Facilities: 2 restaurants, 3 bars, health club, pool, beach, tennis courts, water sports. AE, D, DC, MC, V. $$$$*

★ **Pavilions & Pools.** Simple, tropical-cool decor and privacy set the mood here, where each island-style room has its own very private 20-by-14-foot or 18-by-16-foot pool and a small sunning deck. The

So, you're getting away from it all.

Just make sure you can get back.

AT&T Access Numbers
Dial the number of the country you're in to reach AT&T.

ANGUILLA	1-800-872-2881	**COLOMBIA**	**980-11-0010**	JAMAICA††	0-800-872-2881
ANTIGUA (Public Card Phones)	#1	*COSTA RICA	114	MEXICO◊◊◊	95-800-462-4240
ARGENTINA♦	001-800-200-1111	**CURACAO**	**001-800-872-2881**	MONTSERRAT†	1-800-872-2881
BAHAMAS	**1-800-872-2881**	DOMINICA	1-800-872-2881	**NICARAGUA**	**174**
BELIZE♦	555	DOMINICAN REP.††	1-800-872-2881	PANAMA	109
BERMUDA†	1-800-872-2881	ECUADOR†	119	PARAGUAY†	0081-800
*BOLIVIA	0-800-1112	*EL SALVADOR	190	PERU†	191
BONAIRE	**001-800-872-2881**	GRENADA†	1-800-872-2881	ST. KITTS/NEVIS	1-800-872-2881
BRAZIL	**000-8010**	*GUATEMALA	190	**ST. MAARTEN**	**001-800-872-2881**
BRITISH V.I.	1-800-872-2881	***GUYANA††**	**165**	**SURINAME**	**156**
CAYMAN ISLANDS	1-800-872-2881	HAITI†	001-800-972-2883	URUGUAY	00-0410
CHILE	**00◊-0312**	HONDURAS†	123	*VENEZUELA	80-011-120

Countries in bold face permit country-to-country calling in addition to calls to the U.S. **World Connect℠** prices consist of **USADirect®** rates plus an additional charge based on the country you are calling. Collect calling available to the U.S. only. *Public phones require deposit of coin or phone card. †May not be available from every phone. ††Collect calling only. ♦Not available from public phones. ◊Await second dial tone. ◊◊◊When calling from public phones, use phones marked "Ladatel." ©1994 AT&T

Here's a travel tip that will make it easy to call back to the States. Dial the access number for the country you're visiting and connect right to AT&T. It's the quick way to get English-speaking AT&T operators and can minimize hotel telephone surcharges.

If all the countries you're visiting aren't listed above, call **1 800 241-5555** for a free wallet card with all AT&T access numbers. Easy international calling from AT&T. **TrueWorld Connections.**

American Express offers Travelers Cheques built for two.

Cheques *for Two*℠ from American Express are the Travelers Cheques that allow either of you to use them because both of you have signed them. And only one of you needs to be present to purchase them.

Cheques *for Two* are accepted anywhere regular American Express Travelers Cheques are, which is just about everywhere. So stop by your bank, AAA* or any American Express Travel Service Office and ask for Cheques *for Two*.

Travelers Cheques

unpretentious accommodations include air-conditioning, telephones, full kitchens, and VCRs. Water sports are available at Sapphire Beach on the adjacent property. *Rte. 6, 00802, tel. 809/775–6110 or 800/524–2001, fax 809/775–6110. 25 rooms. Facilities: restaurant. AE, MC, V. $$$$*

★ **Point Pleasant Resort.** This is almost an "eco" resort (the natural vegetation has been lovingly preserved and there's a wonderful nature trail). Stretching up a steep, tree-filled hill from Smith Bay, affording a great view of St. John and Drake Passage to the east and north, this resort offers a range of accommodations, from simple bedrooms to multiroom suites. Units (all newly refurbished) are in a number of buildings hidden among the trees, and the highest ones have the best views. The air-conditioned rooms have balconies, and all rooms have kitchens. Three appealing, nice-size pools surrounded by decks are placed at different levels on the hillside. Although there are water sports here, the "beach" is almost nonexistent; guests are granted beach privileges next door at the long beach at the Stouffer Grand resort, a one-minute walk away. Every guest gets four hours' free use of a car daily. (They need only pay the $9.50 per day insurance cost.) *Estate Smith Bay, 00802, tel. 809/775–7200, 800/524–2300, or 800/645–5306, fax 809/776–5694. 135 rooms. Facilities: 2 restaurants, bar, tiny beach, 3 pools, lighted tennis court, water sports. AE, MC, V. $$$$*

★ **Sapphire Beach Resort and Marina.** This resort sits right on Sapphire Beach, one of St. Thomas's prettiest, where on a clear day the lush green mountains of the neighboring B.V.I. seem close enough to touch. There's excellent snorkeling on the reefs to each side of the beach. This is a quiet retreat where you can nap while swinging in one of the hammocks strung between the palm trees in your front yard; but on Sunday the place rocks with a beach party. All units have fully equipped kitchens, air-conditioning, telephones, and cable TV. Children are welcome and may join the Little Gems Kids Klub. Children under age 12 sleep in their parents' accommodations at no extra charge and eat free at the resort's restaurant, when dining with their parents. *Box 8088, Red Hook, 00801, tel. 809/775–6100 or 800/524–2090, fax 809/775–4024. 141 rooms. Facilities: restaurant, bar, beach, marina, 4 tennis courts, water sports. AE, MC, V. $$$$*

Secret Harbour Beach Resort. The white buildings, containing air-conditioned studios and suites, are nestled around an inviting, perfectly framed sandy cove on Nazareth Bay, where you can watch the marvelous sunsets. During the summer children under age 12 stay free. Rates include continental breakfast. *Box 7576, 00801, tel. 809/775–6550 or 800/524–2250, fax 809/775–1501. 60 suite-style rooms. Facilities: 2 restaurants, bar, beach, pool access, 2 tennis courts, water sports. AE, MC, V. $$$$*

Stouffer Grand Beach Resort. This resort's zigzag architectural angles spell luxury, from the marble atrium lobby to the one-bedroom suites with private whirlpool baths. The beach is excellent, and there's a fitness center with Nautilus machines. The lobby is often populated by those lucky business types whose companies favor the resort as a convention-and-conference center. Daily organized activities for children include iguana hunts, T-shirt painting, and sand-castle building. This tends to be a very busy hotel, with lots of people in the restaurants and on the beach. *Smith Bay Rd., Box 8267, 00801, tel. 809/775–1510 or 800/468–3571, fax 809/775–3757. 297 rooms. Facilities: 2 restaurants, beach, 6 lighted tennis courts, 2 pools, water sports. AE, DC, MC, V. $$$$*

Sugar Bay Plantation Resort. From afar, this large cluster of bulky white buildings looks rather overwhelming. Built as a Holiday Inn

Crowne Plaza, the resort is now owned by Carnival (the cruise ship company). Most rooms have water views, and some have great views of the British Virgin Islands. All units have balconies and are spacious and comfortable, with contemporary furnishings and such amenities as hair dryers and coffeemakers. The beach is small for a property of this size, but there's a giant pool with waterfalls, all manner of water sports, tennis courts and a tennis stadium, and plenty of other diversions for people of all ages. Children under 19 stay free in same room with parents. *Estate Smith Bay, 00802, tel. 809/777–7100, fax 809/777–7200. 300 rooms. Facilities: 2 restaurants, 4 bars, 3 pools, health club, beach, 7 tennis courts, snorkeling equipment. AE, D, DC, MC, V. $$$$*

Frenchtown **Admiral's Inn.** This charming inn stretches down a hillside on the point of land known as Frenchtown, just west of Charlotte Amalie. All rooms have wonderful views of either the town and the harbor or the ocean; the four Ocean View rooms have private balconies and refrigerators. All units have rattan furniture, muted gray-and-pink draperies and bedspreads, gray carpeting, and large, tiled vanity areas. The shore is rocky here, but there's a small sandy area and a swimmable salt-water pool that was formed naturally by coral. The inn's man-made pool is surrounded by a large wooden deck; there's bar service and a poolside snack bar open for lunch. *Box 306162, 00802, tel. 809/774–1376, fax 809/774–8010. 16 rooms. Facilities: pool, bar, tiny beach, poolside snack bar. AE, MC, V. $*

South Shore **Bolongo Club Everything.** One-time sister resorts Bolongo Bay Beach and Tennis Club and Limetree Beach Resort (whose beaches sat next to each other) have combined into one mega-resort. Oceanfront and garden-view rooms and villas all have air-conditioning, cable TV, VCR, phone, and electronic safe. All villas have full kitchens and many rooms have kitchenettes. Guests are part of Club Everything, which means the room rate includes full breakfast, airport transfers, shuttle to town, use of tennis courts, snorkel gear, canoes, Sunfish sailboats, windsurfing and paddleboats, a scuba lesson, and vouchers for an all-day sail, a cocktail cruise, and a half-day snorkel tour on one of the resort's yachts. Guests can also choose the All Inclusive-Club-Everything rate (three-night minimum), which includes the above plus lunch, dinner, and some drinks. Kids Corner entertains the young ones all day, complimentary. *50 Estate Bolongo, 00802, tel. 809/779–2844 or 800/524–4746, fax 809/779–2400. 225 units, from hotel rooms to 1–3 bedroom villas. Facilities: 5 restaurants, 2 nightclubs, 3 pools, 2 beaches, 6 tennis courts, extensive health club, water sports, volleyball, shuffleboard. AE, DC, MC, V. $$$$*

★ **Marriott's Frenchman's Reef and Morning Star Beach Resorts.** Sprawling, luxurious, and situated on a prime harbor promontory east of Charlotte Amalie like a permanently anchored cruise ship, these two resorts are St. Thomas's full-service American superhotels. All rooms are spacious and furnished with contemporary furniture in soft pastels. Many Frenchman's Reef rooms have glorious ocean and harbor views, but a few look out over the parking lot. Morning Star rooms are more luxurious, in buildings tucked among the foliage that stretches along the fine white sand of Morningstar Beach; the sound of the surf can lull you to sleep. In addition to various snack and sandwich stops and a raw bar, you can dine alfresco on American or excellent Italian fare, or head to the Japanese Steak House; there's also a lavish buffet served overlooking the sparkling lights of Charlotte Amalie and the harbor. There is also a dinner theater, live entertainment and disco, scheduled activities, branches of several duty free shops, and a shuttle boat to town. This is a property you don't have to leave. *Box 7100, 00801, tel. 809/776–8500 or 800/ 524–2000, fax 809/776–3054. 503 rooms, 18 suites. Facilities: 7 restaurants, 2 snack bars, 6 bars, 2 pools, 4 tennis courts, beach, water sports, helicopter tours. AE, DC, MC, V. $$$$*

Cottages and Condominiums

Anchorage Beach Villas. Next door to the St. Thomas Yacht Club, these 30 air-conditioned two- and three-bedroom villas on the beach have washing machines and dryers. There are two lighted tennis courts, a freshwater pool, and an informal dining room. *Reservations: Property Management Caribbean, Rte. 6, 00802, tel. 809/ 775–6220 or 800/524–2038. 30 rooms. Facilities: restaurant, 2 tennis courts, pool, laundry facilities, maid service. AE, D, MC, V. $$$$*

Crystal Cove. One of the older condominium complexes on the island, Crystal Cove was built as part of a Harvard University–sponsored architectural competition. The unassuming buildings blend into the Sapphire Beach setting so well that egrets and ducks are right at home in the pond in the center of the property. There are studio, one-, and two-bedroom units, each with a porch or balcony. There's also good snorkeling. *Reservations: Property Management Caribbean, Rte. 6, 00802, tel. 809/775–6660 or 800/524–2038. 56 units. Facilities: saltwater pool, 2 lighted tennis courts. AE, DC, MC, V. $$$$*

Secret Harbourview Villas. These units rest on a gentle hill just behind Secret Harbour Resort and the beach, and share all the resort's facilities. All units have air-conditioning and maid service. *Reservations: Ocean Property Management, Box 8529 (office in bldg. #5), 00801, tel. 809/775–2600 or 800/874–7897. 23 units. Facilities: restaurant, 3 tennis courts, beach access, freshwater pool, whirlpool. DC, MC, V. $$$$*

Sign of the Griffin. If it's a house party you have in mind, you might want to consider these privately owned, furnished, one- and two-bedroom homes with great views on a hillside 500 feet above Tutu Bay. Each house has a fully equipped kitchen, telephone, private garden, and covered terrace. You'll need a car to get around from here. *Box 11668, 00801, tel. 809/775–1715. 3 houses. MC, V. $$$–$$$$*

Sapphire Village. A stay in these high-rise units may take you back to the swinging-singles days of apartment-house living, since many of the units are rented out long-term to refugees from northern winters working down here for the season. The best units overlook the marina and St. John; the beach is in sight and just a short walk down the hill. *Reservations: Property Management Caribbean, Rte. 6, 00802, tel. 809/775–7531 or 800/524–2038. 35 units. Facilities: pub, 2 pools, restaurant. AE, DC, MC, V. $$–$$$*

Sea Horse Cottages. These simple cottages, at the eastern end of the island on Nazareth Bay, look across to St. Croix, 40 miles south. Although Hurricane Hugo stole the beach, steps go directly into the sea from a swimming platform. All rooms have kitchens and ceiling fans. *Box 2312, 00801, tel. 809/775–9231. 15 units, from studio to 2-bedrooms. Facilities: pool. No credit cards. $–$$$*

Private Homes and Villas

Private-home rentals may be arranged through various agents, including: **Leisure Enterprises** (Box 11192, 00801, tel. 809/775–9203 or 800/843–3566), which also handles wedding and honeymoon packages and special services; and **McLaughlin-Anderson Vacations** (100 Blackbeard's Hill, 00802, tel. 809/774–6780 or 800/537–6246), which specializes in luxury-end villas. Write for their beautiful brochure containing photographs of the properties they represent.

Nightlife

You'll find quite a variety of nightlife on St. Thomas. On any given night, especially in season, you'll find steel-pan orchestras, rock and roll bands, piano music, jazz, broken-bottle dancing, disco, and karaoke. Pick up a copy of the bright-yellow St. Thomas *This Week* magazine when you arrive (you'll see it at the airport, in stores, and in hotel lobbies); check the back pages for a list of who's playing where.

Nightspots **Bolongo Club Everything** (tel. 809/776–4770). Visitors and locals from all over the island head to Iggies, a casual beach restaurant named after the iguanas that make their home nearby. It's famous for its sing-along sound system that makes anyone want to try a song for the crowd. In addition to darts, fooz ball, air hockey, and video games, there's disco dancing nightly in the Paradise I club.

Barnacle Bill's (tel. 809/774–7444). Bill Grogan has turned this Crown Bay landmark with the bright-red lobster on its roof into a musicians' home away from home. Grogan is one of the organizers of the annual **Virgin Islands Jazz Festival,** and his club sponsors Kool Jazz events. David Bromberg, Bonnie Raitt, Maria Muldaur, and Ry Cooder have performed in this small room with a parachute-covered ceiling. All Mondays are Limelight Mondays, when local or visiting entertainers take their turn at the mike before an audience composed mostly of fellow performers.

Castaways (tel. 809/776–8410). Old friends from anchorages around the world rendezvous here, and there's always room for a new friend or two. Castaways, which features rock, country, and reggae bands, is the watering hole and dance floor for the crews, owners, and those chartering the fleet of boats anchored at Yacht Haven.

Club Z (Contant Hill, above Sub Base, tel. 809/776–4655). This relic of the disco era is still one of the hottest spots on the island. Resembling the sophisticated clubs of the French Riviera, with pounding music and flashing lights, this club can actually get too crowded on Saturday nights. When you stop to catch your breath, be sure to stroll out to the garden for a glittering night view of Charlotte Amalie.

The Greenhouse (tel. 809/774–7998). This place is slowly making a transition from a waterfront bar to something like the Caribbean equivalent of the T.G.I. Friday's chain in the United States. It strives to meet all tastes, starting with a breakfast that's popular with locals before work; then burgers and taco salad for lunch; and then dinner, with Thursday reserved for prime rib and Sunday designated for lobster mania. Once the Greenhouse puts away the salt-and-pepper shakers it becomes a rock-and-roll club with a DJ or live Top-40 bands rousting the weary to their feet six days a week from 10 PM until the last people go home. It's a drink-and-dance place—and a loud one.

Sugar Bay Disco (tel. 809/777–7100). This is now one of the island's most popular night spots, and the dance floor is crowded until the early morning hours six nights a week.

Sugar's Nightclub at the Old Mill (tel. 809/776–3004), located in— you guessed it—an old mill, is a rock-till-you-drop late-night spot. Whatever the tunes, the place is lively, and there's a small dance floor, as well as a good sound system.

Top of the Reef at Marriott's Frenchman's Reef Resort (tel. 809/776–8500). There are two "Calypso Carnival" shows each Monday through Saturday. Have dinner or drinks and take in the music and rhythms of the Caribbean.

Jazz/Piano Bars
Blackbeard's Castle (tel. 809/776–1234), has live jazz every night except Monday from 8 to midnight. Stateside artists (usually a singer and a piano player) head here for three- to four-week gigs. Sit at the bar, in the comfortable lounge, or outside on the terrace overlooking the sparkling lights of Charlotte Amalie and the harbor—or listen while having dinner in the adjoining fine restaurant.

You'll find piano bars at **Fiddle Leaf** (tel. 809/775–2810), on Government Hill; **Grand Palazzo** (tel. 809/775–3333); and **Raffles** (tel. 809/775–6004), on the East End. The player at Raffles has been entertaining with his show "Gray, Gray, Gray" for many years and shouldn't be missed.

St. Croix

Introduction

By Fredreka Schouten

Updated by Jordan Simon

St. Croix, the largest of the three U.S.V.I., lies 40 miles to the south of St. Thomas and St. John and is only 30 minutes away from Charlotte Amalie by plane. But unlike the bustling island-city of St. Thomas, its harbor teeming with cruise ships and its shopping district crowded with bargain hunters, St. Croix lives at a slower pace and with a more diverse economy, mixing tourism with light and heavy industry on its 84 square miles of rolling land that was once covered with waving carpets of sugarcane.

St. Croix's population has grown dramatically over the last 30 years, and its diversity reflects the island's varied history. The cultivation of sugarcane was more important here than on St. Thomas or St. John and continued as an economic force into the 1960s. After the end of slavery, in 1848, the need for workers brought waves of immigrants from other Caribbean islands, particularly nearby Vieques, Puerto Rico. St. Croix was divided into plantation estates, and the ruins of plantations' great houses and more than 100 sugar mills that dot the island's landscape are evidence of an era when St. Croix rivaled Barbados as the greatest producer of sugar in the West Indies.

Tourism began and boomed in the 1960s, bringing visitors—as well as migrants—from the mainland United States (referred to by locals as "Continentals"). In the late 1960s and early 1970s industrial development brought St. Croix yet another wave of immigrants. This time they came mostly from Trinidad and St. Lucia, to seek work at the Hess oil refinery or at the aluminum-processing plants that dominate the South Shore.

St. Croix is a study of contrasting beauty. The island is not as hilly as St. Thomas or St. John, and a lush rain forest envelops the northwest; the East End is dry and barren, and palm-lined beaches with startlingly clear aquamarine water ring the island. The island's capital, Christiansted, is a restored Danish port on a coral-bound bay on the northeastern shore. The tin-roofed, 18th-century buildings in both Christiansted and Frederiksted, on the western end of the island, are pale yellow, pink, and ochre, resplendent with bright blazes of bougainvillea and hibiscus. The prosperous Danes built well (and more than once—both towns were devastated by fire in the 19th century), using imported bricks or blocks cut from coral, fashioning covered sidewalks (called galleries here) and stately colonnades, and leaving an enduring cosmopolitan air as their legacy. St.

Croix was hit hard in 1989 by Hurricane Hugo, which left behind widespread destruction. Although the island was slow to bounce back, and there are still several roofless cottages dotting the hillsides, most historic edifices have finally been fully restored.

Important Addresses and Numbers

Tourist Information
The **U.S. Virgin Islands Division of Tourism** has offices in St. Croix at the Old Scale House in Christiansted (Box 4538, 00822, tel. 809/773–0495) and on the pier in Frederiksted (Strand St., 00840, tel. 809/772–0357).

Emergencies
Police
To reach the police dial 915. The number is the same for all three islands.

Hospitals
In Christiansted there is the **St. Croix Hospital and Community Health Center** (6 Diamond Bay, north of Sunny Isle Shopping Center, on Rte. 79, tel. 809/778–6311.

Ambulance
Dial 922 for emergency ambulance service.

Air Ambulance
Bohlke International Airways (tel. 809/778–9177) operates out of the St. Croix airport. **Air Medical Services** (tel. 800/443–0013) and **Air Ambulance Network** (tel. 800/327–1966) also service the area from Florida.

Pharmacies
People's Drug Store, Inc. has two branches on St. Croix: on the Christiansted Wharf (tel. 809/778–7355) and at the Sunny Isle Shopping Center (tel. 809/778–5537), located just a few miles west of Christiansted on Centerline Road. In Frederiksted, try **D & D Apothecary Hall** at 50 Queen Street (tel. 809/772–1890).

Coast Guard
To reach the Coast Guard in St. Croix, dial 809/773–7614. The Rescue Coordination Center in San Juan, Puerto Rico, is at 809/772–2943.

Getting Around

By Car
Unlike St. Thomas and St. John, where narrow roads wind through hillsides, St. Croix is relatively flat, and even boasts a four-lane highway. On the Melvin H. Evans Highway, the speed limit is 55 mph, and ranges from 35 to 40 mph elsewhere on the island. Seat belts are mandatory. Roads are often unmarked as well as unpaved, so be patient as you explore the island, and remember that getting lost is often half the fun!

Call **Atlas** (tel. 809/773–2886), **Avis** (tel. 809/778–9355), **Budget** (tel. 809/778–9636), **Caribbean Jeep & Car** (tel. 809/773–4399), **Hertz** (tel. 809/778–1402), **Olympic** (tel. 809/773–2208), and **Thrifty** (tel. 809/773–7200).

By Taxi
Taxis, generally station wagons or minivans, are a phone call away from most hotels and available in downtown Christiansted, at the Alexander Hamilton Airport, and at the Frederiksted pier during cruise-ship arrivals. Rates, set by law, are prominently displayed at the airport. Try the **St. Croix Taxi Association** (tel. 809/778–1088) at the airport, and **Antilles Taxi Service** (tel. 809/773–5020) or **Cruzan Taxi Association** (tel. 809/773–6388) in Christiansted.

By Public Transportation
St. Croix has no public bus system. Rather, privately owned taxi-vans crisscross the island regularly, providing reliable service between Frederiksted and Christiansted along Centerline Road. This inexpensive ($1.50) mode of transportation is favored by local residents. Because of the many stops on the 20-mile drive between the

two main towns, the taxi-vans offer a slower—albeit more interesting—ride.

Guided Tours

Van tours of St. Croix are offered by **St. Croix Safari Tours** (tel. 809/773–6700) and **St. Croix Transit** (tel. 809/772–3333). The tours, which depart from Christiansted and last about three hours, cost from $20 per person.

Exploring St. Croix

Numbers in the margin correspond to points of interest on the St. Croix map.

1 This tour starts in the historic, Danish-style town of **Christiansted,** St. Croix's commercial center. Many of the structures, which are built from the harbor up into the gentle hillsides, date from the 18th century. An easy-to-follow walking tour begins at the **visitor's bureau,** set at the harbor. The building was constructed in 1856, and once served as a scale house, where goods passing through the port were weighed and inspected. Directly across the parking lot, at the edge of D. Hamilton Jackson Park (the park is named for a famed labor leader, journalist, and judge), is the **Old Customs House.** Built in 1734, this building now houses the island's national park offices. To the east stands yellow **Fort Christiansvaern.** In 1749 the Danish built the fort to protect the harbor, but the structure was repeatedly damaged by hurricane-force winds, and was partially rebuilt in 1771. It is now a National Historic Site, and the best preserved of the five remaining Danish-built forts in the Virgin Islands. Hurricane Hugo, which swept through in 1989, also took its toll on the structure. The 200-mile-per-hour winds lifted boats out of the water and flung them onshore, damaging one of the fort's exterior walls. *Box 160, Christiansted 00822, tel. 809/773–1460. Admission (includes admission to Steeple Building, below); $2; free to children under 16 and senior citizens. Open weekdays 8–5, weekends and holidays 9–5. Closed Christmas.*

Cross Hospital Street from the customs house to reach the **post office building.** Built in 1749, it once housed the Danish West India & Guinea Company warehouse. The Old Customs House and the post office building were once one structure, and an archaeological dig beneath Hospital Street unearthed an unusual building technique: The 18th-century builders had constructed their floors over a layer of conch shells.

To the south of the post office, across Company Street, stands the maroon-and-white **Steeple Building,** which was built by the Danes in 1735, and once housed the first Danish Lutheran church on St. Croix. It is now a national-park museum and contains exhibits documenting the island's habitation by the native population. There is also an extensive array of archaeological artifacts, and displays concerning the black experience on St. Croix. *Box 160, Christiansted 00822, tel. 809/773–1460. Admission (includes admission to fort, above): $2. Open Wed. and weekends 9–4.*

Continue down Company Street and you will find the **Christian "Shan" Hendricks Market,** built in 1735 as a slave market. Today, farmers and others sell their goods under the wood-and-galvanized-aluminum structure, Wednesday and Saturday 8–5.

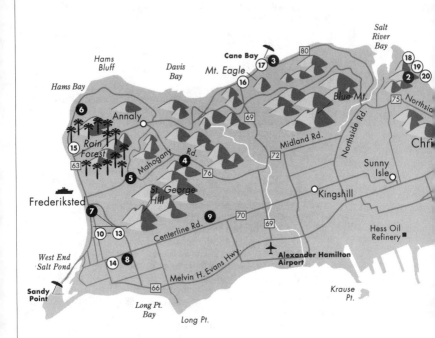

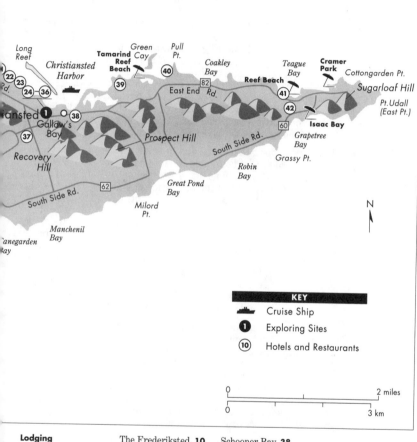

Buck Island

Buck Island Beach

Long Reef

Christiansted Harbor

Tamarind Reef Beach

Green Cay

Pull Pt.

Coakley Bay

Teague Bay

Cramer Park

Cottongarden Pt.

Reef Beach

Sugarloaf Hill

22 23 24 36

39

40

East End Rd.

82

41

42

Pt. Udall (East Pt.)

ansted

1

38

Gallow's Bay

60

37

Prospect Hill

South Side Rd.

Isaac Bay

Recovery Hill

Grapetree Bay

Grassy Pt.

62

Robin Bay

Great Pond Bay

South Side Rd.

Milord Pt.

N

Manchenil Bay

Canegarden Bay

KEY

⚓ Cruise Ship

1 Exploring Sites

10 Hotels and Restaurants

0 ——————————————— 2 miles
0 ——————————————— 3 km

Lodging

The Buccaneer, **39**
Carambola Beach Resort, **16**
Chenay Bay Beach Resort, **40**
Club St. Croix, **23**
Colony Cove, **21**
Cormorant Beach Club, **20**

The Frederiksted, **10**
Hibiscus Beach Hotel, **19**
Hilty House, **37**
Hotel Caravelle, **34**
King Christian Hotel, **35**
The Pink Fancy, **36**
St. Croix by the Sea, **18**

Schooner Bay, **38**
Sprat Hall, **15**
Sugar Beach, **22**
Villa Madeleine, **42**
Waves at Cane Bay, **17**

Double back to Queen Cross Street and turn left; go one block toward the waterfront to reach King St. and **Government House,** one of the town's most elegant buildings. Built as a home for a Danish merchant in 1747, the building today houses U.S.V.I. government offices and the U.S. district court. Slip into the peaceful inner courtyard to admire the still pools and gardens. A sweeping staircase leads visitors to a second-story ballroom, still the site of official government functions.

To leave Christiansted, drive up Hospital Street from the tourist office and turn right onto Company Street. Follow Company Street for several blocks and turn right with the flow of traffic, and pass the police station. Make a quick left onto King Street, and follow it out of town. At the second traffic light, make a right onto Route 75, Northside Road. A few miles up the road, you can make a side trip by turning right just past the **St. Croix Avis** building, onto Route 751. On the right is the entrance to **St. Croix by the Sea,** a hotel with one of the most spectacular sea views on St. Croix. Stroll through the lobby and outside to the 154-foot ocean-fed swimming pool, the largest saltwater pool in the Caribbean. The view of Christiansted and Buck Island, to the east, is terrific.

❷ A bit farther down this road is **Judith's Fancy,** where you can see the ruins of an old great house and the tower left from a 17th-century château that was once home to the governor of the Knights of Malta. The "Judith" comes from the first name of a woman buried on the property. From the guardhouse at the entrance to the neighborhood, follow Hamilton Drive past a number of St. Croix's loveliest homes. At its conclusion, Hamilton Drive overlooks Salt River Bay, where Christopher Columbus anchored offshore in 1493. A skirmish between members of Columbus's crew and a group of Arawak-speaking Indians resulted in the first bloody encounter between Europeans and West Indians. The peninsula on the east side of the bay is named for the event: Cabo de las Flechas (Cape of the Arrows). On the way back, make a detour left off Hamilton Drive onto Caribe Road, for a close look at the neighborhood's ruins.

Salt River Landing National Historic Park and Ecological Preserve was dedicated in November 1993. In addition to such sites of cultural significance as a prehistoric ceremonial ball court and burial site, it encompasses a biodiverse coastal estuary that hosts the largest remaining mangrove forest in the U.S.V.I., a submarine canyon, and several endangered species, including the hawksbill turtle and roseate tern. At present, few sites are of more than archaeological interest to laypeople, but plans call for a museum, interpretive walking trails, and a replica of a Carib village.

After driving back to Route 75, continue west for 2 miles and turn right at Tradewinds Road onto Route 80. Follow this road to the **Salt River Marina,** on the right-hand side of the road. This lush lagoon is home to the Anchor Dive Shop (tel. 809/778–1522) and a couple of casual eateries catering to yachties. The road that veers to the left behind the marina leads to the beach where Columbus landed.

Return to Route 80, which curves along the north coast of the island. The road dips inland briefly, and at the next intersection, you must turn right to continue on Route 80. On the southwest corner of the intersection is the Cane Bay Dive Shop (tel. 809/773–9913), a popular spot for visitors on their way to nearby Cane Bay.

Time Out Also popular with visitors to Cane Bay is **Picnic In Paradise** (tel. 809/778–1212), the gourmet delicatessen and restaurant located next door to the dive shop. Pick up their popular quiche, pasta, or salad to bring to the beach for lunch, or dine alfresco at one of their outdoor tables.

❸ Continue along Route 80, which quickly returns to the grassy coastline and **Cane Bay.** This is one of St. Croix's best launches for scuba diving, and near the small stone jetty you may see a few wet-suited, tank-backed figures making their way out to the drop-off (a bit farther out there is a steeper drop-off to 12,000 feet).

Rising behind you is Mt. Eagle, St. Croix's highest peak, at 1,165 feet. Leaving Cane Bay and passing North Star beach, follow the beautiful coastal road that dips briefly into the forest, then turn left. There is no street sign, but you'll know the turn: The pavement is marked with the words "The Beast" and a set of giant paw prints. The hill you're about to climb is the location of the infamous Beast of the America's Paradise Triathlon, an annual St. Croix event in which participants must bike up this intimidating slope.

Follow this road, Route 69, as it twists and climbs up the hill and south across the island. The golf course you'll pass on the right is a Robert Trent Jones course, part of the Carambola resort complex. Eventually you'll bear right to join Route 76, Mahogany Road. Follow Mahogany Road into the heart of the rain forest, where the thick tangle of turpentine and mahogany trees in places forms a canopy over the road.

❹ On the right you'll pass the **Mt. Pellier Domino Club.** This sprawling palm frond-and-bamboo hut, nestled in the rain forest, features cold drinks, fried chicken, pork chops, and johnnycakes. But the real attraction is Miss Piggy, a beer-guzzling sow who scurries across her pen like Pavlov's dogs at the sound of an Old Milwaukee beer can opening. (Actually, she's switched to nonalcoholic beer for her health!)

❺ Continue along Mahogany Road to reach **St. Croix Leap** (tel. 809/772–0421) on the left, a workshop where you can purchase handsome articles of mahogany, saman, or thibet wood crafted by local artisans.

Mahogany Road ends at Ham's Bluff Road (Route 63), which runs along the west coast of the island. Turn right and, after a few miles,
❻ look to the right side of the road for the **Estate Mount Washington Plantation** (tel. 809/772–1026). Several years ago, while surveying the property, the owners discovered the ruins of an historic sugar plantation buried beneath the rain forest brush. The grounds have since been cleared and opened to the public. A free, self-guided walking tour of the animal-powered mill, rum factory, and other ruins is available daily, and the antiques shop located in the old stables is open on Saturdays.

❼ Double back along Ham's Bluff Road to reach **Frederiksted,** founded in 1751. A single long cruise-ship pier juts into the sparkling sea from this historic coastal town, noted less for its Danish than for its Victorian architecture (dating from after the uprising of former slaves and the great fire of 1878). A stroll around will take you no more than an hour.

Begin your tour at the **visitor's center** (tel. 809/772–0357) on the pier. From here, it's a short walk across Emancipation Park to **Fort Frederik** where, in 1848, the slaves of the Danish West Indies were freed by Governor General Peter van Scholten. The fort, completed in 1760, houses a number of interesting historical exhibits as well as an art gallery. *Tel. 809/772–2021. Admission free. Open weekdays 8:30–4:30.*

Cross through the park again and head up Strand Street. The buildings on the left house a variety of shops, as well as the tiny **St. Croix Aquarium** (tel. 809/772–1345). The aquarium is open Friday–Sunday and its tanks are home to an ever-changing variety of local sea creatures.

At Market Street (Torvegade) turn left. Two blocks east at Queen Street is the **Market Place,** where fresh fruits and vegetables are sold early in the morning, just as they have been for over 200 years. One block farther on the left is the coral-stone St. Patrick's Church, a Roman Catholic church built in 1843. Double back to King Street and turn left.

Time Out   Set back in a hidden courtyard on the corner of Market and King streets is **Tradewinds Bar and Deli** (tel. 809/772–0718). Serving well-built sandwiches (great subs and clubs) and well-priced daily specials, Tradewinds is an ideal spot for casual lunches on the west end.

Stroll along King Street for two blocks to King Cross Street. A left turn here will take you past **Apothecary Hall,** built in 1839, to **St. Paul's Episcopal Church,** a mixture of classic and Gothic Revival architecture, built in 1812. Double back along King Cross Street and follow it west to Strand Street and the waterfront. Turn right and walk along the water to the pier, where the tour began.

Take Strand Street south to its end, turn left, then bear right before the post office to leave Frederiksted. Make a left at the first stop light to get on Centerline Road (Queen Mary Highway). A few miles along this road, on the right, is the **Estate Whim Plantation Museum.** The lovingly restored estate, with a windmill, cook house, and other buildings, will give you a true sense of what life was like on St. Croix's sugar plantations in the 1800s. The oval-shaped great house has high ceilings, antique furniture, decor, and utensils well worth seeing. Notice that it has a fresh and airy atmosphere. (The waterless stone moat around the great house was used not for defense but for gathering cooling air.) Its apothecary exhibit is the largest in all the West Indies. You will also find a museum gift shop. *Box 2855, Frederiksted 00841, tel. 809/772–0598. Admission: $5 adults, $1 children. Open Tues.–Sat. 10–4.*

Continue along Centerline Road to the St. George Estate. Turn left here to reach the **St. George Village Botanical Gardens,** 17 acres of lush and fragrant flora amid the ruins of a 19th-century sugarcane plantation village. You'll find miniature versions of each ecosystem on St. Croix, from a semi-arid cactus grove to a verdant rain forest. *Box 3011, Kingshill 00851–3011, tel. 809/772–3874. Admission: $3 adults, $1 children. Open Tues.–Sat. 10–3. Closed holidays.*

Continue east along Centerline Road all the way back to Christiansted.

St. Croix for Free

There are miles and miles of sandy beaches ringing this island, and swimming, shell collecting, and sun bathing cost only the price of your picnic lunch. Other free activities include the walking tour at Estate Mount Washington Plantation and a visit to see Miss Piggy at the Domino Club (*see* Exploring, *above*).

What to See and Do with Children

St. Croix offers much to children by way of exploration. Introduce them to the underwater world by renting an inexpensive set of snorkeling gear and visiting Buck Island, Cane Bay, or the waters around the Frederiksted pier. The St. Croix Aquarium (*see* Exploring, *above*) does a wonderful job of presenting sea life to children. Youngsters will enjoy learning about plantation life on the island with a visit to the Estate Whim Plantation Museum (*see* Exploring, *above*), where they are free to roam around the grounds and explore inside the sugar mill. Several hotels, such as the Buccaneer, often organize special activities for young guests.

Off the Beaten Track

One of St. Croix's most popular attractions isn't even on St. Croix. **Buck Island,** along with the underwater reef that surrounds it, is a national monument under the protection of the National Park Service. Off St. Croix's northeast shore, the island's pristine beaches are lovely, and the snorkeling trail set in the reef allows visitors the opportunity for a close-up study of coral formations and tropical fish. Visits to the island are available with any of St. Croix's charter services (*see* Diving and Snorkeling in the Virgin Islands, Chapter 3).

Follow Route 82 out of Christiansted for a leisurely tour of the island's **East End.** In stark contrast to the lush greenery of most of St. Croix, the East End is arid. Its gentle wheat-color slopes are dotted with cacti. Head past Cramer's Park, a popular recreational spot, to **Point Udall,** a rocky promontory that juts into the Caribbean Sea and the easternmost point of the United States. The climb to this point, by a rutted dirt road, may be slow, but it's worth the effort. On the way back, look for "The Castle," an enormous mansion atop the cliffs that resembles a cross between a Moorish mosque and the Taj Mahal. It was built by a flamboyant recluse known only as the Contessa.

A ritual that began millions of years ago is played out annually on St. Croix's **Sandy Point Beach** between March and June. That's when the majestic **leatherback turtles** come ashore to lay their eggs. These creatures, which can weigh up to 800 pounds and are of an older species than the dinosaurs, are oblivious to onlookers when they lay their eggs in the sand. With only the moonlight to guide them, Earthwatch volunteers patrol the beach nightly during the turtles' nesting season to protect the eggs from predators and poachers. The beach is a federal wildlife preserve and is closed to the public at night, but the Earthwatch volunteers will take groups of up to 10 people with them. Call the **St. Croix Environmental Association** (tel. 809/773–1989) to reserve a space.

Shopping

Although St. Croix doesn't offer as many shopping opportunities as St. Thomas, the island does provide an array of smaller stores with unique merchandise. In Christiansted, the best shopping areas are the Pan Am Pavilion and Caravelle Arcade off Strand Street, and along King and Company streets. These streets give way to arcades filled with small stores and boutiques. Stores are often closed on Sundays.

Books **The Bookie** (1111 Strand St., Christiansted, tel. 809/773–2592) carries paperback novels as well as a line of stationery, newspapers, and greeting cards.

China and **Little Switzerland** (Hamilton House, 56 King St., Christiansted, tel.
Crystal 809/773–1976). The St. Croix branch of this Virgin Islands' institution features a variety of Rosenthal flatware, Lladro figurines, Waterford and Baccarat crystal, Lalique figurines, and Wedgwood and Royal Doulton china.

The Royal English Shop (5 Strand St., Frederiksted, tel. 809/772–2040). Saint-Louis and Beyer crystal and Wedgwood china are carried here at prices significantly lower than those on the mainland. Store hours vary, depending on the cruise-ship schedule, so check ahead.

Clothing **Caribbean Clothing Company** (55 Company St., Christiansted, tel. 809/773–5012). This fashionable store features contemporary sportswear by top American designers, and they also carry Bally shoes for men.

From the Gecko (1233 Queen Cross St., tel. 809/778–9433). Come here for the hippest clothes on St. Croix, from superb batik sarongs to hand-painted silk scarves and hammocks.

Gold Coast (3 AB Queen Cross St., Christiansted, tel. 809/773–2006). Fashionable swimsuits and casual sports clothes for both men and women fill the shelves at this pleasant shop.

Java Wraps (Company St., Christiansted, tel. 809/773–3770). Indonesian batik cover-ups and resort wear for men, women, and children are featured here.

Polo/Ralph Lauren Factory Store (52 C Company St., Christiansted, tel. 809/773–4388). The factory outlet for this popular, upscale clothing line presents men's and women's clothes at huge discounts.

Simply Cotton (36 C Strand St., Christiansted, tel. 809/773–6860). The Caribbean branch of this popular California chain sells cool, comfortable, cotton, women's activewear, perfect for this climate, at reasonable prices.

Wayne James Boutique (42 Queen Cross St., tel. 809/773–8585). This engaging Crucian has designed vestments for the Pope and eveningwear for the Queen of Denmark. His bright, savvy clothes are inspired by island traditions and colors. Proud of his Crucian heritage, he also makes and sells Carnival, a sensational (and secret) seasoning from an old family recipe.

Crafts and **American West India Company** (1 Strand St., Christiansted, tel. 809/
Gifts 773–7325). In the market for some Jamaican allspice, or perhaps a piece of Haitian metalwork? Goods gathered from around the Caribbean are available here, as are some produced right here on St. Croix, including Cruzan ceramics, locally produced spices, and hand-painted clothing.

Designworks (53 King St., Christiansted, tel. 809/773–5355). This new store features "everything for the home," from Danish candles and hand-woven palm baskets to heavy Mexican glassware and Marimekko fabrics imported from Finland.

1870 Town House Shoppes (52 King St., Christiansted, tel. 809/773–2967) carries handcrafted jewelry, casual wear for men and women, and a selection of gift items.

Folk Art Traders (1 B Queen Cross St. at Strand St., Christiansted, tel. 809/773–1900). Owners Patty and Charles Eitzen travel to Haiti, Jamaica, Guyana, and throughout the Caribbean to find treasures to sell in their shop. The baskets, ceramic masks, pottery, and sculpture found here are unique examples of the area's folk-art tradition.

Only in Paradise Gifts (5 Company St., Christiansted, tel. 809/773–0331). True to its name, this place features one-of-a-kind wood-, silver-, and glass-bead jewelry, plus Indian cotton scarves and skirts, ceramic vases, and leather- and patterned-fabric purses. They've recently added a lingerie and leather handbag shop behind the store.

The Royal Poinciana (38 Strand St., Christiansted, tel. 809/773–9892). This attractively designed store carries island seasonings and hot sauces, West Indian crafts, bath gels, and herbal teas.

Jewelry **Colombian Emeralds** (43 Queen Cross St., Christiansted, tel. 809/773–1928 or 809/773–9189). Specializing—of course—in emeralds, this store also carries diamonds, rubies, sapphires, and gold. A branch store, featuring watches, is slated to open across the street. The chain, the Caribbean's largest jeweler, offers certified appraisal and international guarantees.

Crucian Gold (57 A Company St., Christiansted, tel. 809/773–5241). This store, located in a small courtyard in a West Indian–style cottage, carries the unique gold creations of St. Croix native Brian Bishop. His trademark piece is the Turk's Head ring, made of an interwoven gold strand.

Karavan (5 Gallows Bay, tel. 809/773–9999). This shop is just east of downtown Christiansted, in the residential Gallows Bay neighborhood that retains traces of its 200-year-old fishing village heritage. The owner designs her own funky jewelry and also sells an assortment of tchatchkes, including handmade Christmas ornaments and magical beads, from amber to amethyst.

Sonya's (1 Company St., Christiansted, tel. 809/778–8605). A 28-year-old business run by Sonya Hough, with husband David and daughters Diane and Shelley, features Sonya's own jewelry creations. Hough invented the hook bracelet, popular among locals. Hurricane Hugo's visit to the island in 1989 inspired a "hurricane" bracelet. Its unique clasp features a gold strand shaped like the storm's swirling winds, with a gemstone eye.

Leather Goods **Kicks** (57 Company St., Christiansted, tel. 809/773–7801). This upscale shop carries a good, if small, selection of shoes and leather goods.

Liquor **Cruzan Rum Distillery** (West Airport Rd., tel. 809/772–0280). A tour of the company's rebuilt factory culminates in a tasting of its products, all of which are sold here at bargain prices.

Grog and Spirits (59 Kings Wharf, Christiansted, tel. 809/778–8400 and Chandlers Wharf, Gallows Bay, tel. 809/773–8485). A good selection of liquor is available at these conveniently located shops.

Woolworth's (Sunny Isle Shopping Center, Centerline Rd., tel. 809/778–5466). This department store carries a huge line of discount, duty-free liquor.

Perfumes **La Parfumerie** (43 A Queen Cross St., Christiansted, tel. 809/778–7799). Here you'll find a variety of fragrances for men and women, at duty-free prices.

St. Croix Shoppes (53 AB Company St., Christiansted, tel. 809/773–2727). One of these side-by-side shops specializes solely in Estée Lauder and Clinique products, while the other carries a full line of fragrances.

St. Croix Perfume Center (53 King St., Christiansted, tel. 809/773–7604). An extensive array of fragrances, including all the major brands, is available here.

Violette Boutique (Caravelle Arcade, 38 Strand St., Christiansted, tel. 809/773–2148). A large selection of perfume, skin-care, and makeup products is featured here.

Toys **The Land of Oz** (52 A Company St., Christiansted, tel. 809/773–4610). This shop caters to both the young and the young at heart, with everything from classic board games to the latest novelty items.

Sports and the Outdoors

Fishing In the past quarter-century, some 20 world records—many for blue marlin—have been set in these waters. Sailfish, skipjack, bonito, tuna (allison, blackfin, and yellowfin), and wahoo are abundant.

Ruffian Enterprises (St. Croix Marina, Christiansted, tel. 809/773–6011 day, or 809/773–0917 night) will take you out on a 41-foot Hatteras. Half- or full-day charters are also available on **Cruzan Diver's** *Afternoon Delight* (tel. 809/772–3701) and **Mile Mark**'s *Shenanigans* (tel. 809/773–2628).

Golf **The Buccaneer's** (tel. 809/773–2100) 18-hole course is conveniently close to (east of) Christiansted. Yet more spectacular is **Carambola** (tel. 809/778–5638), in the valleyed northwestern part of the island, designed by Robert Trent Jones. **The Reef Club** (tel. 809/773–8844), at the northeastern part of the island, has nine holes.

Horseback At Sprat Hall, near Frederiksted, Jill Hurd runs **Paul and Jill's**
Riding **Equestrian Stables** (tel. 809/772–2880 or 809/772–2627) and will take you clip-clopping through the rain forest (explaining the flora, fauna, and ruins along the way), along the coast, or on moonlit rides. Costs range from $50 to $75 for the three-hour rides.

Sailing See Sailing in the Virgin Islands, Chapter 4, for information.

Snorkeling/ See Diving and Snorkeling in the Virgin Islands, Chapter 3, for in-
Diving formation.

Tennis The public courts found in Frederiksted and out east at Cramer Park are in pretty questionable shape: It's better to pay the fees to play at the many hotel courts around the island.

There are a pro, a full tennis pro shop, and eight courts (two lighted) at the **Buccaneer Hotel** (tel. 809/773–2100); a resident pro and four courts (two lighted) at the **Carambola Beach Resort** (tel. 809/778–3800); a resident pro and three lighted courts at **Club St. Croix** (tel. 809/773–4800); a pro, pro shop, and two lighted courts at **St. Croix by the Sea** (tel. 809/778–5639); and two courts at the **Chenay Bay Beach Resort** (tel. 809/773–2918).

Windsurfing Most of the major water-sports centers on the three islands can accommodate the Windsurfer.

Tradewindsurfing Inc. (Hotel on the Cay and Club St. Croix, tel. 809/773–7060) offers windsurfing rentals, sales, and rides, along with a wide range of water-sports equipment, like aquabikes, kayaks, and catamarans. Terry Merrigan operates **Virgin Territory Surf**

and Sail (Box 3793, Christiansted, tel. 809/773–4810 or 809/773–8665) out of the Chenay Bay Beach Resort. Windsurfing lessons are offered, as well as rental of ocean kayaks and windsurfing and snorkeling gear.

Beaches

Buck Island and its reef, which is under environmental protection, can be reached only by boat; nonetheless, it is a must outing on any visit to St. Croix. Its beach is beautiful, but its finest treasures are those you can see when you plop off the boat and adjust your face mask, snorkel, and flippers. Get there with one of the island's many charter boat companies (*see* Daysail Boats in Sailing in the Virgin Islands, Chapter 4).

The waters are not always gentle at **Cane Bay,** a breezy north shore beach, but the scuba diving and snorkeling are wondrous, and there are never many people around. Just swim straight out to see elkhorn and brain corals. Less than 200 yards out is the drop-off or so-called Cane Bay Wall.

Tamarind Reef Beach is a small but attractive beach east of Christiansted. Both Green Cay and Buck Island seem smack in front of you and make the view arresting. Snorkeling is good.

There are several popular West End beaches found along the coast north of Frederiksted. The beach at the **West End Beach Club** features a bar, water sports, and volleyball. South of Frederiksted, try the beach at the **King Frederik Hotel,** where palm trees can provide plenty of shade for those who need it, and there is a fine beachside restaurant for a casual lunch on weekends.

Isaac Bay, at St. Croix's East End, is almost impossible to reach without a four-wheel drive vehicle, but worth it if you want some seclusion and calm swimming plus a barrier reef for snorkeling. You can get here via footpaths from Jacks Bay.

Dining

Seven flags have flown over St. Croix, and each has left its legacy in the island's cuisine. Visitors can feast on Italian, French, Danish, and American dishes; there are even Chinese and Mexican restaurants in Christiansted. Seafood, taken fresh from the waters around the island, is plentiful and always good; wahoo, mahimahi, and conch are popular dishes. For a true island experience, stop in a local Cruzan restaurant to feast on stew goat, curry chicken, or fried pork chops. Dining out on St. Croix is an informal affair. Several hotels offer worthwhile "all-inclusive" packages with dine-around options at top island restaurants.

Christiansted **Kendricks.** This restaurant is a tranquil oasis of civility in the heart
★ of Christiansted. Jazz plays softly in the background, waiters in bow ties dote on customers seated in three elegant, air-conditioned dining rooms where the walls are painted Wedgwood blue, mango, and scarlet, and the tables are laid with crisp linens and fine china. The menu is stylish Continental, and dishes are lovingly presented. Try the coconut shrimp with jalapeño-and-chive aioli to start, or the silken cream of shiitake soup. Move on to the house specialty, roasted pecan-crusted pork loin with ginger mayonnaise, or the grilled rack of lamb with roasted garlic and fresh thyme sauce. The owners have opened a hole-in-the-wall directly across the street called Simply Lobster. Open daily for lunch, it presents a cornucopia of reasonably

priced lobster dishes, including Kendricks's signature lobster spring rolls. *Queen Cross St., Christiansted, tel. 809/773–9199. Reservations advised. AE. No lunch, closed Sun. and Mon. $$$$*

The Chart House. A tropical mood prevails in the large dining room, where trees vault through openings in the ceiling, and a friendly, efficient waitstaff wears splashy Caribbean prints. Ideally located on Christiansted's Kings Wharf, this is one of St. Croix's most popular restaurants. Try any of their fresh seafood dishes, or one of the prime rib dinners, all consistently high quality. Save room for dessert, though: One order of mud pie, a concoction of coffee ice cream, fudge, and whipped cream, can feed three people. *Kings Wharf, tel. 809/773–7718. Reservations accepted. AE, DC, MC, V. Closed lunch. $$$*

Club Comanche. The atmosphere is very friendly and casual at this upstairs terrace restaurant, where the decor includes an outrigger canoe hanging from the ceiling. The curry of beef fillet is a popular dish, as are the stuffed shrimp Savannah and such reliable old standbys as lobster louis and filet mignon bearnaise. There are about 15 appetizers on the varied menu. The personable owners also operate an appealing little inn on the premises and a perfect honeymoon hideaway in a converted 18th-century sugar mill right on the harbor. *Strand St., tel. 809/773–2665. Reservations advised. AE, MC, V. Closed Sun. $$$*

★ **Dino's.** Homemade Italian food, often with an innovative West Indian twist, is found at this intimate trattoria, one of the island's best. The hip ambience is accentuated by wildly colored handpainted tablecloths juxtaposed with rustic still lifes on the walls. Pasta is made fresh daily by chefs/owners Dwight DeLude and Dino Natale. Its hot antipasto appetizer features bacon-wrapped and grilled shrimp; broiled tomato with a veil of fresh pesto; fried eggplant in a tomato-butter sauce; and grilled, succulent scallops. Sweet-potato- or eggplant-ravioli and boldly flavored fettuccine Caribbean (tossed with chicken, rum, black beans, ginger, cilantro, and peppers) are just two of the unusual but surprisingly tasty dishes. *4 C Hospital St., tel. 809/778–8005. Reservations advised. No credit cards. Closed Sept. Closed Wed. $$$*

★ **Pangaea.** The name—meaning all earth—is certainly reflected in the ambitious, eclectic menu, which synthesizes African, Caribbean, and Middle Eastern influences and ingredients with aplomb. You'll start off with wonderful home-baked banana whole-wheat bread. Specials might include mahimahi in two salsas (mango and tomato cilantro) and seven-hour slow-roasted duck breast in honey-raspberry glaze. Finish it off with delectable homemade ice creams or sinful chocolate pâté with strawberries. The ambience is best described as Peace Corps bohemian: incense, wind chimes, and artifacts culled from the owners' world travels like Hawaiian coconut masks and Japanese watercolors. The waitstaff is hip and very friendly; the house cat, Shadow, even more so. Pangaea is an unexpected delight. *2203 Queen Cross St., tel. 809/773–7743. Reservations accepted. No credit cards. No lunch, closed Tues. and Wed. Hours vary; call ahead. $$$*

Top Hat. Owned by a delightful Danish couple, this restaurant has been in business for 20 years, serving international cuisine with an emphasis on Danish specialties—roast duck stuffed with apples and prunes, *frikadeller* (savory meatballs in a tangy cocktail sauce), fried camembert with lingonberries, and smoked eel. The old West Indian structure, complete with gingerbread trim, is nicely accented in gray, white, and pink. The photographs on the walls are the work of owner and European-trained chef Hans Rasmussen. *52*

Company St., tel. 809/773-2346. Reservations advised. AE, MC, V. Closed May-Oct.; closed Sun. and lunch. $$$

Tutto Bene. Its yellow walls, brightly striped cushions, and painted trompe l'oeil tables make Tutto Bene look more like a sophisticated Mexican cantina than an Italian cocina. A quick inspection of the menu, however, will clear up any confusion. Written on hanging mirrors is the daily-changing menu which incorporates such standard Italian fare as veal parmigiana with inventive creations such as veal chop with sun-dried tomatoes, crabmeat ravioli, and the seafood gondola, a hollowed-out eggplant stuffed with scallops, herbs, and vegetables. Desserts, prepared by one of the island's finest pastry chefs, are top-notch. *2 Company St., tel. 809/773-5229. Reservations accepted. No credit cards. Closed Mon. and Tues. $$-$$$*

Bombay Club. This dimly lit boîte plastered with bright local artworks is set in a historic pub. The bar, with its cool, exposed stone walls, is a favored haven for expatriates. The typical pub grub includes fine salads, nachos, scrumptious onion rings, pastas, and simple chicken and steak dishes. Don't pass up the heavenly stuffed crabs with roast garlic herb sauce. *5A King St., tel. 809/773-1838. Reservations advised. AE, V. No lunch on weekends. $$*

Camille's. This tiny, lively spot, whose warm, exposed brick walls are splashed with colorful island prints, is perfect for lunch or a light supper. Sandwiches and burgers are the big draw here, though the daily seafood special, often wahoo or mahimahi, is also popular. *Corner of Company and Queen Cross Sts., tel. 809/773-2985. Reservations advised for groups of 5 or more. No credit cards. No lunch Sun. $*

Harvey's. The plain, even dowdy room contains just 12 tables, whose plastic, flowered tablecloths constitute the sole attempt at decor. Who cares? The delicious local food ranks among the island's best. Daily specials such as mouth-watering stew goat and melting whelks in butter, served with heaping helpings of rice, fungi, and vegetables, are listed on the blackboard. Genial owner Sarah Harvey takes great pride in her kitchen, bustling out from behind the stove to chat and urge you to eat up. *11 Company St., tel. 809/773-3433. Reservations not necessary. No credit cards. Lunch only, closed Sun. (call for dinner hours during high season). $*

East End **Cafe Madeleine.** This elegant restaurant, part of the Villa Madeleine resort nestled in the hills on St. Croix's East End, features such diverse cuisine as lamb and polenta soup, swordfish medallions sautéed with green tomato and asparagus, and a number of fine beef dishes. The wine list is extensive. In high season, the enterprising management brings in top stateside chefs on a two-week rotation. *Teague Bay (take Rte. 82 out of Christiansted and turn right at the Reef Condominiums), tel. 809/778-7377. Reservations advised. AE, DC, MC, V. Closed Mon. and Tues. $$$$*

Duggan's Reef. A favorite spot with visitors to the East End, this beachside restaurant, draped with dozens of pennants celebrating New England pro and college sports teams (yup, owner Frank Duggan hails from Boston), offers casual, open-air dining at wicker tables and chairs. The lunch menu features burgers, sandwiches, and numerous fish dishes. Dinner choices are more extensive and ambitious; try the lobster-stuffed chile relleños or grouper in parchment with arugula, pesto, tomato, lemon, and chardonnay. *Teague Bay, Star Route 00864, Christiansted, tel. 809/773-9800. Reservations accepted. AE, MC, V. Closed Sept. $$-$$$*

Frederiksted **Blue Moon.** This terrific little bistro, popular for its live jazz on Friday nights, has an eclectic, often-changing menu that draws heavily on Asian, Cajun, and French influences. Try the delicious seafood chowder or satays as an appetizer; the sweet-potato ravioli in mushroom sauce as an entrée; for dessert, the hot fudge rum cake is heavenly. *17 Strand St., tel. 809/772–2222. AE. Closed July–Sept. Closed Mon. and lunch. $$–$$$*

Café du Soleil. This upstairs terrace eatery bills itself as "the perfect place to watch the sunset," and it's no exaggeration. Even the mauve walls and maroon and salmon napery cleverly duplicate the sun's pyrotechnics. The food understandably takes a backseat to the main event, but you won't go wrong with gravlax or charcuterie as an appetizer, followed by seafood panache (shrimp, scallops, and the catch of the day swimming in a leek, tomato, and saffron broth). *625 Strand St., tel. 809/772–5400. Reservations advised. AE, MC, V. Closed Thurs., no dinner Sun. $$*

Le St. Tropez. A ceramic-tiled bar and soft lighting add to the Mediterranean atmosphere at this pleasant bistro, tucked into a courtyard off Frederiksted's main thoroughfare. Diners, seated either inside or on the adjoining patio, enjoy French fare such as salads, brochettes, and grilled meats in delicate sauces. The menu changes daily, often taking advantage of fresh local seafood. *67 King St., tel. 809/772–3000. Reservations accepted. AE, MC, V. Closed Sun. $$*

Villa Morales. This simple family-run eatery is a popular spot for locals, with dancing in the cavernous back room. The kitchen turns out well-prepared Cruzan and Spanish dishes like stew goat and baked chicken, all served with heaping helpings of fungi, rice, and vegetables. *Plot 82C, off Rte. 70, Estate Whim, tel. 809/772–0556. Reservations required on weekends. No credit cards. Closed Sun. and Mon.; and dinner Tues. and Wed. $*

Lodging

From plush resorts to simple beachfront digs, and everything in between, St. Croix's variety of accommodations is bound to suit every type of traveler. In 1989 Hurricane Hugo damaged most of the island's hotels; as a result, almost all of them underwent renovation in the months that followed and reopened as new and improved versions of their old selves.

Room rates on St. Croix are competitive with those on other islands, and those who choose to travel off-season will enjoy substantial price reductions. Many properties offer honeymoon and dive packages that are also big money savers.

All hotels have air-conditioning and cable television, unless otherwise noted.

Christiansted   **Hotel Caravelle.** The charming three-story Caravelle is an excellent bet for moderately priced lodging in Christiansted. All rooms have refrigerators and were recently redone in tasteful dusky blues and whites, with floral-print bedspreads and curtains and vaulted ceilings. Baths are clean and new, though the unique tile in the showers is a holdover from when the hotel was built, 22 years ago. Superior rooms overlook the harbor, but most rooms do have some sort of ocean view. Owners Sid and Amy Kalmans are friendly and helpful. The fine Banana Bay Club restaurant is also on the premises. *44 A Queen Cross St., 00820, tel. 809/773–0687 or 800/524–0410; fax 809/778–7004. 43 rooms. Facilities: restaurant, bar, pool, water sports, conference room, gift shops, guest parking. AE, D, DC, MC, V. $$*

King Christian Hotel. This centrally located Christiansted inn, a bright-yellow, 250-year-old former warehouse, houses a row of shops and restaurants on the first floor, with guest rooms occupying the second and third floors. Pass through the small, nondescript lobby to reach a freshwater swimming pool ringed with yellow-and-white patio furniture. The new sun deck overlooks the pool on one side and the harbor on the other. White wicker furniture and bright pastels strike a pleasant note in the guest rooms, which are equipped with coffeemakers and refrigerators. Rooms on the south side overlook a noisy main street, but those facing the water are quiet and have balconies (for the best view, request Room 201, 202, 301, or 302). One of Christiansted's finest restaurants, the Chart House, is connected to the hotel. *59 King's Wharf, Box 3619, 00822–3619, tel. 809/773–2285 or 800/524–2012; fax 809/773–9411. 39 rooms. Facilities: restaurant, bar, pool, sun deck, water sports. AE, DC, MC, V. $$*

The Pink Fancy. This homey, restful place is a few blocks west of the center of town in a much less touristy neighborhood. The oldest of the four buildings here is a 1780 Danish town house, and old stone walls and foundations enhance the setting. The inn's efficiency rooms are basic but clean and well tended; all feature hardwood floors, tropical-print fabrics, and wicker furniture. The hotel is laid out around the pool, where pink-and-white awnings throw shade over the patio, hammock, and small bar. Complimentary breakfast and cocktails are included in room rates. *27 Prince St., 00820, tel. 809/773–8460 or 800/524–2045. 13 rooms. Facilities: bar, pool. MC, V. $*

The East End   **Carambola Beach Resort.** This superb resort has finally reopened its
★ doors after Hugo's devastation, and it's better than ever. The 25 quaint, two-story red-roofed villas connected by lovely arcades seem hacked from the luxuriant undergrowth. The rooms are identical; the only difference is the view—ocean or garden. Decor is Laura Ashley–style English country house, with rocking chairs and sofas upholstered in soothing floral patterns, terra-cotta floors, rough-textured ceramic lamps, and mahogany ceilings and furnishings. All boast private patios and huge baths (showers only). There are two fine restaurants (the Sunday buffet brunch is already legendary for its munificent table, featuring everything from sushi to blackened shark, pork stew to pasta puttanesca), an exquisite ecru beach, and lots of quiet nooks for a secluded drink. *Box 3031, Kingshill, tel. 809/778–3800, fax 809/778–1682. 151 rooms. Facilities: 2 restaurants, deli, lounge, pool, water-sports center, 4 tennis courts (2 lighted), library, gift shop. AE, D, DC, MC, V. $$$$*

★ **Villa Madeleine.** This exquisite hotel opened in 1990 and has quickly earned a reputation as one of St. Croix's best. The main building was patterned after a turn-of-the-century West Indian plantation great house. Richly upholstered furniture, Oriental rugs, teal walls, and whimsically painted driftwood set the mood in the billiards room, in the austere library and sitting room, and at Cafe Madeleine, the resort's highly praised Continental restaurant, which seem straight from the pages of *Architectural Digest*. The great house sits atop a hill, on which private guest villas are scattered in both directions, affording views of the north and south shores. The villas' decor is modern tropical, with rattan and plush cushions, and many bedrooms have bamboo four-poster beds. Each villa has a full kitchen and a private swimming pool. Special touches in the rooms include 5-foot-square pink-marble showers and, in many cottages, hand-painted floral borders along the walls, done in splashy tropical colors. *Box 3109, Christiansted 00822, tel. 809/778–7377 or 800/548–4461; fax 809/773–7518. 43 villas. Facilities: restaurant, bar, private pools, billiards room, library, tennis court, concierge, nearby golf course. AE, D, DC, MC, V. $$$$*

★ **The Buccaneer.** If you want a self-contained tropical beach resort offering golf, all water sports, tennis, a nature/jogging trail, shopping arcade, health spa, and several restaurants, this 300-acre property is the place for you. A palm-tree–lined main drive leads to the large pink hotel at the top of a hill, and a number of smaller guest cottages, shops, and restaurants are scattered throughout the property's rolling, manicured lawns. Stroll through the elegant lobby, with its green-and-white marble checkerboard floor, into the open-air terrace, where guests can relax and take in the view. Most of the guest rooms in this former sugar plantation have been renovated to incorporate eye-catching marble or colorful tile floors; they also feature four-poster beds and massive wardrobes of pale wood, pastel fabrics, and locally produced artworks, along with such modern conveniences as refrigerators and cable TVs. Spacious bathrooms are noteworthy for their marble bench showers and double sinks. *Box 218, Christiansted 00821–0218, tel. 809/773–2100 or 800/223–1108. 150 rooms. Facilities: 4 restaurants, beach, golf, health spa, 2 pools, 8 tennis courts (2 lighted), jogging trail, water sports, shopping arcade, in-room safes, holiday activities for children. AE, DC, MC, V. $$$–$$$$*

Chenay Bay Beach Resort. These family-oriented bungalow-style accommodations are situated on Chenay Bay. Rooms have red-tile floors, bright-peach or yellow walls, and rattan furnishings. Kitchenettes and porches add versatility to each room; cable TV and minibars have recently been added. Gravel paths connect the terraced gray-and-white-wood cottages with the shore, where you'll find a large L-shape pool, a protected beach, a picnic area with barbecues, and a casual restaurant. Families with children may find this an ideal setting. The hotel also offers a one-week all-inclusive package that incorporates accommodations, meals at Chenay Bay and local restaurants, rental car, admission to local attractions, windsurfing lessons, a two-tank dive, golf, a boat trip, and all tips. *Box 24600, Christiansted 00824, tel. 809/773–2918 or 800/548–4457. 50 rooms. Facilities: restaurant, bar, pool, picnic area with barbecue, TV lounge, 2 tennis courts, shuttle to Christiansted, water sports, nearby golf course. AE, MC, V. $$$*

Frederiksted **The Frederiksted.** Don't be put off by the neat but unprepossessing exterior: This modern four-story inn is your best bet for lodging in Frederiksted. In the inviting, outdoor tile courtyard, the glass tables and yellow chairs of the hotel's bar and restaurant crowd around a small freshwater swimming pool where live music can be enjoyed Friday and Saturday nights. Yellow-striped awnings and tropical greenery create a sunny, welcoming atmosphere. Steps at one side of the courtyard lead to the second floor's main desk and sun deck. The bright, pleasant guest rooms are outfitted with bar refrigerators and microwaves, and are decorated with light-color rattan furniture and print bedspreads. Bathrooms are on the small side but are bright and clean. The nicest rooms are those with an ocean view; these are also the only rooms that have a bathtub in addition to a shower. *20 Strand St., 00840, tel. 809/773–9150 or 800/524–2025; fax 809/778–4009. 40 rooms. Facilities: restaurant, bar, outdoor pool, sun deck, live entertainment. AE, D, DC, MC, V. $*

The North **Cormorant Beach Club.** Breeze-bent palm trees, hammocks, the
Shore thrum of North Shore waves, and a blissful sense of respected priva-
★ cy rule here. The open-air public spaces are filled with tropical plants and comfy wicker furniture in cool peach and mint-green shades. Ceiling fans and tile floors add to the atmosphere at this top-shelf resort, which resembles a series of connected Moorish villas. The beachfront rooms are lovely, with dark wicker furniture, pale-

peach walls, white-tile floors, and floral-print spreads and curtains; all rooms have a patio or balcony and telephone (at press time, cable TV and safe were being installed). Bathrooms stand out for their coral-rock–wall showers, marble-top double sinks, and brass fixtures. Morning coffee and afternoon tea are set out daily in the building breezeways, and you'll receive a "CBC" terry robe to wear when you walk to the beautifully ledged polygonal pool. The airy, high-ceiling restaurant is one of St. Croix's best. *4126 La Grande Princesse, Christiansted 00820, tel. 809/778–8920 or 800/548–4460; fax 809/778–9218. 34 rooms, 4 suites. Facilities: restaurant, bar, beach, pool, snorkeling, 2 tennis courts, library with TV and VCR, croquet lawns. AE, DC, MC, V. $$$$*

St. Croix by the Sea. The hotel's coastal landscape and view east to Christiansted and Buck Island are spectacular, as is its huge, curved, seawater pool. The ceiling fans and comfortable wicker chairs in the spacious hotel lobby set an inviting mood. The simple but comfortable rooms are done in rattan and dark floral prints; some have balconies. The rocky coast in front of the hotel doesn't have a beach, but an artificial beach has been created next to the pool. *Box 248, Christiansted 00820, tel. 809/778–8600 or 800/524–5006. 65 rooms. Facilities: 2 restaurants, 2 lounges, saltwater pool, 4 tennis courts, gift shop, conference rooms. AE, DC, MC, V. $$$*

Waves at Cane Bay. Owners Kevin and Suzanne Ryan have done wonders with this 25-year-old property since purchasing it in 1989. The two peach-and-mint-green buildings house enormous, balconied guest rooms done in cream and soft pastel prints, all with kitchens or kitchenettes. The small inn caters to couples and to divers who take advantage of the fine reef located just offshore. The hotel is rather isolated, and its beachfront is rocky, but Cane Bay Beach is right next door and there is a small patch of sand at poolside for sunbathing. The pool itself is unusual, having been carved from the coral along the shore: The floor and one wall are concrete, but the seaside wall is made of natural coral, and the pool water is circulated as the waves crash dramatically over the side, creating a foamy jacuzzi on blustery days. *Box 1749, Kings Hill 00851, tel. 809/778–1805 or 800/545–0603. 12 rooms, 1 suite, 8 with air-conditioning. Facilities: bar, pool, complimentary snorkeling gear, in-room safes. AE, MC, V. $$–$$$*

Hibiscus Beach Hotel. This affordable, appealing property is set on the same stretch of palm-tree–lined beach as its sister hotel, the Cormorant. Guest rooms at the Hibiscus Beach are divided among five two-story pink buildings, each named for a tropical flower. All have views of the oceanfront, thanks to the staggered placement of the buildings at strategic angles, but request a room in the Hibiscus building—it's closest to the water. Rooms have welcome amenities like cable TV, safe, and minibar, and are tastefully furnished: White tiled floors and white walls are brightened with pink-striped curtains; bright, flowered bedspreads; and fresh-cut hibiscus blossoms. Bathrooms are nondescript but clean—both the shower stalls and the vanity mirrors are on the small side. Every unit has a roomy balcony that faces the sea. The staff is friendly and helpful, and the Tuesday night manager's party in the open-air bar-restaurant is a pleasant gathering. *Box 4131, La Grande Princesse 00820–4441, tel. 809/773–4042. 38 rooms with bath. Facilities: restaurant, bar pool, complimentary snorkel equipment, minibar, room safes, one kitchenette-equipped room. AE, D, DC, MC, V. $$*

★ **Hilty House.** This small bed-and-breakfast, tucked away on a hilltop, is a tranquil alternative to the island's many beach resorts. Follow a rutted dirt road up the hill to a shaded courtyard, and pass through picturesque iron gates to reach the inn's gardens. The house is a rambling, one-story affair that was once a rum distillery: patios surround the place and numerous doors allow cool breezes throughout. The immense, high-ceilinged living room has a Mediterranean flavor: Handpainted Italian tile lines the walls, and the giant fireplace accommodates a spit. Of the five guest rooms, the master suite is the largest, with a four-poster bed and a sunken shower over which is suspended a chandelier. The other bedrooms, each based on a specific color theme, are all lovely as well (the peach bedroom is the roomiest). The green bedroom has a bath across the hall; other rooms have their own adjacent bathrooms. A cozy efficiency cottage sits next to the main house. Affable owners Jacqueline and Hugh Hoare-Ward have a gift for detail: It is their tiny decorative touches that make the rooms here so special. On the other side of the house is a large pool with handpainted tile. *Box 26077, Gallows Bay 00824, tel. 809/773–2594. 5 rooms. Facilities: pool, complimentary breakfast. No credit cards. $*

The West End **Sprat Hall.** This 20-acre seaside Frederiksted property is a restored 1670 plantation estate, the oldest in the U.S.V.I. The homey, antiques-filled great house (no smoking, please) has guest rooms that harken back to more genteel days, with high-standing four-poster beds, antique furniture, bowls of fresh-cut bougainvillea and ginger thomas, and no air-conditioning. There are also family cottages on the grounds, but these are rather dingy and not in the same class as the great house rooms. The Hurd family also operates extensive horseback riding facilities here, as well as serving complimentary continental breakfast daily and fine dinners upon request for guests only. *Box 695, Frederiksted 00841, tel. 809/772–0305 or 800/843–3584. 9 rooms, 8 suites. Facilities: restaurant, beach, horseback riding, water sports. AE. $$–$$$*

Cottages and **Colony Cove.** Next door to Sugar Beach, Colony Cove offers a condo-
Condominiums minium-style resort alternative. The resort was completely rebuilt after the hurricane, and apartments here are sunny, tropical retreats done in pastel prints, rattan, and white tile. Each has two bedrooms, two baths, a balcony, full kitchen (so complete, it even has lasagna pans), and a washer/dryer. You'll find a large pool, water-sports center, and tennis courts on the grounds, and you can walk along the beach to reach the restaurant next door. The most compelling reason to stay here, though, is owner Susan Ivey, a dedicated naturalist who grows herbal gardens throughout the grounds and often leads nature walks and informal ecology seminars. *221A Golden Rock, Christiansted 00820, tel. 809/773–1950 or 800/524–2025; fax 809/778–4009. 59 apartments. Facilities: snack bar, pool, 2 tennis courts, water sports. AE, MC, V. $$$–$$$$*

Schooner Bay. This red-roof condominium village climbs the hillside above Gallows Bay, just outside Christiansted. The modern apartments were all completely renovated in 1990 and have balconies, full kitchens, and two or three bedrooms. The decor features floral fabrics and rattan or wicker, and the floors are covered in beige tile. All apartments have ceiling fans, air-conditioning in the bedrooms, washer/dryer, microwave oven, and dishwasher. The three-bedroom units have spiral staircases. Sun worshippers might be disappointed that the nearest beach is east, at the Buccaneer, but those with a yen to explore historic Christiansted will find this location ideal—within walking distance, yet at some remove from the bustle of downtown. *Schooner Bay, Gallows Bay, Christiansted 00820, tel. 809/773–9150 or 800/524–2025; fax 809/778–4009. 30 apartments. Facilities: 2 pools, whirlpool, tennis court, complimentary snorkeling gear. AE, MC, V. $$$*

Sugar Beach. Situated on the beach on the north side of the island,

Sugar Beach is just five minutes outside Christiansted. The air-conditioned apartments here, which range from studios to three-bedrooms, are immaculate and breezy. Each has a large patio or balcony, all with good views of the ocean. The larger apartments have washer/dryer units, and all have full kitchens with microwaves. Though the exteriors of these condos are done in an ordinary beige stucco, the white interiors, all done with cool, tropical furnishings, are lovely. The pool is built around the ruins of a 250-year-old sugar mill. *Estate Golden Rock, Christiansted 00820, tel. 809/773–5345 or 800/524–2049; fax 809/773–1359. 46 apartments. Facilities: pool, 2 tennis courts, conference room, beach. AE, MC, V. $$$*

★ **Club St. Croix.** Popular with honeymooners, this condominium resort made a strong comeback from Hurricane Hugo: Newly refurbished inside and out, the studio, one-, and two-bedroom apartments are spacious and bright. Indian-print throw rugs and cushions complement the bamboo furniture and rough, white-tile floors; the modern decor is further highlighted by glass-top tables and mirrored closet doors. Penthouses have loft bedrooms reached by spiral staircases, and studios enlist Murphy beds in the sitting rooms. Every room has a full kitchen and a sun deck, with waterfront views of Christiansted and Buck Island. On the beach you'll find a poolside restaurant and bar and a dock. Guests can take a sunset sail or go snorkeling via the hotel's 42-foot catamaran, the *Cruzan Cat. Estate Golden Rock, Christiansted 00820, tel. 809/773–4800 or 800/635–1533; fax 809/773–4805. 54 suites. Facilities: restaurant, bar, 3 tennis courts, conference room, dock, pool, whirlpool, laundry room, water sports. AE, MC, V. $$*

Private Homes and Villas Several real estate companies handle short-term rental of private homes. Try **Island Villas** (tel. 809/773–8821) or **Farchette, Hanley, & Johnson** (tel. 809/773–4665) in Christiansted and **Richards & Ayer** (tel. 809/772–0420) in Frederiksted.

The Arts and Nightlife

Christiansted **Island Center for the Performing Arts** (tel. 809/778–5272), located mid-island, hosts St. Croix's major concerts, plays, and performances by visiting entertainers.

Christiansted has a lively and eminently casual club scene near the waterfront. At **Mango Grove** (53 King St., tel. 809/778–8103) you'll hear live guitar and vocals in an open-air courtyard with a bar and Cinzano umbrella-covered tables. The upstairs **Moonraker Lounge** (43A Queen Cross St., tel. 809/773–1535) presents a constant calendar of live music, usually a singer with any acoustic guitar playing all your favorites from Jimmy Buffett, Bob Dylan, and the like. Milder piano music can be heard on the broad veranda of **Club Comanche** (1 Strand St., tel. 809/773–0210). To party under the stars in a very, very informal setting, head to the **Wreck Bar** (tel. 809/773–6092), on Christiansted's Hospital Street, for crab races as well as rock and roll. At **Calabash** (Strand St., tel. 809/778–0001) you'll find steel band music from Wednesday through Saturday, and on Friday there's a broken bottle dancer. **Hotel on the Cay** (Protestant Cay, tel. 809/773–2035) has a West Indian Buffet on Tuesday nights that features a broken bottle dancer and Mocko Jumbie. On Thursday nights, the **Cormorant** (La Grande Princesse, tel. 809/778–8920) throws a similar event. The **2 Plus 2 Disco** (17 La Grande Princesse, tel. 809/773–3710) spins a great mix of calypso, soul, disco, and reggae, with live music on weekends.

Frederiksted Although less hopping than Christiansted, Frederiksted restaurants and clubs have a variety of weekend entertainment. **Blue Moon** (17 Strand St., tel. 809/772–2222), a waterfront restaurant, is the place to be for live jazz on Friday 9 PM–1 AM. The island's premiere calypso band, Blinky and the Roadmasters, performs every Sunday night at **Stars of the West** (14 Strand St., tel. 809/772–9039). The **Lost Dog Pub** (King St., tel. 809/772–3526) is a favorite spot for a casual drink, a game of darts, and occasional live rock and roll on Sunday nights. Head up to Mahogany Road to the **Mt. Pellier Domino Club** (50 Mt. Pellier, tel. 809/772–9914). Piro, the one-man band, plays on Sunday.

St. John

Introduction

By Margaret Enos Kearns and Janet E. Bigham

Updated by Jordan Simon

About 20 minutes by ferry, 3 miles east of St. Thomas across Pillsbury Sound from Red Hook on St. Thomas, the island of St. John comes close to realizing that travel-folder dream of "an unspoiled tropical paradise." Beautiful and largely undisturbed, St. John is covered with tropical vegetation, including a bay-tree forest that once supplied St. Thomas with the raw material of its fragrant bay rum. Clean, gleaming, white-sand beaches fringe the many bays scalloped out along the northern shore, and the iridescent water is perfect for swimming, fishing, snorkeling, and underwater photography. There are two state-of-the-art campgrounds, two luxury resorts, and plenty of guest houses, condominiums, and small inns in between. Two-thirds of St. John's 21 square miles were donated to the United States as a national park in 1956 by Laurance Rockefeller, founder of Caneel Bay Plantation.

Today there are only about 3,000 permanent residents on St. John, most of them native Virgin Islanders. Most Continentals are in the tourist and boating business or are permanent residents who've chosen the island for retirement. Cruz Bay, the administrative capital, is still a small West Indian village, even with the advent of the National Park Service facilities and the reconstruction of small shopping centers and other buildings in recent years.

The activity level has increased, and when the occasional cruise ship ferries in its passengers, Cruz Bay can get crowded. While Coral Bay and the east end of the island are feeling the pressure of development, for the most part the island still has a wild feel to it. Perhaps because there is so much beauty preserved on St. John, the community is active in curbing excesses on private land, as well. One example is the only successful effort in the U.S.V.I. to recycle aluminum cans—which a coalition of St. John citizens began with the help of the national park in 1990.

The Danes acquired St. John in 1675, when Governor Jorgen Iverson claimed the unsettled island. The British residents of nearby Tortola, however, considered St. John theirs, and when a small party of Danes from St. Thomas moved onto the island they were "invited" to leave by the British, and they did. In 1717 a group of Danish planters took formal possession of the island and formed the first permanent settlement, at Coral Bay. The question of who owned St. John wasn't settled until 1762, when Britain—which had continued to dispute the Danes' claim to the island—decided that keeping up good relations with Denmark was more important than keeping St. John.

By 1728 St. John had 87 plantations and a population of 123 whites and 677 blacks. In 1733 St. John was hit by a drought, hurricanes, and a plague of insects that destroyed the summer crops. There were by this time more than 1,000 slaves working more than 100 plantations. The Africans on St. John were recent arrivals, and many had been noblemen and landowners—even slave holders—themselves and felt threatened now with famine. Conditions for slaves on the island were already unusually severe, and the white population, sensing the slaves' growing desperation, enacted even harsher measures to keep them in line. On November 23 the slaves revolted, surprising the Danes with their military prowess, and captured the fort at Coral Bay. They controlled the island for six months, during which time nearly a quarter of the island's population—black and white—was killed. The rebellion was finally put down by 100 Danish militia and 220 Creole troops brought in from Martinique.

St. John today is perhaps the most racially integrated of the three U.S.V.I.; the people here, black and white, share a stronger sense of community than is found on St. Thomas or St. Croix. This may be due to St. John's small size and to the consensus among residents that the island's beauty is sacrosanct and must be protected.

Sightseeing is best done by jeep, with or without a driver or guide. Guides are useful, sometimes indispensable, for exploring the scenic mountain trails, the secret coves, and the sobering bush-covered ruins of old forts and palatial plantation houses.

Secure in its protection as a national park, St. John offers respite and refuge to the traveler who wants to escape from the pressures of 20th-century life for a day, a week, or perhaps forever.

Important Addresses and Numbers

Tourist Information Information about the U.S.V.I. is available on St. John through the **U.S. Virgin Islands Government Tourist Office** (Box 200, Cruz Bay, St. John 00830, tel. 809/776–6450). The **National Park Service** (Box 710, Cruz Bay, St. John 00831, tel. 809/776–6201) also has a visitor center near the docks in Cruz Bay.

The telephone exchange throughout St. John was slated to be switched to 693 by 1994. However, at press time, the change had not been fully implemented. When you dial the current listing a recording will redirect you, if necessary.

Emergencies
Police To reach the police dial 915.

Hospitals For medical emergencies on St. John contact the **Clinic** (Cruz Bay, tel. 809/776–6400), or call an **emergency medical technician** directly (tel. 809/776–6222).

Air Ambulance The only U.S.V.I.-based air ambulance service is **Bohlke International Airways** (tel. 809/778–9177), which operates out of the airport in St. Croix. **Air Medical Services** (tel. 800/443–0013) and **Air Ambulance Network** (tel. 800/327–1966) also service the area from Florida.

Coast Guard For emergencies call the **Marine Safety Detachment** (tel. 809/776–3497) on St. Thomas from 7 AM to 3:30 PM weekdays. If there is no answer, call the **Rescue Coordination Center** (tel. 809/722–2943) in San Juan, open 24 hours a day.

Pharmacies The **St. John Drug Center** (tel. 809/776–6353) is located in the Boulon shopping center, up Centerline Road in Cruz Bay.

Getting Around

By Car Use caution when driving on St. John. The terrain is very hilly, the roads winding, and blind curves are numerous. You may suddenly come upon a huge safari bus careening around a corner, or a couple of hikers strolling along the side of the road. Major roads are well paved, but once you get off a specific route, dirt roads filled with potholes are common. For such driving, a four-wheel drive vehicle is your best bet.

On St. John, call **Avis** (tel. 809/776–6374), **Budget** (tel. 809/776–7575), **Cool Breeze** (tel. 809/776–6588), **Delbert Hill Taxi Rental Service** (tel. 809/776–6637), **Hertz** (tel. 809/776–6695), **O'Connor Jeep** (tel. 809/776–6343), **St. John Car Rental** (tel. 809/776–6103), or **Spencer's Jeep** (tel. 809/776–7784).

By Bus and On St. John buses and taxis are the same thing: open-air safari
Taxi buses. Technically the safari buses are private taxis, but everyone uses them as an informal bus system. You'll find them congregated at the Cruz Bay Dock, ready to take you to any of the beaches or other island destinations, but you can also pick them up anywhere on the road by signaling. You're likely to travel with other tourists en route to their destinations. Typical rates from Cruz Bay (for two people) are $3.75 each to Trunk Bay, $4 each to Cinnamon Bay Campground, and $6 each to either Annaberg Plantation or Coral Bay.

Guided Tours

St. John Along with providing trail maps and brochures about St. John Na-
National Park tional Park, the park service also gives a variety of guided tours on- and offshore. For more information or to arrange a tour contact the **St. John National Park Visitor Center** (Cruz Bay, tel. 809/776–6201). Fees charged cover the cost of transportation. The availability of the tours listed below varies, so contact the Cruz Bay visitor center (tel. 809/776–6330) to check. Tours should be reserved through the center.

The following tours require that you make reservations:

Reef Bay Hike. After busing to the trail head, this vigorous hike at Reef Bay visits petroglyph carvings and an old sugar-mill factory. You'll need your serious walking shoes, and it's up to you to bring food and drink. An optional return-trip by boat ($10) saves you a hike back up the hill (making this a walk of only average difficulty) and will have you back in Cruz Bay by 3:30 PM. *$5.*

Around-the-Island Snorkel Tour. A motorboat makes a six-hour trip around the island with three stops for snorkeling. You provide your own snorkeling gear and lunch. *$40.*

Bird Walks. Birders are bused to Francis Bay for a two-hour trail walk with a park-ranger guide. *$3.*

The following tours do not require that you make reservations, but you will need to check in advance to verify the times and days tours are given:

Seashore Walk. This 1-hour walk along the coral flats and Mangrove Lagoons meets at the shoreline below the Annaberg Plantation parking lot. You'll need wading shoes. *No fee.*

Snorkel Trips. Beginner trips (1½ hours) are run at Trunk Bay, advanced (1 hour) start from the beach on Cinnamon Bay. Bring your own snorkeling gear and a T-shirt for protection from the sun. *No fee.*

During the evenings two to three days a week at **Cinnamon Bay,** rangers hold informal talks on park history, marine research, and other topics. Confirm times, because schedules change often in the islands.

Exploring St. John

Numbers in the margin correspond to points of interest on the St. John map.

St. John may be small, but the roads are narrow and wind up and down steep hills, so don't expect to get anywhere in a hurry. Except for cozy Cruz Bay, places to go and things to do are spread across the island, and, if you plan to do a lot of touring, renting a car (or best of all a jeep) will be cheaper, give you more freedom, and be a lot more fun than depending on taxis.

Many of its southern-coast beaches and other sites can be reached only on foot or by boat, but most of the island's famed beaches are easily accessible by car or jeep. This suggested itinerary takes you along much of the scenic northern coast before a trip over a paved road on the central, mountainous ridge of St. John. Bring along your swimsuit for stops at some of the most beautiful beaches in the world.

❶ **Cruz Bay** town dock is the starting point for just about everything on St. John. Take a leisurely stroll through the streets of this colorful, compact town: There are plenty of shops in which to browse and numerous watering holes where you can stop to take a breather.

Follow the waterfront out of town (about 100 yards) to another dock at the edge of a parking lot. On the far side of this lagoon you'll find the **National Park Service Visitors Center** (tel. 809/776–6201), where you can pick up a handy guide to St. John's hiking trails or see various large maps of the island. If you see a "St. John Map" featuring Max the Mongoose, grab it; it's full of information. The apartment complex partially hidden by the trees behind the park center gives you an idea of the style with which St. John residents approach the world—the attractive, balconied complex is low-income housing.

Begin your tour traveling north out of Cruz Bay. You'll pass **Mongoose Junction,** recently expanded to include Mongoose Junction II, one of the prettiest shopping areas to be found. Its West Indian–style architecture and native stone blend into the surrounding woods, making it a widely touted example of good development in a community grappling with growth problems. There's a bakery with great pastries and limited supplies for a picnic here.

Time Out If you'd rather relax over a sit-down meal, the **Mongoose Restaurant** (tel. 809/776–7586) is a tranquil, open-air eatery nestled amid banana trees and noted for its sumptuous breakfast and brunch spreads, as well as for top-notch soups and salads at lunch and steaks and chops at dinner.

As you pass Mongoose Junction, head up the hill (on Route 20) and along the northern coast. One gorgeous vista follows another, so don't despair if you miss one or two. At the ½-mile mark you'll come to the well-groomed gardens and beaches of **Caneel Bay,** purchased

St. John

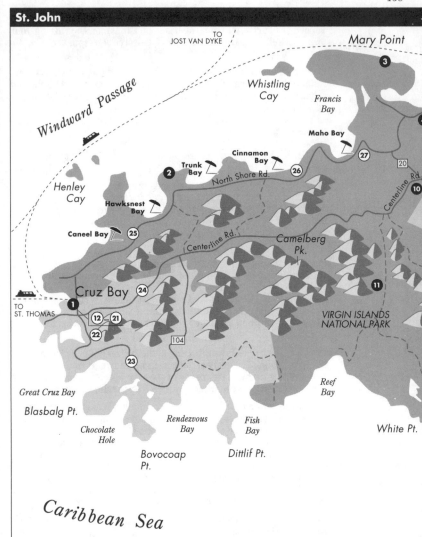

TO JOST VAN DYKE

Mary Point

Windward Passage

Whistling Cay

Francis Bay

Henley Cay

Maho Bay

Cinnamon Bay

Trunk Bay

North Shore Rd.

Hawksnest Bay

Caneel Bay

Centerline Rd.

Camelberg Pk.

Centerline Rd.

Cruz Bay

TO ST. THOMAS

VIRGIN ISLANDS NATIONAL PARK

Great Cruz Bay

Blasbalg Pt.

Chocolate Hole

Rendezvous Bay

Fish Bay

Reef Bay

White Pt.

Bovocoap Pt.

Dittlif Pt.

Caribbean Sea

Exploring

Annaberg Plantation, **4**
Bordeaux Mountain, **9**
Christ of the Caribbean statue, **2**

Coral Bay, **5**
Cruz Bay, **1**
East End, **6**
Fortsberg, **7**
King Hill Road, **10**
Minna Neger Ghut, **3**
Reef Bay Trail, **11**
Salt Pond, **8**

Dining

Le Chateau de Bordeaux, **29**
Chow Bella, **23**
Don Carlos, **30**
Ellington's, **12**
Etta's, **13**
The Fish Trap, **14**

Lime Inn, **15**
Luscious Licks, **16**
Miss Lucy's, **28**
Morgan's Mango, **17**
Paradiso, **18**
Pusser's, **19**
Shipwreck Landing, **31**

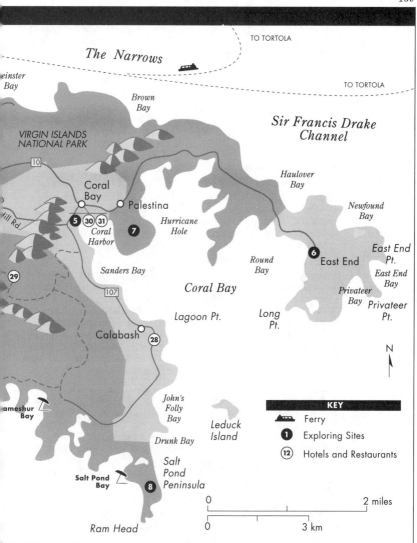

TO TORTOLA

The Narrows

TO TORTOLA

einster Bay

Brown Bay

VIRGIN ISLANDS NATIONAL PARK

Sir Francis Drake Channel

10

Coral Bay

Palestina

5 30 31

Coral Harbor

7

Hurricane Hole

Haulover Bay

Newfound Bay

6 East End

East End Pt.

East End Bay

ill Rd.

29

Sanders Bay

107

Round Bay

Coral Bay

Privateer Bay

Privateer Pt.

Calabash 28

Lagoon Pt.

Long Pt.

N

John's Folly Bay

ameshur Bay

Leduck Island

Drunk Bay

KEY

Ferry

1 Exploring Sites

12 Hotels and Restaurants

Salt Pond Bay

8

Salt Pond Peninsula

0   2 miles

Ram Head

0   3 km

Lodging

Caneel Bay Resort, **25**

Cinnamon Bay Campground, **26**

Cruz Views, **21**

Gallows Point Suite Resort, **12**

Hyatt Regency St. John, **23**

The Inn at Tamarind Court, **13**

Lavender Hill Estates, **20**

Maho Bay Camp, **27**

Pastory Estates, **24**

Raintree Inn, **14**

Serendip, **22**

from the Danish West India Company and developed by Laurance Rockefeller in the 1950s, who then turned over much of the island to the U.S. government as parkland. Visitors are welcome at one of its seven beaches and at two of the three excellent restaurants.

Continue east on North Shore Road; you are about to see, one after another, four of the most beautiful beaches in all of the Caribbean. The road is narrow and hilly (it was actually expanded not too long ago, believe it or not) with switchbacks and steep curves that make driving a challenge. **Hawksnest,** the first beach you will come to, is where Alan Alda shot scenes for his film *The Four Seasons.* The beach is narrow, and the sea calm here. Sea-grape branches arch into the water, and there are plenty of nooks and crannies, providing an ideal hideaway for an afternoon.

Just past Hawksnest Hill swing left to Peace Hill, sometimes called Sugarloaf Hill, to the *Christ of the Caribbean* **statue** and an old sugar-mill tower. Park in the small unmarked parking lot and walk about 100 yards up a rocky path. The area is grassy, and views do not get much better than this. *Christ of the Caribbean* was erected in 1953 by Colonel Julius Wadsworth and donated, along with 9 acres of land, to the national park in 1975.

Your next stop, and that of quite a few tourist-filled safari buses, is **Trunk Bay.** Trunk Bay is a beautiful beach, but it is where the cruise ships' shore excursions bring passengers for a day's outing, and it's sometimes a little busy with snorkeling instruction and the distribution of rum punch. Trunk Bay is a good place to learn to snorkel. The underwater trail is a little the worse for wear from all the traffic, but it can be comforting, when you are first starting out, to see other people in the water with you. Trunk Bay has changing rooms, a snack bar, equipment rentals, and lifeguards.

Continuing on the beach hunt, you'll come to **Cinnamon Bay,** with its wide beach. The snorkeling around the point to the right is good— look for the big angelfish and the swarms of purple triggerfish that live here. Afternoons on Cinnamon Bay can be windy, so you may want to get an early start, in case the wind picks up. The national-park campground is at Cinnamon Bay and includes a snack bar, bathhouse, boutique, restaurant, general store, water-sports equipment rental, and a self-guided museum. Across the road from the beach parking lot is the beginning of the Cinnamon Bay hiking trail: Look for the ruins of a sugar mill that mark the trailhead.

As you leave Cinnamon, the road flattens out and you'll find yourself on a shaded lane running under flowering trees. **Maho Bay** comes almost to the road here, and you might want to stop and take a dip. The Maho Bay Campground is here, too—a wonderful mélange of open-air, rustic tent cottages nestled in the hillside above. Maho Bay Campground offers programs featuring informal talks and slide and film presentations. In spring, jazz and jungle harmonize when Maho sponsors a series of jazz and classical music in its outdoor pavilion.

Past Maho Bay, keep to the left and head north. Follow signs for Annaberg Plantation. When you run out of road, turn right toward the plantation, and at the first break in the trees, look left. The body of land that you see jutting out into the water is **Mary Point,** site of the historic **Minna Neger Ghut.** In this rocky ravine, in 1733 rebelling slaves are said to have jumped to their deaths rather than capitulate to French troops brought in by the Danes.

❹ The partially restored **Annaberg Plantation** at Leinster Bay, built in the 1780s and once an important sugar mill, is just ahead on North Shore Road. (Self-guided tour pamphlets are available at the National Park Visitors Center for 95¢.) As you stroll around, look up at the steep hillsides and imagine cutting sugarcane against that grade in the hot sun. Slaves, Danes, and Dutchmen toiled here to harvest the sugarcane that produced sugar, molasses, and rum for export. There are no official visiting hours, no charge for entry, and no official tours, although some well-informed taxi drivers will show you around. Daily from 9 to noon, artisans give demonstrations of island crafts and local ladies bake luscious johnnycakes (the Caribbean Egg McMuffin). The roofless buildings are dramatic under moonlight. *For more information on talks and cultural demonstrations, contact the National Park Service Visitors Center, tel. 809/776–6201.*

From Annaberg keep to the left and go south, then head uphill and bear left at the junction to go east, on Route 10, to Coral Bay.

As you turn off Route 20 and head along Route 10 to Coral Bay the road becomes a little rougher, an indication that you are heading toward the quieter side of the island.

❺ **Coral Bay** is named for its shape rather than for its underwater life. The word *Coral* comes from *krawl*, Danish for *corral*. The community at the dry, eastern end of the island is the ultimate in laid-back style. It's quiet, neighborhoody, local, and independent. The small wood-and-stucco West Indian homes house everyone from families born here to newer residents who offer palm readings and massage. This is a place to get away from it all. If you want to stay on this end of the island there are several private homes for rent (*see* Homes and Villas and Condominiums, in Lodging, *below*). You'll also need a jeep, unless you plan to drop out of civilization completely.

Time Out **Seabreeze Cafe** (Rte. 107, ¼ mi west of the intersection of Rte. 10, tel. 809/776–7824) is the kind of place where you can sit for a long, long time. The walls provide exhibition space for local artists, and the mostly open front looks out to Coral Bay. There's eggs Florentine on the menu, Joni Mitchell on the sound system, and friendly folks at your service. There are also burgers and homey lunch specials such as meatloaf and tuna melts, as well as ethnic theme nights, with a jazzed-up menu.

❻ The road forms a loop around Coral Bay. Head northeast along Route 10 to Hurricane Hole at the remote and pristine **East End,** only a 15- to-20-minute ride from Coral Bay, where Arawak Indians are believed to have first settled on the island 2,000 years ago. At **Haulover Bay** only a couple of hundred yards separate the Atlantic Ocean from the Caribbean.

❼ South of the ball field at Coral Bay is **Fortsberg.** This is the site of Fort Frederik, which was overtaken and held by rebellious slaves for six months during the bloody uprising of 1733. Many of the fierce battles in that conflict took place here.

❽ Route 107 takes you south to the peninsula of **Salt Pond,** which is only about 1 foot above sea level. If you're weary of driving you can hike the trail south to the spectacular cliffs of **Ram's Head.** In any case you or your rented car can't proceed much farther on 107 without venturing onto a truly rocky road that heads west. Be sure at least to get a view of **Lameshur Bay,** one of the best snorkeling places on St. John and an area used for underwater training by the U.S. Navy.

Once you've run out of road on Route 107 retrace your steps to Coral Bay and go west (left) on Route 10 again, which takes you over the heights of the island toward Cruz Bay. On your left is the turnoff for **⑨ Bordeaux Mountain,** at 1,277 feet St. John's highest peak. This is also an area of rain forest. Stop for a moment hereabouts and crackle a leaf from one of the bay trees: You'll get a whiff of the spicy aroma that you may recognize from the bay rum for which St. John is fa-**⑩ mous.** One mile ahead stop on the right at **King Hill Road** for a view of some of the B.V.I. to the northeast, including Peter Island, Tortola, and Norman and Cooper islands.

To appreciate the Bordeaux Mountain region fully, save some time **⑪** during your stay to hike the **Reef Bay Trail.** Unless you are a rugged individualist who wants a physical challenge (and that describes a lot of people who stay on St. John) you'll probably get the most out of the trip if you join a hike led by a National Park Service ranger who can identify the trees and plants on the hike down, fill you in on the history of the Reef Bay Plantation, and tell you about the carvings you'll find in the rocks at the bottom of the trail. The National Park Service provides a boat ($10) to take you back to Cruz Bay, saving you the uphill return climb (*see* Guided Tours, *above*).

The Reef Bay Plantation, according to architectural historian Frederik C. Gjessing, is the most architecturally ambitious plantation structure on St. John. The great house is largely intact, though gutted, and its classical beauty is still visible from what remains. You'll also see the remnants of a cook house, servants' quarters, stable, and outhouse. Reef Bay was the last working plantation on St. John when it stopped production in 1920.

Time Out   At a widening of Route 10 is a business that started out as an ice cooler on the back of a pickup truck, grew to a hotdog vendor's stand, and is now a full-fledged bar and restaurant with a sweeping view of Coral Bay. **Cheeseburger in Paradise** (8A–1 Carolina, tel. 809/776–6611) offers lunch and dinner on the terrace or inside in Le Chateau de Bordeaux, the small, formal dining room. It's the only building of its size on this section of Route 10.

Return to Cruz Bay on Route 10.

St. John For Free

St. John is known for some of the most exquisite, unspoiled beaches in the world, and they are all free. Whether it's snorkeling along the trail at Trunk Bay or lounging under a sea-grape tree at Hawksnest Beach, there is plenty of variety.

St. John National Park offers a range of free guided hikes and seashore walks as well as nature lectures (*see* Guided Tours, *above*). They're popular and fill up fast, so call ahead for reservations. Self-guided tours are available at **Annaberg Plantation** and the **museum** at Cinnamon Bay. Pick up brochures at the National Park Visitors Center in Cruz Bay.

What to See and Do with Children

St. John was designed for the delights of children, young and old. The National Park Service has a listing of all the ways you can explore nature. Some of the most popular for children include the cultural demonstrations at Annaberg Plantation, such as baking bread and basket weaving; seashore walks; evening nature lectures at Cinnamon Bay; and an afternoon snorkel safari especially designed for beginners.

Off the Beaten Track

Outside Cruz Bay (up the hill by the Texaco station and across from the Tradewinds office) is the **Enighed Estate Great House,** built in 1757. Enighed is the Danish word for "concord," meaning unity or peace. The great house and its surrounding buildings (a sugar-production factory and horse-driven mill) have been destroyed by fire and hurricanes, and the house sat in ruins until it was restored in 1982. Today it is home to the **Elaine Ione Sprauve Library and Museum,** and houses a small collection of Indian pottery, colonial artifacts, and contemporary craftwork by local artisans. The library hosts occasional craft demonstrations and classes. *Tel. 809/776–6359. Open weekdays 9–1 and 2–5.*

Shopping

With so much natural beauty to offer, the pleasures of shopping on St. John are all but overlooked in travel literature, but the blend of luxury items and handcrafts found in the shops on St. John offers excellent opportunities. Two new shopping areas have widened the choices. Two levels of cool, stone-wall shops, set off by colorfully planted terraces and courtyards, make **Mongoose Junction** one of the prettiest shopping malls in the Caribbean. **Wharfside Village,** on the other side of Cruz Bay, is a painted-clapboard community with shops and restaurants.

There's no bookstore on St. John, but the national park headquarters sells several good histories of St. John, including *St. John Back Time,* by Ruth Hull Low and Rafael Valls, and for linguists, *What a Pistarckle!,* by Lito Valls.

Cruz Bay and Mongoose Junction *Arts and Crafts*

Bamboula (Mongoose Junction, tel. 809/776–7699). Owner Jo Sterling travels the Caribbean and the world to bring back clothing, accessories, and housewares for this multicultural boutique.

The Canvas Factory (Mongoose Junction, tel. 809/776–6196). If you're a true shopper, you may need an extra bag to carry all your treasures home; this shop offers every kind of tote and carrier imaginable, some fancifully hand-decorated.

Caravan (Mongoose Junction, tel. 809/776–8677). Buyers scour the marketplace worldwide to supply this shop with its unique treasures. You'll find everything from Brazilian coconut masks to African trading beads here. In addition, much of the finely worked jewelry is crafted right in the shop.

Donald Schnell (Mongoose Junction, tel. 809/776–6420). Choose from the unique selection of hand-blown glass, pottery, and dinnerware made from crushed coral. Whether you opt for wind chimes, kaleidoscopes, or fanciful water fountains, your choice can be shipped worldwide.

Fabric Mill (Mongoose Junction, tel. 809/776–6194). Shop here for handmade island animals and dolls, as well as place mats, napkins, and batik wraps. Or take home a bolt of tropical brights from the upholstery-fabric selection.

Mongoose Trading Company (Mongoose Junction, tel. 809/776–6993). A bit of the Cotswalds and Provençe in the Caribbean. Available here are Crabtree and Evelyn soaps, lacework pillows, all kinds of cookbooks and kitchen accessories, and hand-painted dinnerware reminiscent of a French country inn.

Clothing **Big Planet Adventure Outfitters** (Mongoose Junction, tel. 809/776–6638 or 800/238–8687). Somehow you knew when you got off the boat that someone on St. John would sell Birkenstock sandals. This outdoor-clothing store is where you'll find them, as well as other colorful and durable cotton clothing and accessories, including designs by Patagonia, The North Face, and Sierra Designs. The adjacent Little Planet section sells children's clothes, often recycled from such unlikely materials as plastic bottles.

Jewelry **Colombian Emeralds** (Mongoose Junction, tel. 809/776–6007). A beautiful store in which curving balconies lead you through the showcases of gems. This is one of two branches on St. John; the other is at Wharfside Village (tel. 809/776–6999). Both carry high-quality jewelry, unset gems, and perfumes.

Pink Papaya (Lemon Tree Mall, Cruz Bay, tel. 809/776–7266). Home of M.L. Etre's exclusive geometric designs and Jumbie Jewels, spirited accessories, and unique tropical jewelry.

R&I Patton Goldsmiths (Mongoose Junction, tel. 809/776–6548). Rudy and Irene Patton design most of the unique silver and gold jewelry in this shop. The rest comes from various jeweler friends of the Pattons. Sea fans (those large, lacy plants that sway with the ocean's currents) in filigreed silver, lapis set in long drops of gold, and starfish and hibiscus pendants in silver or gold are tempting choices. To commemorate your Reef Bay hike (or your stay at Caneel), there are petroglyphs of every size and metal.

Wharfside Village You'll see this island shopping center as your ferry pulls into the Cruz Bay dock. It's the cluster of pastel pink-and-blue clapboard buildings at the edge of the bay to your right. Wharfside shops tend to be slightly less expensive and a little more on the T-shirts–and–imported–jewelry side than the pricey, elegant shops at Mongoose Junction. In addition to several restaurants and bars, there is a terrific deli: **Barracuda Bistro** (tel. 809/779–4944) serves homestyle cooking and will prepare beach picnics.

For bathing suits and casual island wear, try **Cruz Bay Clothing Co.** (tel. 809/776–7611); **Let's Go Bananas** (tel. 809/776–7055) for cool 100%-cotton tropical clothing; and **Free Bird Creations** (tel. 809/776–7512) for unique handcrafted jewelry. **Blue Carib Gems** (tel. 809/776–5268) has custom-made jewelry, loose gemstones, old coins, and an art gallery.

Sports and Outdoor Activities

Fishing Sport-fishing trips can be arranged by calling the **St. Thomas Sportfishing Center** (tel. 809/775–7990), at Red Hook on St. Thomas, or **American Yacht Harbor** (tel. 809/775–0685), also in Red Hook. The fishing boats will pick you up on St. John. **Gone Ketchin'** (tel. 809/776–7709) is an informal St. John–based outfit. For light-tackle fishing, ask around Cruz Bay, or check with your hotel's activities desk.

Hiking The National Park Service maintains more than 20 trails on the north and south shores. They vary in difficulty and length, but there is something for almost everyone. These trails are not garden paths, however, and the park service recommends that you wear long pants to protect yourself against insects and thorny vegetation; sturdy and comfortable walking shoes, rather than sandals or flip-flops (even if the trail ends up at the beach); and a head covering. The park service publishes a trail map, detailing the points of interest, dangers, trail lengths, and estimated hiking times. Check in at the visitor center in Cruz Bay on St. John (*see* Important Addresses and Numbers, *above*).

Sailing See Sailing in the Virgin Islands, Chapter 4, for information.

Sea Kayaking Trips are led by professional guides and use traditional kayaks to ply coastal waters. They are run by **Big Planet Adventure Outfitters** (tel. 809/776–6638 or 800/238–8687) and **Low Key Water Sports** (tel. 809/776–7048). Prices start at $40 for a ½-day trip.

Snorkeling/ Diving See Diving and Snorkeling in the Virgin Islands, Chapter 3, for information.

Tennis The public courts near the fire station in Cruz Bay are lighted until 10 PM and are available on a first-come, first-served basis. **Caneel Bay** (tel. 809/776–6111) has 11 courts (none lighted) and a pro shop. The **Hyatt Regency** (tel. 809/776–7171) has six lighted courts and a pro shop.

Windsurfing Try **Cinnamon Bay Campground** (tel. 809/776–6330), where rentals are available for $12–$15 per day. In Coral Bay, **Coral Bay Watersports** (tel. 809/776–6850) charges $30 for a 1½-hour lesson.

Beaches

Unlike most islands, where there is a good-better-best scale in rating beaches, St. John is blessed with so many great beaches that the scale is good, great, and why-tell-anyone-else-about-this-place? Most of the good beaches, popular with locals and day-trippers from St. Thomas, are along the north shore of the island, within the boundaries of the national park. Although some are more developed than others, all are under park-service supervision. They can get crowded on weekends, holidays, and during high season, but by and large the beaches retain a pristine quality. Those along the south shore and the eastern half of the island are still quiet and isolated.

The most popular—and most developed—beaches are:

Caneel Bay. This is actually seven white-sand beaches on the north shore, six of which can be reached only by water if you are not a hotel guest. (Public access to beaches is a civil right in the U.S.V.I., but public access across the land to the beach is not.) The main beach (ask for directions) provides easy access to the public. Visitors are welcome and nonguests can dine at the hotels' three restaurants (jacket required at dinner during winter season), cruise the gift shop, and roam the more interesting parts of the resort's 170 acres, including the ruins of the old plantation.

Hawksnest Beach. This beach is becoming more popular every day; it's narrow and lined with sea-grape trees. There are restrooms, cooking grills, and a covered shed for picnicking. It's popular for group outings but most of the time it's quiet.

Trunk Bay. Probably St. John's most-photographed beach, this is also the most popular spot for beginning snorkelers, because of its underwater trail. It's the St. John stop for cruise-ship passengers who choose a snorkeling tour for the day, so if you're looking for seclusion, check cruise-ship listings in *St. Thomas This Week* to find out what days the highest number are in port. Crowded or not (and crowded is a relative term here, because beaches in the U.S.V.I. rarely get as packed as some stateside or European shores) it's a stunning beach and sure to please. There are changing rooms, a snack bar, picnic tables, and snorkeling equipment for rent.

Cinnamon Bay. A long, sandy beach facing beautiful cays serves the adjoining national-park campground. Facilities (showers, toilets, commissary, restaurant, beach shop) are open to all. There's good snorkeling off the point to the right and rental equipment available.

Salt Pond Bay, on the southeastern coast of St. John, is a scenic area to explore, next to Coral Bay and rugged Drunk Bay. This beach is for the adventurous. It's a short hike down a hill from the parking lot, and the only facility is an outhouse. There is little shade since Hurricane Hugo destroyed most of the trees, but a few picnic tables are scattered about. The beach is a little rockier here, but there are interesting tide pools and the snorkeling is good. Take special care to leave nothing valuable in the car, as reports of thefts are numerous.

Dining

You don't come to St. John for the cuisine, but you'll find it's surprisingly good. Often the surroundings make the meal, as in the case of Caneel Bay's Turtle Bay restaurant (open to guests only) or a home-cooked meal on the grill outside your campsite. Food on St. John is expensive, as it is throughout the U.S.V.I., and usually the best bet is to keep it simple.

At the restaurants listed below, the dress code is informal and reservations are unnecessary, unless otherwise mentioned.

If you're renting a house or condo and doing your own cooking, you'll find the best selection and prices at the **St. John's Supermarket and Deli** (tel. 809/776–7373) or the **Marina Market** (tel. 809/779–4401).

Bordeaux Mountain ★ **Le Chateau de Bordeaux.** The best view you're going to find to dine by is on the terrace here or in the air-conditioned dining room (go at sunset). The rustic cabin is practically a glorified tree house, magically transformed into an ultraromantic, elegant aerie by wrought-iron chandeliers, lace tablecloths, and antiques. The chefs merrily blend several culinary traditions; their creations appeal equally to the eye and palate. You might start with velvety carrot soup, perfectly contrasted with roasted ancho chile, or pasta sautéed with smoked salmon, capers, leeks, and white wine and infused with saffron. Then try the superb rack of lamb perfumed with rosemary in a honey dijon crust in shallot and port wine sauce, or the macadamia-coated salmon with crème fraîche dill glaze. The comprehensive, moderately priced wine list is predictably strong on Bordeaux reds. *Rte. 10, just east of Centerline Rd., tel. 809/776–6611. AE, MC, V. $$$–$$$$*

Coral Bay **Shipwreck Landing.** Start with one of the house drinks, perhaps a fresh-squeezed concoction of lime, coconut, and rum, then move on to hearty taco salads, fried shrimp, teriyaki chicken, and conch fritters. The birds keep up a lively chatter in the bougainvillea that surrounds the open-air restaurant, and there's live music on Sunday nights in season. *Coral Bay, tel. 809/776–8640. MC, V. $–$$*

Don Carlos. This rollicking spot is little more than a rickety shack—painted in desert colors and hung with ponchos and serapes—built right over the water. The conch fritters and margaritas are lethal in the best way. Try the fiery shrimp cocktail, tasty *enchiladas de* *jaibe* (crab and ancho chile), and the most authentic mole sauce this side of Cozumel. If you're lucky, there might be a mariachi band patrolling the premises. *Coral Bay, tel. 809/776–6866. AE, MC, V. $*

Cruz Bay **Ellington's.** Extending out onto the second-story veranda of the Gallows Point Suite Resort's central building, Ellington's is a pleasant surprise—still informal yet a cut above Cruz Bay's typical ultracasual fish-fry joint. The menu leans heavily toward fish, nevertheless: Start with the jumbo shrimp cooked in sweet coconut and served with mango sauce, or the seafood chowder. Entrées include flawlessly presented sea scallops and pesto, swordfish scampi, and filet mignon. Save room for dessert, though, perhaps the banana–chocolate-chip cake or the white-chocolate brownie. *Gallows Point Suite Resort, tel. 809/776–7166. Reservations accepted. AE, MC, V. $$$*

Paradiso. This bright, happening place was brought to St. John by the owners of Andrea's, in Martha's Vineyard. It strives to create a European ambience, with vaulted ceilings and cross beams, stone walls, and polished hardwood floors, but the casually attired crowd gives it a decidedly American feel. Stick with the salad and pasta dishes, and you won't be disappointed (unless you were hoping for quick service). *Mongoose Junction, tel. 809/776–8806. AE, DC, MC, V. No lunch. Closed Mon. $$$*

The Fish Trap. Resting on a series of open-air wooden balconies among banana trees and coconut palms, this favorite of locals serves up six kinds of fresh fish nightly, along with tasty appetizers such as conch fritters and Fish Trap chowder. The menu also includes steak, pasta, and chicken. *Downtown, tel. 809/776–9817. AE, D, MC, V. No lunch. Closed Mon. $$*

Lime Inn. This busy, roofed, open-air restaurant has an ornamental garden and beach-furniture chairs. There are several shrimp and steak dishes and such specials as sautéed chicken with artichoke hearts in lemon sauce. On Wednesday night there's an all-you-can-eat shrimp feast, and prime rib is the specialty every Saturday night. *Downtown (turn right at Chase Manhattan Bank), tel. 809/776–6425. Reservations advised. AE, MC, V. $$*

Morgan's Mango. Everything about this restaurant strives to appeal to all tastes—that's the problem. The partially alfresco setting is lovely, with interlocking aqua, peach, and white gazebos; the soothing atmosphere is augmented by live music—everything from classical guitar to samba combos. The menu, however, bites off more than it can chew, offering literally everything from the Caribbean basin: Cajun shrimp, Bajan conch fritters, Jamaican jerk chicken, and so on. Morgan's Mango is frankly best for drinks (an astonishing full page of tropical concoctions) or hi-test desserts, but it gets high marks for trying, and with time it may settle in. Morgan, by the way, is the owner's pet iguana. You might catch him darting about, but he *is* nervous in crowds. *Downtown, across from National Park dock near Mongoose Junction, tel. 809/693–8141. AE, D, DC, MC, V. $$*

Pusser's. With dark paneling and brass rails, the decor is very like any good old British pub, but diners and drinkers here won't be fooled for a minute—tropical temperatures, lazily rotating ceiling fans, and menu items with Caribbean twists are quick reminders that this is Cruz Bay, not Cambridge. Step outside the bar area to the covered deck, take a seat, soak in the fine view, and order up some terrific conch chowder or a lobster club sandwich. Rum Painkillers pack a punch, and while the menu isn't the most memorable, you certainly will go away satisfied. *Wharfside Village, tel. 809/*

774–5489. *Reservations advised for 6 or more. Dress: casual. AE, MC, V. $–$$*

★ **Etta's.** This simple courtyard eatery (with a touching excuse for a gurgling fountain) in the Inn at Tamarind Court has long been a popular locals' hangout. They come not only for the scrumptious island food (sublime kalaloo—similar to slightly bitter spinach—soup with okra and fungi, mouth-watering chicken, conch and grouper fritters served with hot and only-for-the-brave sauces, and true curries), but also for the lively happy hours and tremendous live music on weekends. *Downtown, bear right at the Texaco, tel. 809/776–6378. AE, D, MC, V. $*

Luscious Licks. This funky hole-in-the-wall serves up mostly healthy foods such as all-natural fruit smoothies, veggie pita sandwiches, and homemade muffins. Try the BBQ tofu in sweet and sour sauce or the spinach and olive fettuccine. With a nod to the yuppies, it also sells specialty coffees and Ben & Jerry's ice cream. Nothing on the menu is more than $8. For a real treat, stop by weekdays between 6 PM and 9 PM and get a relaxing 15-minute neck and shoulder massage for $10. *Next door to Mongoose Junction, tel. 809/776–6070. No credit cards. $*

Friis Bay **Miss Lucy's.** This delightful local eatery is in the middle of nowhere;
★ taxi rates are prohibitive, so you need a rental car to get here—but it's worth the drive. The lilac and maroon trellised restaurant, adorned with local artworks, is swept by cooling sea breezes; you can also eat outside on a tiny beach anchored by sea-grape trees. Dinners are served with complimentary johnnycakes and soup (try the superlative fish chowder or spicy black bean), not to mention mounds of rice, potatoes, fungi, plantains, yams, and carrots. Try the meltingly tender conch fritters to start, then curried goat stew or steamed kingfish Creole. Wash it down with one of the addictive fresh fruit drinks (ask for the passionfruit dacquiri). *Calabash, Friis Bay, tel. 809/779–4404. AE, MC, V. Open for lunch and dinner daily in winter; call for summer hours. $–$$*

Great Cruz **Chow Bella.** The menu here, says the maître d', is "trans-cultural"—
Bay Chinese and Italian, as you might have surmised from the name. Order from one side of the menu and you'll have pot stickers; from the other side you'll have pasta. Chow Bella is casually elegant and fun, with striking, contemporary decor, a piano bar every night, and nightclub entertainment and dancing on weekends. *Hyatt Regency Beach Hotel, tel. 809/776–7171. Reservations advised. Dress: No shorts or collarless shirts. AE, MC, V. No lunch. Closed Mon. $$$–$$$$*

Lodging

You're not going to find a lot of beachfront hotel properties on St. John; that's why you've got all those pristine beaches, and miles of tranquil roads through forest and greenery. Development is limited to the one-third of the island not owned by the national park, and the steep terrain discourages development on much of the rest of the island. However, the two luxury hotels that do exist—Caneel Bay and the Hyatt Regency—are world class and expensive. But because Caneel and Hyatt offer all-inclusive packages with three meals a day and all water sports included, you might decide the hotels are not as expensive as they seem at first glance.

If you don't opt for one of these, your choice of accommodation will be from three categories: One of two campgrounds, both at the edge of beautiful beaches; in-town inns where you can quickly become part of the friendly local routine; or one of the luxurious villas or condominiums for rent, almost always with stunning views, and often with pools.

Many of the accommodations have kitchens, and if you're planning on cooking, it's advisable to bring along some basics from home that travel well—dry goods, canned goods, paper products, etc.—as there's no large supermarket on St. John.

Hotels and Inns
★

Caneel Bay Resort. This incredibly lush 170-acre peninsula resort was originally part of the Durloo plantation owned by the Danish West India Company and at one time extended as far as Cinnamon Bay (*Caneel* is Danish for cinnamon). It was opened as a resort in 1936, was bought by Laurance Rockefeller in the 1950s, and joined Rosewood Resorts in 1991. Attention is paid to every detail, and the grounds are immaculately maintained. The flamboyant trees here even seem to shed their blossoms neatly. There are seven beaches, three restaurants, and an 18th-century sugar mill. Serenity reigns at Caneel Bay: Guests come here to relax, find privacy, and indulge, so while guest rooms are spacious and their bathrooms boast every amenity, you'll find that these are simply but tastefully decorated rooms that do not have TV, telephone, or air-conditioning. Jackets are requested for men (during winter season) in restaurants after 6 PM. Formerly an all-inclusive resort, Caneel Bay now offers a choice of rooms with all meals or none; meals are added to room rate. *Box 720, Cruz Bay 00830, tel. 809/776–6111 or 800/223–7637. 171 rooms. Facilities: 7 beaches, 3 restaurants, 11 tennis courts, water sports, boutique, conference facilities. AE, MC, V. $$$$*

★ **Hyatt Regency St. John.** This 34-acre property at Great Cruz Bay shuns the weathered, old-money elegance of Caneel, and lays on the gloss and glitz to the point that even the landscaping looks freshly polished. It's a beautiful place, the grounds are positively iridescent, and the pool area is a sybarite's delight, with waterfalls and islands, and a poolside bar. Spacious, well-appointed guest rooms line the beach and encircle the pool, while some suites and luxurious town houses are set back slightly from the water. Try the on-site Chow Bella restaurant's "trans-cultural" menu of Italian and Chinese specialties. There are morning, afternoon, and evening children's and teen's programs that include beach olympics, stargazing, island tours, and arts and crafts. *Box 8310, Great Cruz Bay 00830, tel. 809/776–7171 or 800/323–7249. 285 rooms. Facilities: beach, marina, 3 restaurants, pool, water sports, fitness room, tennis. AE, DC, MC, V. $$$$*

★ **Gallows Point Suite Resort.** These soft-gray buildings with peaked roofs and shuttered windows grace the peninsula south of the Cruz Bay ferry dock. The garden apartments have kitchens and sky-lit, plant-filled showers big enough to frolic in. The upper-level apartments have loft bedrooms. There's no air-conditioning; the harborside villas get better tradewinds, but they're also noisier. Daily maid service is included. The entranceway is bridged by Ellington's restaurant. *Box 58, Cruz Bay 00831, tel. 809/776–6434 or 800/323–7229, fax 809/776–6520. 60 rooms. Facilities: pool, snorkeling. AE, DC, MC, V. $$$*

Raintree Inn. If you want to be right in the center of the action in town and bunk at an affordable, island-style place, go no farther. The dark-wood rooms, some with air-conditioning, have a nicely simple, tropical-cabin decor. Three efficiencies here have kitchens and—if you don't mind climbing an indoor ladder—a comfortable sleeping loft. The Fish Trap restaurant is next door. *Box 566, Cruz Bay 00831, tel. 809/776–7449 or 800/666–7449. 11 rooms. AE, D, MC, V. $–$$*

The Inn at Tamarind Court. If you can just barely afford a vacation on St. John, try this inexpensive hostelry on the east side of town. It's especially suited to singles. Decor reflects the prices, with mismatched furnishings and somewhat shabby decor, but the helpful staff and youthful, fun-loving clientele compensate somewhat. Choose among traditional hotel rooms (some with shared bath), suites, or a one-bedroom apartment. The front-courtyard bar is a friendly hangout, as well as home to one of Cruz Bay's best West Indian restaurants. Continental breakfast is included. *Box 350, Cruz Bay 00831, tel. 809/776–6378. 20 rooms, some with shared bath. Facilities: restaurant and bar. AE, D, MC, V. $*

Homes and Villas   **Caribbean Villas and Resorts** (Box 458, Cruz Bay 00830, tel. 809/776–6152 or 800/338–0987, fax 809/779–4044) is the island's largest short-term villa rental agent, with some 60 homes available on St. John. Their luxury properties are usually within a mile or two of Cruz Bay and are often found right on the beach. **Vacation Vistas** (Box 476, Cruz Bay 00831, tel. 809/776–6462) has a smaller roster of select water-view properties, ranging from the extravagant (an indoor swimming pool and retractable living room walls that draw back to bring the outdoors inside) to the merely lovely. **Villa Portfolio** (tel. 809/693–5050) represents several charming properties, including Battery Hill, Villas Caribe, and Coconut Coast Villas, all just outside Cruz Bay. **Destination St. John** (Box 37, Cruz Bay 00831, tel. 809/774–3843 or 800/562–1901) represents a number of properties, all perched high on hills overlooking fine views. **Hawksbill Vacation Villas** (Box 8316, Cruz Bay 00831, tel. 809/776–1550) rents a cluster of delightful homes that share a swimming pool on a hillside overlooking Great Cruz Bay. **Catered To, Inc.** (Box 704, Cruz Bay 00831, tel. 809/776–6641, fax 809/779–6191) offers luxury homes, many of which have pools and beach access. At **Jaden Cottages** (tel. 809/776–6423) you'll find two inexpensive cottages just five minutes outside Cruz Bay. Other home rental agents on the island include **Private Homes for Private Vacations** (Mamey Peak 00830, tel. 809/776–6876), **Paradise Hideaways** (Box 149, Cruz Bay 00831, tel. 809/776–6518), and **Vacation Homes** (Box 272, Cruz Bay 00831, tel. 809/776–6094).

Condominiums   Among the condominiums controlled by Caribbean Villas and Resorts (*see above*) are **Cruz Views, Pastory Estates,** and **Cruz Bay Villas,** all of which have dynamite ocean views from their one- and two-bedroom units. The 12 units at **Lavender Hill Estates** (Box 3606, Cruz Bay 00831, tel. 809/776–6969) are just a few-minutes' walk into the center of town. Affordable **Serendip** (Box 273, Cruz Bay 00831, tel. 809/776–6646), just a short drive outside town, has been remodeled and is a good budget option. The luxurious **Virgin Grand Villas** (Great Cruz Bay 00830, tel. 809/775–3856, fax 809/779–4760) are somewhat removed from the Virgin Grand Resort, though guests at these one-, two-, and three-bedroom town houses and villas have full use of the facilities at the Hyatt.

Campgrounds   **Cinnamon Bay Campground.** Tents, cottages with four one-room units in each cottage, and bare sites are available at this National Park Service location surrounded by jungle and set at the edge of big, beautiful Cinnamon Bay Beach. The tents are 10 feet by 14 feet, with flooring, and come with living, eating, and sleeping furnishings and necessities; the 15-by-15-foot cottages have twin beds. Bare sites, which come with a picnic table and a charcoal grill, must be reserved no earlier than eight months prior to arrival. You can reserve by phone with a credit card. The bare sites are cheap—at press time they were $14 a site—but, if you're thinking of this option for budgetary reasons alone, be warned: The tent sites and cottages range from about $65 to $87 for two people per night in season. *Cruz Bay 00830–0720, tel. 809/776–6330. 44 tents, 40 cottages, 26 bare sites. Facilities: beach, commissary, bathhouses (showers and toilets), cafeteria, water sports. AE, MC, V. $*

Maho Bay Camp. Eight miles from Cruz Bay, this private campground is a lush hillside community of rustic tent cottages (canvas and screens) linked by boardwalks, stairs, and ramps, which also lead down to the beach. The 16-by-16-foot shelters have beds, dining table and chairs, electric lamps (and outlets), propane stove, ice cooler, kitchenware, and cutlery. The camp has the chummy feel of a retreat and is very popular, so book well in advance. *Box 310, Cruz Bay 00830, tel. 212/472–9453 or 800/392–9004. 113 tent cottages. Facilities: beach, restaurant, commissary, barbecue areas, bathhouses (showers, sinks, and toilets), water sports. No credit cards. $*

Nightlife

St. John is not the place to go for glitter and all-night partying. Still, after-hours Cruz Bay can be a lively, cozy little village in which to dine, drink, dance, chat, or flirt.

After a sunset drink at **Ellington's** (at Gallows Point Suite Resort, tel. 809/776–7166) up the hill from Cruz Bay, you can stroll here and there in town, where everything is clustered around the small waterfront park. You'll find many of the young people from the U.S. mainland who live and work on St. John out sipping and socializing, too.

Some friendly hubbub can be found at the rough and ready **Backyard** (tel. 809/776–8553), *the* place for sports watching as well as grooving to Bonnie Raitt et al. If you want to kill some time and wine before eating Italian, the bar at second-floor **Cafe Roma** (tel. 809/776–6524) is a convivial nook. There's calypso and reggae on Wednesday and Friday at **Fred's** (tel. 809/776–6363), as well as some live island sounds at the **Rock Lobster** (tel. 809/776–6908), next door to the Backyard. **Etta's** at The Inn at Tamarind Court (tel. 809/776–6378) serves up a blend of jazz and rock on Friday and reggae on Saturday.

A bit out of town, the two big hotels, **Caneel Bay** and the **Hyatt Regency St. John,** have frequent entertainment. Caneel's offerings run more toward the piano bar and quiet calypso; the Hyatt occasionally hosts top-name Caribbean stars who draw big crowds. On the other side of the island, check out the action at Coral Bay's **Skinnylegs** and **Seabreeze,** popular with the sailing set.

Notices posted across from the **U.S. Post Office** and at **Connections** (and on telephone poles) will keep you apprised of special events: comedy nights, movies, and the like.

6 The British Virgin Islands

Introduction

By Robert Grodé

Updated by Pamela Acheson

Serene, seductive, and spectacularly beautiful even by Caribbean standards, the British Virgin Islands are happily free of the runaway development that has detracted from the charm of so many West Indian islands. The pleasures to be found here include sailing around the multitude of tiny, nearby islands; diving to the wreck of the RMS *Rhone*, sunk off Salt Island in 1867; snorkeling in one of hundreds of wonderful spots; walking along deserted beaches; taking in spectacular views from the islands' peaks; and settling down on some breeze-swept terrace to admire the sunset.

Much of the credit for this blissful simplicity must go to the B.V.I.'s sensitive tourism policies. No building can rise higher than the surrounding palms—two stories is the limit. Also, you won't have to compete for sidewalk space with hordes of cruise-ship day-trippers, since only one or two liners visit here each week.

The lack of direct air flights from the mainland United States also helps the British islands retain the endearing qualities of yesteryear's Caribbean. One first has to get to Puerto Rico, 60 miles to the west, or to nearby St. Thomas in the United States Virgin Islands and catch a small plane to the little airports on Beef Island/Tortola or Virgin Gorda. Many of the travelers who return year after year prefer arriving by water, either aboard their own ketches and yawls or on one of the convenient ferryboats that cross the turquoise waters between St. Thomas and Tortola. No doubt the passage provides a fine prelude to a stay in these unhurried tropical havens. Departing from the clamor of St. Thomas's brash and bumptious Charlotte Amalie, ferry passengers find their cares vanishing with the ship's wake. From the upper deck of the *Native Son*, one of the ferries that make the one-hour St. Thomas–Tortola crossing, passengers can view the tiny islands as they slip past, some velvety green, others rocky and wild. Some islands sport thickets of swaying masts marking favored moorings, serving as reminders of the superb sailing to be found hereabouts.

Sailing has always been a popular activity in the B.V.I. The first arrivals here were a romantic seafaring tribe, the Siboney Indians, who wandered among these islands living off the indigenous plant and marine life. About the year 900, the peaceable Arawak Indians sailed north from their home in South America and established settlements throughout the island chain. For 500 years the Arawaks subsisted on farming and fishing. Eventually they were overwhelmed by the warlike Caribs who slaughtered (and ate) their enemies. The Caribbean Sea is named after this group—and the word cannibal is a derivation of *Carib*.

Christopher Columbus was the first European to visit, during his second voyage to the New World, in 1493. The redoubtable "Admiral of the Ocean Seas," impressed by the number of islands dotting the horizon, named them *Las Once Mil Virgines* (The 11,000 Virgins) in honor of the 11,000 virgin-companions of Saint Ursula, martyred in the 4th century. Columbus's arithmetic might have been weaker than his navigational skills, or else he was given to exaggeration; there are, in fact, just over 50 islands in the archipelago. Tortola, about 10 square miles, is the largest, and Virgin Gorda, with 8 square miles, ranks second. Scattered around them are the islands of Jost Van Dyke; Great Camanoe; Norman; Peter; Salt; Cooper; Ginger; Dead Chest; the low-lying, coral Anegada; and others.

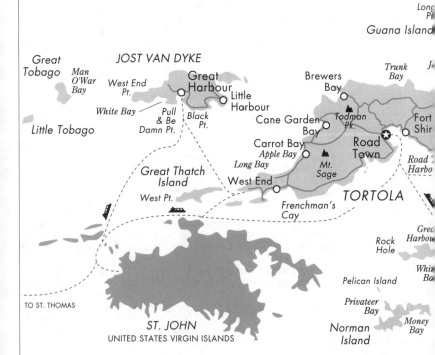

ATLANTIC

Long
Pi
Guana Island

*Great
Tobago*

*Man
O'War
Bay*

JOST VAN DYKE

*West End
Pt.*

**Great
Harbour**

Little
Harbour

Brewers
Bay

*Trunk
Bay*

J

Little Tobago

White Bay

*Pull
& Be
Damn Pt.*

*Black
Pt.*

Cane Garden
Bay

*Todman
Pk.*

Fort
Shir

Carrot Bay

Road
Town

Apple Bay

Long Bay

▲
*Mt.
Sage*

*Road
Harbo*

*Great Thatch
Island*

West End

*Frenchman's
Cay*

TORTOLA

West Pt.

Gre
Harbou

*Rock
Hole*

Whi
Ba

TO ST. THOMAS

Pelican Island

*Privateer
Bay*

Norman
Island

*Money
Bay*

ST. JOHN
UNITED STATES VIRGIN ISLANDS

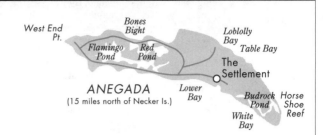

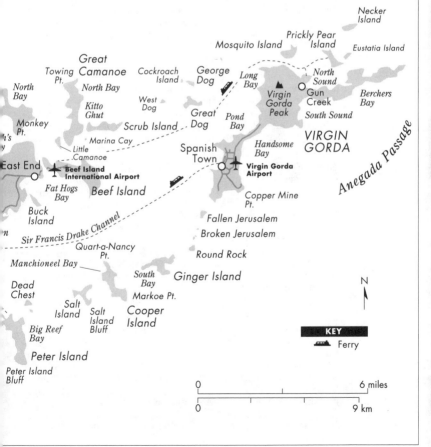

In the ensuing years, the Spaniards passed through these waters seeking gold, and, finding none, they quickly moved on to the richer pastures of Mexico. The haunting ruins of a copper mine on Virgin Gorda's east coast serve as evidence of the Spaniards' aborted search for the yellow ore. The next seafarers to arrive were a number of pirates who found the islands' hidden coves and treacherous reefs an ideal base from which to prey on passing galleons crammed with Mexican and Peruvian gold, silver, and spices. Among the most notorious of these predatory men were Blackbeard Teach, Bluebeard, Captain Kidd, and Sir Francis Drake, who lent his name to the channel that sweeps through the two main clusters of the B.V.I.

In the 17th century, these colorful cutthroats were replaced by the Dutch. They, in turn, were soon sent packing by the British, who retained control of the islands for nearly three centuries. They established a plantation economy and for the next 150 years the British developed the sugar industry, an occupation that proved most profitable for the island group. African slaves were brought in to work the cane fields while the plantation owners and their families reaped the benefits.

It wasn't until 1807 that public sentiment on the islands began to turn against slavery. In that year, Arthur Hodge, a plantation owner, beat one of his slaves to death for eating a mango. Even his fellow slaveholders were revolted by this act of wanton cruelty, and Hodge was tried and hanged. In 1838 slavery was finally abolished throughout the British West Indies. The Emancipation Proclamation freed 5,133 slaves in the B.V.I.

Without slave labor the plantation economy quickly faltered, and the majority of the white population returned to Europe. By 1893, there were only two whites on Tortola and Virgin Gorda, the deputy governor and the doctor. The islands came under control of the former slaves, many of whom bought their own parcels of land. Small-scale farming and fishing supported the island residents, and any excess produce was sent to St. Thomas to be sold.

The islands dozed, a forgotten corner of the British empire, until the early 1960s. In 1966, a new constitution, granting greater autonomy to the islands, was approved. While the governor is still appointed by the Queen of England, his limited powers concentrate on external affairs and local security. Other matters are administered by the Legislative Council, consisting of representatives from nine island districts. General elections are held every four years. The arrangement seems to suit the British Virgin Islanders just fine: The mood is serene, with none of the occasional political turmoil found on other islands. Having had tacit control over their destinies for more than a century and a half, local residents have no reason to feel that visitors are more than welcome guests.

The 1960s also saw the arrival of a few profit-seeking souls, notably Laurance Rockefeller and American-expatriate Charlie Cary, who became convinced that the islands' balmy weather, powder-soft beaches, and splendid sailing would make them an ideal holiday destination. Attempts at building a small tourist industry began in 1965, when Rockefeller set about creating the Little Dix resort on Virgin Gorda. Dedicated to preserving the natural beauty of the island while providing its guests with unpretentious, yet elegant surroundings, Little Dix set the standard that still prevails in the B.V.I. A few years later, Cary and his wife, Ginny, established The Moorings marina complex on Tortola, and sailing in the area burgeoned.

Today, tourism accounts for most of the B.V.I.'s income. The majority of jobs on the islands are tourism-related, as light industry is practically nonexistent and, for the present, is unlikely to appear. British Virgin Islanders love their unspoiled tropical home and are determined to maintain its easygoing charms, for both themselves and the travelers who are their guests.

Essential Information

Government Tourist Offices

Information about the B.V.I. is available through the **British Virgin Islands Tourist Board** (370 Lexington Ave., Suite 416, New York, NY 10017, tel. 212/696–0400 or 800/835–8530) or at the **British Virgin Islands Information Offices** in San Francisco (1686 Union St., Suite 305, San Francisco, CA 94123, tel. 415/775–0344; nationwide, tel. 800/232–7770). British travelers can write or visit the **BVI Information Office** (110 St. Martin's La., London WC2N 4DY, tel. 071/240–4259).

Arriving and Departing

From the U.S. by Plane
Airports and Airlines

No nonstop service is available from the United States to the B.V.I.; connections are usually made through San Juan, Puerto Rico, or St. Thomas, U.S.V.I. Airlines serving both San Juan and St. Thomas include **American** (tel. 800/433–7300), **Continental** (tel. 800/231–0856), and **Delta** (tel. 800/323–2323). **American Eagle** (tel. 800/433–7300) flies from San Juan to Tortola. **Sunaire Express** (809/495–2480) flies from San Juan and St. Thomas to both Beef Island/Tortola and Virgin Gorda, as well as between St. Croix and Beef Island/Tortola. Regularly scheduled service between the B.V.I. and most other Caribbean islands is provided by **Leeward Islands Air Transport (LIAT)** (tel. 809/495–1187). Many Caribbean islands can also be reached via **Gorda Aero Service** (Tortola, tel. 809/495–2271), a charter service.

Both the Beef Island/Tortola and Virgin Gorda airports are classic Caribbean studies: sleepy, and all but dead when there are no flights. Service desks can be slow at Beef Island when the airport gets crowded before departures: Give yourself at least an hour.

Most hotels will provide transport if you call prior to arrival. At the Beef Island/Tortola airport, there is usually a group of taxi drivers hovering at the exit from customs to meet flights. Fares are officially set and are not negotiable, and are lower per person for more than one passenger. Figure about $15 for up to three people, $5 for each additional passenger, for the 20-minute ride to Road Town and around $20–$30 for the 45-minute ride to the West End. Expect to share your taxi, and be patient if your driver searches for people to fill his cab—only a few flights land each day and this could be your driver's only run. You can also call the **B.V.I. Taxi Association** (tel. 809/495–2378). On Virgin Gorda call **Mahogany Taxi Service** (tel. 809/495–5469). Rates will vary depending on your destination. If you're staying anywhere on the North Sound in Virgin Gorda, you can fly to Beef Island/Tortola and catch the nearby North Sound Express (*see* Getting Around, *below*), or you can fly to Virgin Gorda and take a taxi to North Sound. From there a hotel launch will meet you, but you must have made arrangements with your hotel before your arrival. Don't get nervous if your land taxi leaves you by yourself on a deserted dock and tells you to wait for your skipper. They are very reliable and someone will show up. If your destination is Leverick Bay, your land taxi will take you there directly.

From the U.S. Mostly smaller ships, and occasionally larger ones, call at the Brit-
by Ship ish Virgin Islands. The most popular ports are Tortola, Virgin Gorda, and Jost Van Dyke. Smaller ships often stop at more than one of the islands; larger ones usually only make one port call during the course of an eastern Caribbean sailing. Among the few ocean liners that call in the B.V.I. are ships from **Cunard Line** (555 5th Ave., New York, NY 10017, tel. 800/528–6273) and **Princess Cruises** (10100 Santa Monica Blvd., Los Angeles, CA 90067, tel. 310/553–1770). Many luxury yachts visit the islands. Contact **Renaissance Cruises** (1800 Eller Dr., Suite 300, Box 350307, Fort Lauderdale, FL 33335, tel. 800/525–5350), **Royal Viking Line** (95 Merrick Way, Coral Gables, FL 33134, tel. 800/422–8000), or **Seabourn Cruise Line** (55 San Francisco St., San Francisco, CA 94133, tel. 800/351–9595). Sail-powered ships also frequent the B.V.I. Contact **Club Med** (40 W. 57th St., New York, NY 10019, tel. 800/258–2633), **Tall Ship Adventures** (1010 S. Joliet St., Suite 200, Aurora, CO 80012, tel. 800/662–0090), **Windjammer Barefoot Cruises** (Box 190120, Miami Beach, FL 33119, tel. 800/327–2602) or **Windstar Cruises** (300 Elliot Ave. W, Seattle, WA 98119, tel. 800/258–7245). Itineraries and ship deployments change frequently, so contact your cruise line for the latest scheduled sailings.

For more information on cruising, *see* Fodor's *Cruises & Ports of Call 1995.*

From the U.S. Various ferries connect St. Thomas, U.S.V.I., with Tortola and Vir-
Virgin Islands gin Gorda. **Native Son, Inc.** (tel. 809/495–4617), operates three fer-
by Ferry ries (*Native Son, Oriole,* and *Voyager Eagle*), and offers service between St. Thomas and Tortola (West End and Road Town) daily and between St. Thomas and Spanish Town, Virgin Gorda on Wednesday and Sunday. **Smiths Ferry Services** (tel. 809/494–4430 or 809/494–2355) carries passengers between downtown St. Thomas and Road Town and West End on Monday through Saturday; offers daily service between Red Hook on St. Thomas and Tortola's West End; and travels between St. Thomas and Spanish Town on Sunday. **Inter-Island Boat Services'** *Sundance II* (tel. 809/776–6597) connects St. John and West End on Tortola daily.

Getting Around

By Boat **Speedy's Fantasy** (tel. 809/495–5240) makes the run between Road Town, Tortola, and Spanish Town, Virgin Gorda, daily. Running daily between Virgin Gorda's North Sound and Beef Island/Tortola are **North Sound Express** (tel. 809/494–2746) boats. There are also daily boats between Peter Island's private dock on Tortola (just east of Road Town) and Peter Island. **Jost Van Dyke Ferry Service** (tel. 809/494–2997) makes the Jost Van Dyke–Tortola run several times daily via the *When* ferry.

By Plane **Sunaire Express** flies between Beef Island/Tortola and Virgin Gorda. Call for fares and schedules. **Gorda Aero Service** flies between Tortola and Anegada Monday, Wednesday, and Friday and offers charter flights between Tortola, Virgin Gorda, and Anegada, and to other Caribbean islands.

By Car Driving on Tortola and Virgin Gorda is not for the timid. Roller-coaster roads with breathtaking ascents and descents and tight turns that give new meaning to the term "hairpin curves" are the norm but the ever-changing views of land, sea, and neighboring islands are among the most spectacular in the Caribbean. Most people will strongly recommend renting a four-wheel-drive vehicle. Roads tend to be named by where they lead to (i.e., Joe's Hill) but don't count on them being marked with signs. Since the numerous curves can trick even the greatest of pathfinders into taking a wrong turn (and heading down ever-narrowing dirt roads to a final dead end) be sure to get a map at the rental agency and ask for suggested routes. Some roads are in better shape than others. It helps to keep track on the map of where you think you might be, so you'll know when to look for a turn.

Driving is *à l'Anglais*, on the left side of the road. It's easy if you drive slowly, think before you make a turn, and pay attention when driving in and out of the occasional traffic circle, locally called "round-a-bouts." Speed limits are 30–40 mph outside of town, 10–15 mph in residential areas. Just ignore any tailgating locals and drive at your own speed, or pull over and let them go by. A valid B.V.I. driving license is required and can be obtained for $10 at car rental agencies. You must be at least 25 and have a valid driver's license from another country.

Telephones and Mail

Telephones The area code for the B.V.I. is 809. To call anywhere in the B.V.I. once you've arrived, dial only the last five digits: Instead of dialing 494–1234, just dial 4–1234. A local call from a public pay phone costs 25¢. Pay phones are frequently on the blink but a handy alternative (if you will be in the islands long enough) is a Caribbean Phone Card, available in $5, $10, and $20 denominations. It's sold at most major hotels and many stores, and can be used all over the Caribbean (except on the French islands) in special phone card telephones.

For credit card or collect long-distance calls to the United States, look for special **USADirect** phones, which are linked directly to an ATT operator. For access dial 1/800/872–2881, or dial 111 from a pay phone and charge the call to your Master Card or Visa. **USADirect** and pay phones can be found at most hotels and in towns.

Mail There are post offices in Road Town on Tortola and in Spanish Town on Virgin Gorda. Postage for a first-class letter to the United States is 35¢ and for a postcard 20¢. (It might be noted that postal efficiency is not first class in the B.V.I.) For a small fee **Rush It In Road Town** (tel. 809/494–4421) or **Rush It In Spanishtown** (tel. 809/495–5821) offers most U.S. mail and UPS services (via St. Thomas the next day).

Opening and Closing Times

Stores are generally open from 9 to 5 Monday through Saturday. Bank hours are Monday through Thursday 9–2:30 and Friday 9–2:30 and 4:30–6.

Tipping

Service charges are generally added to the hotel bill. Porters and bellhops should be tipped $1 per bag. A tip is usually not necessary for cabbies since most taxis are owned independently; add 10%–15% if they exceed their duties. Service is often included at restaurants; if not, 15% is customary.

Dining

The most popular choices in B.V.I. restaurants are seafood dishes. Unfortunately, some restaurants have found that it's cheaper to serve fish imported frozen from Miami than local fresh fish. You'll find a greater range of eateries on Tortola than on more remote Virgin Gorda and the other islands, where most hotels offer a meal plan.

Category	Cost*
$$$$	over $35
$$$	$25–$35
$$	$15–$25
$	under $15

per person for three courses, excluding drinks and service; there is no sales tax in the B.V.I.

Highly recommended restaurants are indicated by a star ★.

Lodging

There is a reassuring sense of intimacy about B.V.I. resorts. None are large—only four have more than 50 rooms. The soaring lobbies, anonymous guest rooms, and long check-in lines found in the high-rise behemoths on other Caribbean islands don't exist here. Guests are treated as more than just room numbers.

Don't be surprised if your room—even those at the more expensive resorts—is missing some of the amenities taken for granted, such as a television or telephones. Some visitors find this a minor inconvenience, but for others it's a welcome surprise. Indeed, many, many visitors return to the B.V.I. year after year. In fact, booking a room at many of the more popular resorts is even difficult during the off-season, although nearly half the island visitors stay aboard their own boats during their holidays.

Some hotels also do not have air-conditioning but rely on ceiling fans to capture the almost constant trade winds. Nights are cool and breezy, even in midsummer, and never reach the temperatures or humidity levels that are so common in major U.S. cities during the summer.

Category	Cost*
$$$$	over $225
$$$	$150–$225
$$	$75–$150
$	under $75

All prices are for a standard double room in high season, excluding 7% hotel tax and 10% (sometimes 12% or higher on Virgin Gorda) service charge.

Highly recommended lodgings are indicated by a star ★.

Tortola

Introduction

Unwinding can easily become a full-time occupation on Tortola, where the leisurely pace of the island's inhabitants makes even traffic lights unnecessary. Though Tortola offers a wealth of things to see and do, visitors can just loll about on a deserted beach or linger over lunch at one of the island's many delightful restaurants: Even the scenery seems to have been created with the idea of inspiring the poet in us. The neighboring islands glimmer like emeralds in a sea of sapphire. Beaches are never more than a few minutes away, and the steeply sloping green hills that form Tortola's spine are continuously fanned by gentle trade winds. It's a world far removed from the hustle of modern life.

Though 10-square-mile Tortola can be explored in a few hours, opting for such a whirlwind tour is surely a mistake. Life in the fast lane has no place among some of the Caribbean's most breathtaking panoramas and prettiest beaches.

Important Addresses and Numbers

Tourist Information On Tortola there is a **BVI Tourist Board Office** at the center of Road Town near the ferry dock, just south of Wickham's Cay I (Box 134, Road Town, Tortola, tel. 809/494–3134). For all kinds of useful information about these islands, including rates and phone numbers, get a free copy of *The Welcome Tourist Guide*, available at hotels and other places.

Emergencies Dial 999 for all emergencies.

Hospitals On Tortola there is **Peebles Hospital** in Road Town (tel. 809/494–3497).

Pharmacies Pharmacies in Road Town include **J.R. O'Neal Drug Store** (tel. 809/494–2292) and **Lagoon Plaza Drug Store** (tel. 809/494–2498).

Getting Around

By Car Rentals are available from **Avis** (tel. 809/494–3322), **Budget** (tel. 809/494–2639), **Hertz** (tel. 809/495–4405), and **National** (tel. 809/494–3197).

By Taxi Your hotel staff will be happy to summon a taxi for you when you want one. There is a B.V.I. Taxi Association stand in Road Town near the ferry dock (tel. 809/494–2875) and Wickham's Cay I (tel. 809/494–2322), and one on Beef Island, where the airport is (tel. 809/495–2378). You can also usually find a taxi at the ferry dock at Sopers Hole, West End, where ferries arrive from St. Thomas.

By Bus For information about rates and schedules, call **Scato's Bus Service** (tel. 809/494–2365). Taking the bus is a great way to meet locals, albeit at a bumpy snail's pace.

By Moped and Bicycle Scooters and bicycles can be rented on Tortola from **Hero's Bicycle Rental** (tel. 809/494–3536).

Guided Tours

If you'd like to do some chauffeured sightseeing on Tortola, get in touch with the **B.V.I. Taxi Association** (minimum three persons, tel.

809/494–2875 or 809/495–2378), **Style's Taxi Service** (tel. 809/494–2260 during the day or 809/494–3341 at night), or **Travel Plan Tours** (tel. 809/494–2872). **Scato's Bus Service** (tel. 809/494–2365), in Road Town, provides public transportation, special tours with group rates, and beach outings.

Exploring Tortola

Numbers in the margin correspond to points of interest on the Tortola map.

The drives on Tortola are dramatic, with dizzying roller-coaster dips and climbs and glorious views. Leave plenty of time to negotiate the hilly roads and drink in the irresistible vistas at nearly every hairpin turn. Distractions are the real danger here, from the glittering mosaic of azure sea, white skies, and emerald islets to the ambling cattle and grazing goats roadside.

❶ Before setting out on your tour of Tortola, you may want to devote an hour or so to strolling down Main Street and along the waterfront in **Road Town,** the laid-back island capital. If at any point on your tour you should need directions, you'll do best to ask how to get to the attraction or restaurant, rather than to ask for a street. You'll find that locals will be most helpful. A good place to start is at the General Post Office facing **Sir Olva Georges Square,** across from the ferry dock and the customs office. The hands of the clock atop this building permanently point to 10 minutes to 5, rather appropriate in this drowsy town, where time does seem to be standing still.

The eastern side of Sir Olva Georges Square is open to the harbor, and a handful of elderly Tortolans can generally be found enjoying the breeze that sweeps in from the water here. The General Post Office and government offices occupy two other sides of the square, and small shops line the third side. At press time, the government offices were slated to move off the square, to be replaced by more shops. From the front of the post office follow Main Street to the right past a number of small shops housed in traditional pastel-painted West Indian buildings with high-pitched, corrugated tin roofs, bright shutters, and delicate fretwork trim.

On the left, about half a block from the post office, you'll encounter the **British Virgin Islands Folk Museum.** Founded in 1983, the museum has a large collection of artifacts from the Arawak Indians, some of the early settlers of the islands. Of particular interest are the triangular stones called *zemis*, which depict the Arawak gods Julihu and Yuccahu. The museum also has a display of a number of bottles, bowls, and plates salvaged from the wreck of the RMS *Rhone*, a British mail ship sunk off Salt Island in a hurricane in 1867. *Main St., no phone. Admission free. Open Mon., Tues., Thurs., Fri. 10–4; Sat. 10–1, though hours may vary.*

Continue along Main Street and you'll pass stores selling clothing, T-shirts, resort wear, and jewelry, including **Bonker's Gallery** and **Samarkand** (*see* Shopping, *below*). On the right is **The Pusser's Company Store** (*see* Shopping, *below*). This handsome emporium has a nautical theme, and its sporty knickknacks, Pusser's rum mugs, and all-cotton clothes make attractive purchases. As Main Street curves left you'll see **Felix Gold and Silver Ltd.** (*see* Shopping, *below*). Then you'll come to the **Sunny Caribbee Herb and Spice Company** (*see* Shopping, *below*), on the right in a charmingly restored West Indian inn with an entrance off a flower-banked courtyard. The shelves of this bright and airy establishment are chockablock with exotic concoctions—Arawak Love Potion and Island Hangover Cure, for example; teas and spices, hot sauces, hand-painted boxes and coat hooks, and tableware. Next door is the new Sunny Caribbee Art Gallery, with a collection of artwork by local artists and artists from many other Caribbean islands.

If you keep following Main Street, you'll have a chance to stop in **J.R. O'Neal** (*see* Shopping, *below*), which has a wonderful selection of ceramic housewares from Portugal and hand-blown Mexican glass. Retrace your steps to Challwell Street and turn left, cross Waterfront Drive, and proceed a few hundred yards to **Wickham's Cay** to admire the boats moored at **Village Cay Marina**. Enjoy a broad view of the wide harbor, home of countless sailing vessels and yachts and a base of the well-known yacht-chartering enterprise The Moorings. You'll find a **B.V.I. Tourist Board** office to serve you right here as well as banks, and more stores and boutiques.

When you've finished wandering about Wickham's Cay, take Fishlock Road up to the courthouse, and make a right to get back on Main Street. At the police station, turn left onto Station Avenue and follow this to the **J. R. O'Neal Botanic Gardens.** These 2.8 acres of lush gardens include hothouses for ferns and orchids, a bush garden of medicinal herbs and plants, a special Christmas blooming garden, and plants and trees indigenous to the seashore. A number of flower shows and special events are held here during the year. *Station Ave., tel. 809/494–4557. Admission free. Open Mon.–Sat. 8–4, Sun. noon–5.*

Retrace your steps to Sir Olva Georges Square to pick up your car.

Time Out   Before you head around the island, you might stop at **Capriccio di Mare** (tel. 809/494–5369), an indoor-outdoor Italian café across the street from the ferry dock, for a cappuccino and perhaps a fresh pastry.

From Road Town, head southwest along Waterfront Drive. As you round a sharp curve, you'll see a steep driveway leading up to a fortresslike structure tucked into the side of a steep hill. **Fort Burt** was a Dutch fortification during the mid-1600s. Behind the thick stone walls now is a restaurant, a bar, and a simple seven-room hotel.

Just up the road, on the left, you'll spot the turnoff for the B.V.I.'s largest hotel, the **Prospect Reef Resort** (*see* Lodging, *below*). The landscaped grounds, bright with hibiscus and bougainvillea, are laced with canals, and a unique seaside swimming pool has been carved out of the coral reef on which the resort is built. There are fine views of the 20-mile-long Sir Francis Drake Channel, Norman Island, and Peter Island from here, and there are several interesting shops, including the **Pink Pineapple** (*see* Shopping, *below*).

Returning to the shore road follow the coastline for 5 miles or so of the easiest driving in the B.V.I.: no hills, little traffic, lots of curves to keep things interesting, and the lovely, island-studded channel on your left. At Sea Cows Bay the road bends inland just a bit to pass through a small residential area, but it soon rejoins the water's edge. Sir Francis Drake Channel provides a kaleidoscope of turquoise, jade green, and morning-glory blue on your left, and further entertainment is provided by pelicans diving for their supper.

The next development you come to is **Nanny Cay.** Jutting out into the channel, this villagelike complex, with brightly painted buildings trimmed with lacy wood gingerbread, also contains a marina that can accommodate more than 200 yachts.

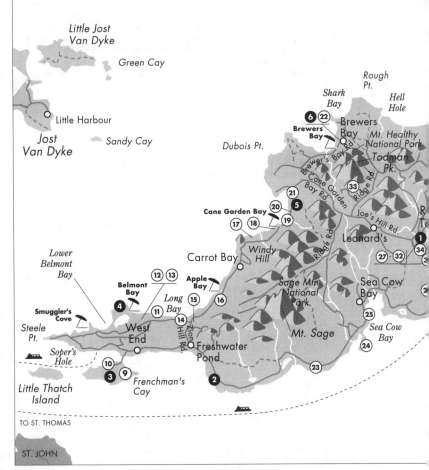

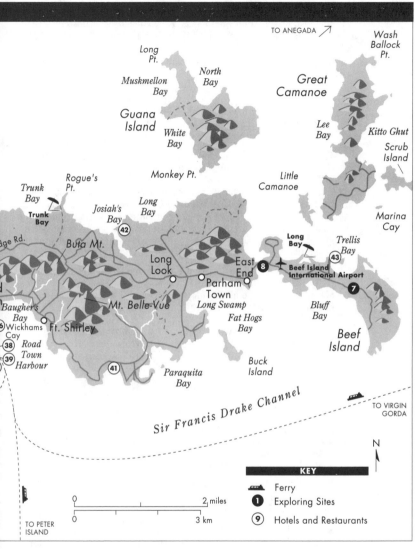

TO ANEGADA ↗

Wash
Ballock
Pt.

Long
Pt.

North
Bay

Great
Camanoe

Muskmellon
Bay

Guana
Island

White
Bay

Lee
Bay

Kitto Ghut

Scrub
Island

Monkey Pt.

Little
Camanoe

Marina
Cay

Trunk
Bay

Rogue's
Pt.

Josiah's
Bay
42

Long
Bay

Long
Bay

Trellis
Bay
43

Trunk
Bay

dge Rd.

Buta Mt.

Long
Look

East
End

8

Beef Island
International Airport

7

Baugher's
Bay
6
Wickhams
Cay
38

Mt. Belle-Vue

Ft. Shirley

Parham
Town

Long Swamp

Bluff
Bay

Beef
Island

Road
Town
Harbour
39

41

Fat Hogs
Bay

Buck
Island

Paraquita
Bay

Sir Francis Drake Channel

TO VIRGIN
GORDA

N

KEY

🚢 Ferry

① Exploring Sites

⑨ Hotels and Restaurants

0 —————— 2 miles
0 —————— 3 km

TO PETER
ISLAND

Nanny Cay Resort and
Marina, **24**

Ole Works Inn, **20**

Prospect Reef
Resort, **26**

Rhymer's Beach
Hotel, **19**

Sebastian's on the
Beach, **14**

Sugar Mill Hotel, **16**

Sunset House and
Villas, **12**

Treasure Isle
Hotel, **32**

Village Cay Hotel &
Marina, **36**

From Nanny Cay the route continues westward as St. John, the smallest of the three main U.S.V.I., comes into view across the channel. The road curves into **West End** past the ruins of the 17th-century Dutch **Fort Recovery,** a 30-foot-diameter historic fort on the grounds of Ft. Recovery Villas. There are no guided tours, but the public is welcome to stop by. The road ends at **Soper's Hole.** The waterfront here is dominated by the boat terminal and customs office that service the St. Thomas, St. John, and Tortola ferries. There is also a small post office where philatelists can purchase unusual B.V.I. stamps to add to their collections.

Time Out Follow the road a bit and you'll come to the **Jolly Roger** (tel. 809/495–4559), a fine place to stop for great pizza or a hamburger and watch the boats come and go in the harbor.

Turn around, head back, and take your very first right over a bridge. Follow signs to **Frenchman's Cay** and bear right on the other side of the bridge. There's a marina and a captivating complex of pastel-hued West Indian-style buildings with shady second-floor balconies, colonnaded arcades, shuttered windows, and gingerbread trim that showcase art galleries, boutiques, and restaurants.

Retrace your route out of West End, turn left and head across the island on Zion Hill Road, a steep byway that rises and then drops precipitously to the other side of the island. Follow the road to the end and then turn left, drive up a steep hill. Be prepared for a dazzling view of **Long Bay,** a mile-long stretch of white sand secured on the west end by **Belmont Point,** a sugar-loaf promontory that has been described as "a giant, green gumdrop." On this stretch of beach is the **Long Bay Hotel,** one of Tortola's more appealing resorts, with one of the island's two pitch-and-putt golf courses (Prospect Reef has the other). The large island visible in the distance is Jost Van Dyke. A detour for the intrepid here is the rocky trek to Smuggler's Cove, among the island's most beautiful and secluded beaches. This is where your four-wheel-drive vehicle becomes essential. Drive past Long Bay, turn left up a twisty dirt road, and take your first right. Persevere, driving slowly (and bumpily) ahead until you reach the small dead-end clearing. There is some good snorkeling a bit offshore, at the west end of this beach.

Retrace your tracks (whispering thanks for the level, paved road past Long Bay).

Time Out A rest might feel good after that bumpy ride! Head over the hill to **Sebastian's on the Beach** (tel. 809/495–4212), a hotel with an excellent restaurant overlooking the water. It's the perfect place for a cold soda, a snack, or an excellent sandwich.

Follow North Coast Road northeast for about three minutes to **Apple Bay** (Capoon's Bay). Tucked away here between the road and the sea is the **Bomba Shack** (no phone), a curious collection of driftwood and thatch that's been fashioned into a bar festooned with everything from paint-daubed license plates and crepe-paper leis to frilly garters and graffiti. In the daytime it is hard to believe it's bustling every night and that hundreds of people gather here every full moon for the famous, multi-band, all-night Bomba Shack "Full Moon" party. If you're lucky enough to be on Tortola during a full moon (and you like music and parties), be sure to stop by. Everyone is welcome.

Just a bit farther on, as the road begins to rise above the shore, look for the **Sugar Mill Hotel.** You'll want to inspect the 360-year-old mill that now serves as the hotel's main dining room and owners Jeff and Jinx Morgan's collection of Haitian primitive art.

Back in the car, follow the North Coast Road over **Windy Hill,** a gripping climb that affords splendid vistas of the sea and sky. You'll descend to sea level at **Cane Garden Bay:** Its crystalline water and silky stretch of sand make this enticing beach one of Tortola's most popular getaways. Its existence is no secret, however, and it can get crowded, though never uncomfortably so.

To return to Road Town, follow Cane Garden Bay Road past the beach and up a steep winding hill.

Time Out **Skyworld** (tel. 809/494–3567), a restaurant, bar, gift shop, and lookout tower, offers the highest 360° view in the B.V.I. of the ocean, neighboring islands, and spectacular sunsets.

Joe's Hill Road, which will take you back to Road Town, is the first right after the sign to Skyworld. Follow this right along a little ridge and bear left when you come to the "Y." The road's steep grade may make you gasp, but the spectacular, nearly aerial view of Road Town and the harbor should assuage your nerves. If you'd rather continue exploring the rest of the island, an interesting but rugged detour is to **Brewer's Bay** and adjacent **Mt. Healthy National Park,** an old plantation site. Take the Brewer's Bay West cutoff on the left from Cane Garden Bay Road. As you head up the hill from Cane Garden Bay, the road you are on bears sharply and steeply to the right. Turn left here, onto a dirt road, and then turn right, and steeply down to Brewer's Bay. The road is rough, but the pristine beach here is usually deserted and ideal for picnics. Continue along Brewer's Bay East Road to **Windmill Ruin,** where one of the best preserved sugar mill remains on Tortola sits in a wild and desolate spot.

Otherwise, go up Cane Garden Bay Road, turn left, and follow the mountainous Ridge Road eastward. The views from this twisting road are breathtaking; the dizzying turnoffs that lead to tranquil bays like **Trunk** and **Josiah's** would make a Grand Prix racer blanch. Ridge Road ultimately winds up at East End, the sleepy village that is the entryway to **Beef Island,** and the Beef Island International Airport. The narrow **Queen Elizabeth II Bridge** connects Tortola and Beef Island, and you'll have to pay a toll to cross (50¢ for passenger cars, $1 for vans and trucks). It's worth it if only for the sight of the tolltaker extending a tin can attached to the end of a board through your car window to collect the fee.

From East End, head back along the south shore by bearing left on Blackburn Highway to Sir Francis Drake Highway, then west along the coast back to Road Town.

Tortola for Free

Beaches. One of Tortola's biggest draws is also its least expensive attraction. Cane Garden Bay, Long Bay on Beef Island, and Smuggler's Cove, to name just a few, are great spots for sun worshipers, snorkelers, and surfers to while away the hours (*see* Beaches, *below*).

J. R. O'Neal Botanic Gardens (*see* Exploring Tortola, *above*).

British Virgin Islands Folk Museum (*see* Exploring Tortola, *above*).

Sage Mountain National Park (*see* Off the Beaten Track, *below*).

What to See and Do with Children

Visitors with children will find several of Tortola's **beaches** particularly worth visiting: The variety of seashells washed up along the beach at Long Bay on Beef Island will provide hours of amusement for young collectors; Cane Garden Bay offers a long beach and very calm water for swimming; and Brewers Bay on the North Shore boasts a campground, sugar-mill ruins, and calm water for swimming, although it is a bit difficult to reach by car (*see* Beaches, below).

Children can expend some of their boundless energy by hiking through **Sage Mountain National Park** (*see* Off the Beaten Track, below), or snorkeling at the many protected areas just a few feet off Tortola's shores (*see* Chapter 3).

Off the Beaten Track

Sage Mountain National Park. At 1,716 feet, Sage Mountain is the highest peak in the B.V.I. The best unobstructed views up here are from the parking area, from which a trail will lead you in a loop not only to the peak itself but also to the island's rain forest, sometimes shrouded in mist. Most of the island's forest was cut down over the centuries to clear land for sugarcane, cotton, and other crops; pastureland; and timber. But in 1964 this park was established to preserve the remaining rain forest, which not only has exotic trees and plants, but also serves an important function in preserving water for Tortola's aquifer. Up here you can see mahogany trees, white cedars, mountain guavas, elephant-ear vines, mamey trees, and giant bulletwoods, to say nothing of such birds as mountain doves and thrushes. As you walk the trail to the main gate, you'll also have good views on your right of the Sir Francis Drake Channel. Hikers and nature lovers can reach Sage Mountain by taxi from Road Town or by driving up Joe's Hill Road and making a left onto Ridge Road toward Chalwell and Doty villages. The road dead-ends at the park. *Ridge Rd., no phone (contact the tourist office for information). Admission free.*

Get yourself some snorkeling gear and hop a dive boat to the wreck of the **RMS *Rhone,*** off Salt Island (just across the channel from Road Town on Tortola). This is your chance to float on crystal-clear water over or near one of the world's best wrecks: a royal mail steamer 310 feet long that sank here in a hurricane in 1867, and was later used in the movie *The Deep.* Its four parts are at various depths from 30 to 80 feet. Nearby Rhone Reef is only 20–50 feet down. Every dive outfit in the B.V.I. runs superlative scuba and snorkel tours here. For timid snorkelers, simple and safe flotation devices are available, and the scuba supervisors will keep an eye on you. Call **Baskin in the Sun** (tel. 809/494–2858), **Underwater Safaris** (tel. 809/494–3235), **DIVE B.V.I.** (tel. 809/495–5513), **Blue Water Divers** (tel. 809/494–2847), **Island Diver, Ltd.** (tel. 809/494–3878), or **Caribbean Images** (tel. 809/495–2563).

A fun excursion for lunch or dinner is to the **William Thornton** (tel. 809/494–2564), a converted Baltic trader schooner anchored off Norman Island, Robert Louis Stevenson's reputed "Treasure Island" of yore. Launch service is available from the Fort Burt Marina on Tortola.

Shopping

The B.V.I. are not known as a shopper's delight, but you can find some interesting items, particularly artwork. Don't be put off by an informal shop entrance. Some of the best finds in the B.V.I. lie behind shopworn doors.

Shopping Districts Most of the shops and boutiques on Tortola are clustered on and off Road Town's Main Street and at Wickham's Cay shopping area adjacent to the marina. There is also an ever-growing group of art and clothing stores at Soper's Hole on Tortola's West End.

Specialty Stores and Antiques Art **Antiquities and Presents Unlimited** (Waterfront Dr., Road Town, tel. 809/495–2439) has a small but rich collection of 18th- and 19th-century furniture, wall hangings, rugs, and pottery from Africa, Asia, and South America, and some pottery made in the B.V.I.

Collector's Corner (Columbus Centre, Wickham's Cay, tel. 809/494–3550) carries antique maps, watercolors by local artists, gold and silver jewelry, coral, and Larimar—a pale blue Caribbean gemstone.

The Courtyard Gallery (Main St., Road Town, no phone) shows its exclusive Carinia Collection, delicate crushed-coral sculptures created on the premises and depicting darting hummingbirds, angelfish, nesting pelicans, and flowers.

Islands Treasures (Soper's Hole Marina, tel. 809/495–4787) is the place to find model ships, coffee-table books on the Caribbean, Caribbean maps and prints, and watercolors, paintings, pottery, and sculpture by island artists.

Caribbean Fine Arts Ltd. (Main St., tel. 809/494–4240) has a wide range of Caribbean art including original watercolors, oils, and acrylics, as well as signed prints, limited-edition serigraphs, and turn-of-the-century sepia photographs.

The Sunny Caribbee Art Gallery (Main St., tel. 809/494–2178) has a large collection of paintings, prints, and watercolors by artists from all over the Caribbean.

Clothing **Bonker's Gallery** (Main St., Road Town, tel. 809/494–2535) carries trendy resort wear for women, including cotton and washable-silk tops and bottoms, and cover-ups. There is also a small collection of pants and shirts for men.

The Pusser's Company Store (Main St. and Waterfront Rd., Road Town, tel. 809/494–2467; Soper's Hole Marina, tel. 809/495–4603) features nautical memorabilia, ship models, marine paintings, an entire line of clothes and gift items bearing the Pusser's logo, and handsome decorator bottles of Pusser's rum.

Sea Urchin (Columbus Centre, Road Town, tel. 809/494–3129 or 809/494–2044; Soper's Hole Marina, tel. 809/495–4850) has a good selection of island-living designs: print shirts and shorts, slinky swimsuits, sandals, and T-shirts.

Turtle Dove Boutique (Flemming St., Road Town, tel. 809/494–3611) is among the best in the B.V.I. for French perfume, international swimwear, and silk dresses, as well as gifts and accessories for the home.

Violet's (Wickham's Cay I, tel. 809/494–6398) has a collection of beautiful silk lingerie and a small line of designer dresses.

Food and | **The Ample Hamper** (Village Cay Marina, Wickham's Cay, tel. 809/
Drink | 494–2494; Soper's Hole Marina, tel. 809/495–4684), the leader in gourmet foods in Tortola, and **The Gourmet Galley** (Wickham's Cay II, Road Town, tel. 809/494–6999) have fine selections of wines, cheeses, fresh fruits and vegetables, canned goods from the United Kingdom and United States and provide full provisioning, including local delicacies, for yachtspeople and villa renters.

Gifts | **J.R. O'Neal, Ltd.** (Main St., Road Town, tel. 809/494–2292) carries fine crystal, Royal Worcester china, a wonderful selection of hand-painted Italian dishes, hand-blown Mexican glassware, ceramic housewares from Spain, and woven rugs and tablecloths from India.

The Sunny Caribbee Herb and Spice Company (Main St., Road Town, tel. 809/494–2178), in a brightly painted West Indian house, packages its own herbs, teas, coffees, herb vinegars, hot sauces, natural soaps, skin and suntan lotions, Caribbean art, and hand-painted decorative accessories. A small branch of this store is at the Skyworld Restaurant (*see* Dining, *below*).

Pink Pineapple (Prospect Reef Hotel, tel. 809/494–3311) offers a remarkable array of gift items, from wearable artwork and hand-painted jewelry to watercolors and batik fabric.

Jewelry | **Felix Gold and Silver Ltd.** (Main St., tel. 809/494–2406) handcrafts exceptionally fine jewelry in their on-site workshop. Choose from island or nautical themes or have something custom made. In most cases, they'll make it for you within 24 hours!

Samarkand (Main St., Road Town, tel. 809/494–6415) features handmade gold and silver pendants, earrings, bracelets, and pins.

Local Crafts | **Caribbean Handprints** (Main St., Road Town, tel. 809/494–3717), creates silk-screened fabric and sells it by the yard. Also sold are dresses, shirts, pants, bathrobes, beach cover-ups, and beach bags.

Perfume | **Flamboyance** (Main St., tel. 809/494–4099; Soper's Hole Marina, tel. 809/495–5946) carries a wide selection of designer fragrances and upscale cosmetics.

Textiles | **Zenaida's of West End** (Soper's Hole Marina, tel. 809/495–4867) displays the fabric finds of Argentinian Vivian Jenik Helm, who travels through South America, Africa, and India in search of batiks, hand-painted and hand-blocked fabrics, and interesting weaves that can be made into pareos or wall hangings. The shop also offers a selection of unusual bags, belts, and sarongs, scarves, and ethnic jewelry.

Sports and Outdoor Activities

Bicycling | You might consider renting a bicycle for an excursion around the flatter sections of Tortola. Try **Hero's Bike Rentals** (Pasea, tel. 809/494–3536), which rents tandems and single bikes by the hour and by the day.

Horseback | On Tortola, equestrians should get in touch with **Shadow Stables**
Riding | (Ridge Rd., tel. 809/494–2262).

Sailboarding | One of the best spots for sailboarding is at Trellis Bay on Beef Island. **Boardsailing B.V.I.** (Trellis Bay, Beef Island, tel. 809/495–2447) offers private and group lessons, and hourly and daily rentals.

Sailing | See Sailing in the Virgin Islands, Chapter 4, for information.

Snorkeling/ | See Diving and Snorkeling in the Virgin Islands, Chapter 3, for in-
Diving | formation.

Sportfishing A number of companies can transport and outfit you for a few hours of reel fun; try **Charter Fishing Virgin Islands** (Prospect Reef, tel. 809/494–3311).

Tennis Tortola's tennis facilities range from simple untended concrete courts to professionally maintained surfaces where organized tournaments and socials are hosted. Listed below are facilities available to the public; some have restrictions for nonguests.

Frenchman's Cay. One artificial grass court with a pretty view of Sir Francis Drake Channel. *West End, tel. 809/495–4844. Available to hotel and restaurant guests free; others at an hourly charge. Lighted. No pro.*

Moorings-Mariner Inn. One all-weather hard court. *Road Town, tel. 809/494–2331. Available to hotel and marina guests and Treasure Isle Hotel guests only. No lights. No pro.*

Prospect Reef Resort. Six hard surface courts. *Road Town, tel. 809/494–3311. Available to hotel guests free (charge for lights) and to nonguests for an hourly charge. Lighted. No pro.*

Peter Island Resort and Yacht Harbour. Four soft-surface Premiere courts hedged with hibiscus and overlooking a beautiful beach. Resident pro Dick Myers gives private and group lessons and runs weekly tournaments in season. Courts are almost always available. *Peter Island (25 minutes by regularly scheduled ferry from Peter Island's private dock just east of Road Town), tel. 809/494–2561. Courts and lessons available to guests; available to nonguests for a fee. Lighted. Pro.*

Spectator Sports

Numerous local **softball** teams play on weekend evenings at the Old Recreation Grounds between Long Bush Road and Lower Estate Road. The season runs from February through August.

Cricket matches are held at the New Recreation Grounds next to the J.R. O'Neal Botanic Gardens on weekends from February through April, and **basketball** fans can catch games here also on any Monday, Wednesday, Friday, or Saturday between May and August.

For further information, contact the B.V.I. Tourist Board (tel. 809/494–3134).

Beaches

Tortola's north side has a number of postcard perfect, palm-fringed white sand beaches that curl luxuriantly around turquoise bays and coves. Nearly all are accessible by car (preferably four-wheel drive), albeit down bumpy roads that corkscrew precipitously. Facilities tend toward the basic, but you can usually find a humble beach bar with rest rooms.

If you want to surf, **Apple Bay** (Capoon's Bay) is the spot, although the beach itself is pretty narrow. Sebastian's, the very casual hotel here, caters especially to those in search of the perfect wave. Good waves are never a sure thing, but January and February are usually high times here. **Josiah's Bay** is another favored place to hang-10. The wide and very often deserted beach is a nice place for a quiet picnic.

The water at **Brewer's Bay** is good for snorkeling. There's a campground here, but in the summer you'll find almost nobody around.

The beach and its old sugar mill and rum-distillery ruins are just north of Cane Garden Bay, just past Luck Hill (*see* Exploring, *above*).

Cane Garden Bay rivals St. Thomas's Magens Bay in beauty but is Tortola's most popular beach. It's the closest one to Road Town—one steep uphill and downhill drive—and is also one of the B.V.I.'s best-known anchorages. It's a grand beach for jogging if you can resist staying out of that translucent water. You can rent sailboards and such, and for noshing or sipping you have a choice of going to Stanley's Welcome Bar, Rhymer's, The Wedding, and Quito's Gazebo, where local recording star Quito Rhymer sings island ballads four nights a week. For true romance, nothing beats an evening of stargazing from the bow of a boat, listening to Quito's love songs drift across the bay.

Long Bay (East) is a stunning mile-long stretch of white sand (have your camera ready for snapping the breathtaking approach). Although Long Bay Hotel sits along part of it, the entire beach is open to the public. The water is not as calm here as at Cane Garden or Brewer's Bay, but it's still swimmable.

Long Bay (West) on Beef Island offers scenery that draws superlatives and is visited only by a knowledgeable few. The view of Little Camanoe and Great Camanoe islands is appealing, and if you walk around the bend to the right, you can see little Marina Cay and Scrub Island. Take the Queen Elizabeth II Bridge to Beef Island and watch for a small dirt turnoff on the left, before the airport. Drive across that dried-up marsh flat—there really is a beach (with interesting seashells) on the other side.

After bouncing your way to the beautiful **Smuggler's Cove** (Lower Belmont Bay) you'll really feel as if you've found a hidden piece of the island, although don't expect to be alone on weekends. Have a beer or a toasted cheese sandwich (the only item on the menu) at the *extremely casual* snack bar. There is a fine view of the island of Jost Van Dyke. The snorkeling is good.

About the only thing you'll find moving at **Trunk Bay** is the surf. It's directly north of Road Town, midway between Cane Garden Bay and Beef Island, and you'll have to hike down a *ghut* gully from the high Ridge Road.

Dining

There's no lack of dining options on Tortola. Seafood is plentiful and, although other fresh ingredients are scarce, the island's chefs are an adaptable lot, and apply creative genius to whatever the weekly supply boat delivers.

Road Town/ **Brandywine Bay.** For the best in romantic dining, don't miss this
East End hillside gem. Candlelit, outdoor tables look out on a sweeping view
★ of neighboring islands. Italian owner/chef Davide Pugliese prepares foods the Tuscan way, grilled with lots of fresh herbs. The remarkable menu, which hostess Cele Pugliese describes tableside, can include homemade mozzarella, grilled portobello mushrooms, grilled local wahoo, and grilled veal chop with ricotta and sun-dried tomatoes, and always includes duck with an exotic sauce (it could be berry, mango, orange and ginger, or passion fruit). The lemon tart and the Tiramisù are irresistible. The wine list is excellent. *Sir Francis Drake Hwy., east of Road Town, tel. 809/495-2301. Reservations advised. Dress: neat but casual. AE, MC, V. Closed for lunch; closed Sun. $$$*

★ **Skyworld.** You'll want to arrive early for dinner at this mountaintop aerie; the sunset views are breathtaking. Watch the western horizon go ablaze with color, then settle back in the casual, but elegant dining room to feast on chef George Petcoff's delectable offerings. Try the veal in lemon caper sauce, the local swordfish with sun-dried tomato pesto, or the passion fruit sorbet. This is also a special place for lunch. Not only are the sandwiches on home-baked bread delicious, but the restaurant and the observation tower above offer the B.V.I.'s highest (and absolutely spectacular) 360° view of numerous islands and cays. Even St. Croix and Anegada (both 20 miles in the distance) can be seen on a clear day. *Ridge Rd., tel. 809/494–3567. Reservations advised. Dress: neat but casual. AE, MC, V. $$$*

★ **The Upstairs.** Ask for a window table where gentle tropical breezes waft by as you gaze out at the stars. Excellent service and food are hallmarks of this elegant and romantic restaurant that overlooks a small marina. The superbly cooked filet mignon with peaches and an outstanding port wine sauce is truly exceptional. Other house specialties include a delicious lobster au gratin appetizer, grilled local fish, roast duck, and key lime pie. A 10% service charge is included in the bill. *Prospect Reef Hotel (turn left just after the entrance), Road Town, tel. 809/494–2228. Reservations accepted. Dress: neat but casual. AE, MC, V. $$$*

The Last Resort. Actually on Bellamy Cay just off Beef Island (free ferry service provided to and from Trellis Bay/Beef Island), this spot features an English buffet, complete with prime rib and Yorkshire pudding—and the inimitable cabaret humor and ribald ditties of owner Tony Snell, the B.V.I.'s answer to Benny Hill. *Bellamy Cay, tel. 809/495–2520. Reservations advised. Dress: casual. AE, MC, V. $$–$$$*

The Pusser's Outpost. On the second floor, above Pusser's Deli and Company Store, is this quiet retreat that features Continental cuisine, including seafood, and pasta dishes. Sit outdoors on the wraparound terrace or inside in the elegantly decorated dining room. The most popular affair here is the lavish champagne brunch, which is held every Sunday from 11 to 3. *Waterfront Dr., Road Town, tel. 809/ 494–4199. Reservations accepted. Dress: casual. AE, MC, V. $$–$$$*

The Fishtrap. Dine alfresco at this restaurant, which serves grilled local fish, steaks, and chicken. Friday and Saturday there's a barbecue with a terrific salad bar, and Sunday features prime rib plus the regular menu. For lunch, there is a buffet as well as burgers and burritos. *Columbus Centre, Wickham's Cay, Road Town, tel. 809/ 494–3626. Reservations accepted. Dress: casual. AE, MC, V. Closed Sun. lunch. $$*

Ft. Burt Restaurant. After years with an excellent reputation, this hillside restaurant with a lovely view of Road Town Harbor went completely downhill. The pendulum is swinging back, though—new management has created a promising menu that includes seafood, curries, and Continental selections. The terrace bar is a peaceful place to relax at the end of a busy day. *Waterfront St., at west edge of Road Town, tel. 809/494–2587. Reservations accepted. Dress: neat but casual. AE, MC, V. $$*

Spaghetti Junction. This funky spot is popular with the boating crowd. Nightly specials complement the tasty and traditional Italian menu (veal or chicken parmigiana, pastas, etc.), and the sundried tomatoes in the Caesar salad are a nice twist. Check out the gorilla in the restroom. *Waterfront Dr., Road Town, tel. 809/494– 4880. Reservations advised. Dress: casual. No credit cards. Closed lunch, Sept., and holidays. $$*

Tavern in the Town. Birds and bougainvillea brighten the garden setting of this "English-style pub." Mixed grills and fish and chips are in the British tradition, though you can also order such entrées as duck in orange and rum sauce and garlic shrimp, as well as hamburgers. *Waterfront Dr., Road Town, tel. 809/494–2790. Reservations accepted. Dress: casual. No credit cards. Closed Sat. $$*

Virgin Queen. The sailing and rugby crowd and locals gather here to play darts, drink beer, and eat Queen's Pizza, which some patrons say is the best pizza in the Caribbean. Also on the menu is excellent West Indian and English fare: Choose from salt fish, barbecued ribs with beans and rice, bangers and mash, shepherd's pie, chili, to name only a selection of delicious menu items. *Fleming St., Road Town, tel. 809/494–2310. No reservations. Dress: casual. No credit cards. Closed Sun. $$*

★ **Capriccio di Mare.** The owners of the well-known Brandywine Bay restaurant (*see above*) have opened this welcome addition to Road Town, an authentic Italian café. People stop by all day long for cappuccino or espresso, a fresh pastry or a Tiramisù, delicious Toast Italiano (grilled ham and swiss-cheese sandwiches), bowls of perfectly cooked linguine or penne with a variety of sauces, and crispy tomato and mozzarella pizzas topped with hot Italian sausage or fresh grilled eggplant. Drink specialities include the Mango Bellini, an adaptation of the famous Bellini cocktail served by Harry's Bar in Venice. *Waterfront Dr., Road Town, tel. 809/494–5369. No reservations. Dress: casual. No credit cards. Closed Sun. No dinner Sat. $–$$*

Outside Road Town

Sugar Mill Restaurant. Candles gleam, and the background music is peaceful in this well-known restaurant. Ranking among America's top food writers, owners Jeff and Jinx Morgan do not disappoint with nicely prepared selections that might include smoked duck breast with honey-lemon glaze, herbed prawns with drawn butter, or His Majesty's West Indian Regimental beef curry. The four-course dinner menu changes nightly and includes soup, salad, your choice of three entrées and one of several desserts. Some might find the menu too limited and the service a bit rushed for the peaceful, romantic setting. *Apple Bay, tel. 809/495–4355. Reservations advised. Dress: casual. AE, MC, V. $$$*

Pusser's Landing. Yachters flock to the two-story home of this popular waterfront restaurant. Downstairs belly up to the large, comfortable, open-air mahogany bar or choose a waterside table for drinks, sandwiches, and light dinners. Head upstairs for quieter alfresco dining and a delightfully eclectic menu that includes homemade black bean soup, freshly grilled local fish, pasta, and such pub favorites as "bubble and squeak." The air-conditioned Dinner Theater, with its 15-foot movie screen, features prix-fixe, three-course meal, and movie combos and sports events. *Soper's Hole, tel. 809/495–4554. Reservations accepted. Dress: casual. AE, MC, V. $$–$$$*

The Apple. This small, inviting restaurant is in a small West Indian house. Soft candlelight complements local seafood dishes such as fish steamed in lime butter and conch or whelks in garlic sauce. There's a traditional West Indian barbecue and buffet every Sunday evening. The excellent new lunch menu includes a variety of sandwiches, meat and vegetarian lasagna, lobster quiche, seafood crêpes, and ham and cheese or spinach and feta croissants. *Little Apple Bay, tel. 809/495–4437. Reservations accepted. Dress: casual. AE, MC, V. $$*

Mrs. Scatliffe's. You'll find the best West Indian cooking on the island here, according to many knowledgeable Tortolans (though some bemoan, "She gone Continental"). Meals are served on the upstairs terrace of Mrs. Scatliffe's home. The food is freshly prepared (vegetables come from the family garden), and the baked chicken in coconut is meltingly tender. After dinner, live entertainment is provided by family members. *Carrot Bay, tel. 809/495–4556. Reservations for dinner required by 5:30 PM. Dress: casual. No credit cards. $$*

Quito's Gazebo. Owned and operated by Quito Rymer, a multitalented B.V.I. recording star, this rustic beachside bar and restaurant offers a Caribbean menu with an emphasis on fresh fish. Try the conch stew or the curried chicken. A Caribbean buffet is featured on Sunday nights, and Friday is Fish Fry Night. Quito plays the guitar and sings Calypso ballads and love songs Tuesday, Thursday, Friday, and Sunday, and a reggae band performs Saturdays. The atmosphere is so convivial that by the time you finish dinner here you are likely to find yourself swapping yarns with some colorful local personalities. *Cane Garden Bay, tel. 809/495–4837. Reservations accepted. Dress: casual. MC, V. Closed Mon. $*

The Struggling Man. Barely more than a roadside shack, this pleasant place with raffish candy-cane decor offers striking views of Drake's Channel and simple, tasty West Indian specialties. *Sea Cow Bay, tel. 809/494–4163. No reservations. Dress: casual. No credit cards. $*

Lodging

Luxury on Tortola is more a state of mind—serenity, seclusion, gentility—than state-of-the-art amenities and facilities. Hotels in Road Town don't have beaches (except Prospect Reef) but do have pools, and are within walking distance of restaurants, nightlife, and shopping. Accommodations outside Road Town are relatively isolated but are on beaches—some of which are exquisite, others are small or artificial.

Hotels and Inns
Road Town

Prospect Reef Resort. Fresh paint (bright pinks, purples, blues, and yellows) has given this sprawling resort, which is near town and overlooks Sir Francis Drake Channel, a much needed face-lift and added a true Caribbean flavor. The 7-acre grounds are neatly manicured, and have creative rock paths and a network of lagoons. The 11 different housing units include small rooms, larger rooms with kitchenettes, and two-story, two-bedroom apartments with private interior courtyards. New light tropical-print fabrics have brightened the rooms. All the rooms have a balcony, patio, or both, and may face either the water or the hotel's gardens. In addition to the hotel's Junior Olympic–size swimming pool and diving pool, there are two adjoining calm saltwater swimming areas created at the edge of a narrow, man-made beach. The resort also boasts its own harbor with sailboats available for day trips or longer excursions. Lighted tennis courts and a rather rustic pitch-and-putt golf course are among the pleasures on the grounds. You may even see one of the local goats moseying around. A bonus at the largest resort in the B.V.I.: splendid views of sunrise over the Drakes Channel. *Box 104, Road Town, tel. 809/494–3311, fax 809/494–5595. 131 rooms. Facilities: man-made beach, 2 restaurants, beachside snack bar, 2 bars, 3 pools (2 freshwater), children's splash pool, 6 tennis courts, pitch-and-putt golf, water sports, gift shop, beachwear shop, commissary, hair salon, conference center. AE, MC, V. $$$–$$$$*

Moorings-Mariner Inn. Headquarters for the Moorings Charter operation and popular with yachting folk who find its full-service facilities convenient and the companionship of fellow "boaties" congenial, this is also a good choice for those who want to be within easy walking distance of town. The atmosphere is a combination of laid-back and lively and the rooms, including four full-size suites, are large and comfortable. The rooms' pale-peach decor is picked up in the peach tiles on the floors, and bright, tropical-print bedspreads and curtains add color. All rooms have a small kitchenette (with sink, refrigerator, and two-burner stove) and a balcony, and most rooms face the water except for eight, which overlook the pool or the tennis court. *Box 139, Road Town, tel. 809/494–2331, fax 809/494–2226. 40 rooms. Facilities: restaurant, bar, pool, tennis court, volleyball court, dive shop, gourmet shop. AE, MC, V. $$–$$$$*

★ **Treasure Isle Hotel.** Owned by The Moorings, this hillside hotel, painted in bright shades of lemon, violet, and mango pink, is one of the prettiest properties on the island. The air-conditioned rooms are spacious and accented with fabrics sporting prints in the manner of Matisse. Set on a hillside overlooking the harbor, Treasure Isle makes a handy base for in-town shopping and visits to nearby marinas. Open to the breezes and the heady aroma of tropical flowers, the Spy Glass Bar with its comfortable lounge is the perfect place to relax and study the stunning view of the harbor and distant islands. There is daily transportation to Cane Garden Bay and Brewers Bay. *Box 68, Road Town, tel. 809/494–2501, fax 809/494–2507. 40 rooms. Facilities: restaurant, 2 bars, pool, water sports. AE, MC, V. $$–$$$$*

Maria's by the Sea. Perched on the edge of Road Harbour, between town and the large, new government building, this simple hotel is an easy walk from restaurants in town. The small rooms are decorated with white rattan furniture, floral-print bedspreads, and murals painted by local artists. All rooms have kitchenettes and balconies, some of which offer harbor views. A freshwater pool is available for cooling dips. *Box 206, Road Town, tel. 809/494–2595. 14 rooms. Facilities: restaurant, bar, freshwater pool. AE, MC, V. $$–$$$*

Village Cay Hotel & Marina. This pleasant, compact hotel looks out on Road Town Harbor and several marinas. It is popular with yachters and those who want to be within easy walking distance of Road Town restaurants and shops. Rooms are nicely decorated in tropical prints and some units have cathedral ceilings. There is a small pool. *Wickham's Cay, Road Town, tel. 809/494–2771, fax 809/494–2773. 20 rooms. Facilities: restaurant, bar, pool, water sports. AE, MC, V. $$–$$$*

Castle Maria. These simple accommodations are ideal for those who are on a budget. Some rooms have kitchenettes, balconies, and air-conditioning. All have refrigerators and cable TV. Close to in-town diversions, Castle Maria also boasts a freshwater pool and a bar. *Box 206, Road Town, tel. 809/494–2553. 30 rooms. Facilities: bar, freshwater pool. AE, MC, V. $–$$*

Outside Road Town **Frenchman's Cay.** This well-maintained resort consists of one- and two-bedroom villas that overlook Drakes Channel. Each unit includes a full kitchen, dining area, and sitting room—ideal for families or couples. Rooms are done in neutral colors, with cream-color curtains and bedspreads and tile floors. Ceiling fans and pleasant breezes keep the rooms cool. There is a small pool and a modest-size man-made beach that is sandy to the water's edge but rocky offshore. It's not good for wading without shoes but does offer good snorkeling. The alfresco bar and dining room are breeze-swept and inviting. Snorkelers will particularly enjoy the offshore reef found here. *Box 1054, West End, tel. 809/495–4844, fax 809/495–4056. 9 units. Facilities: restaurant, bar, tennis court, beach, pool, water sports. AE, D, MC, V. $$$–$$$$*

★ **Long Bay Hotel.** Spectacularly set on a gentle mile-long arc of white sand, this appealing hotel continues to undergo extensive remodeling and now has an elegant lobby and a number of new villas. There is a wide variety of accommodations to choose from, including 32 deluxe beachfront rooms, with two queen-size beds or one king-size four-poster bed, marble-top wet bars, showers with Italian tiles, and balconies. There are also smaller beach cabanas, 10 rustic, tropical hideaways set on stilts at the water's edge. Hillside choices all have balconies and lovely views, and range from small but adequate rooms, to studios with a comfortable seating area, to roomy one- and two-bedroom villas. The use of floral prints and rattan furniture set a tropical mood throughout. The Beach restaurant offers all-day dining, with live island music in the evening. The Garden Restaurant here is highly regarded, and offers a different menu for each night of the week in a romantic, candlelit setting. A small pool, a nine-hole, par-3, pitch-and-putt golf course, and a small tennis court complete the complex. *Box 433, Road Town, tel. 809/495–4252 or 800/729–9599, fax 809/495–4677. 62 rooms, 20 villas. Facilities: 2 restaurants, 2 bars, beach, pool, pitch-and-putt golf, tennis court, gift shop. AE, MC, V. $$$–$$$$*

Nanny Cay Resort and Marina. This hotel continues to need sprucing up. With its pastel-painted, gingerbread-trimmed buildings clustered about overgrown gardens, it exudes the ambience of a small village. The rooms, each with its own patio or balcony, feature kitchenettes, air-conditioning, ceiling fans, telephones, and cable TV. Typically tropical decor includes cane furniture, floral bedspreads, shuttered windows, and a pastel color scheme. There is a nice-size swimming pool, a saltwater pool made out of large boulders at the water's edge, and a man-made beach. *Box 281, Road Town, tel. 809/494–2512, fax 809/494–3288. 41 rooms. Facilities: 2 restaurants, 2 bars, man-made beach, 2 pools (1 freshwater, 1 salt), shopping arcade, marina. AE, MC, V. $$$–$$$$*

Sugar Mill Hotel. The owners of this small, out-of-the-way hotel are Jeff and Jinx Morgan who opened it two decades ago, after becoming well-established as travel and food writers. The reception area, bar, and restaurant are in the ruins of a centuries-old sugar mill and the walls are hung with bright Haitian artwork. Rather plain guest houses are scattered up a hill, and the rooms are simply furnished in soft pastels and rattan and have ceiling fans but no air-conditioning. Light sleepers might find the roosters, who start crowing long before dawn, a bit annoying. There's a circular swimming pool set into the hillside and a tiny beach where lunch is served on a shady terrace. The dinner restaurant by the same name is well known on the island (*see* Dining, *above*). *Box 425, Road Town, tel. 809/495–4355, fax 809/495–4696. 20 rooms. Facilities: 2 restaurants, 2 bars, beach, pool, water sports. AE, MC, V. $$$–$$$$*

★ **Fort Recovery Estates Villas.** This appealing group of one- to four-bedroom bungalows, built around the remnants of a Dutch Fort, stretches along a small, remote beach facing the Sir Francis Drake Channel. All units have excellent views (with sliding glass doors that open onto patios facing the ocean) and fully equipped kitchens. Bedrooms are air-conditioned; living rooms (not air-conditioned) are suitable as an additional bedroom for one child. The grounds are bright with tropical flowers and the management is exceptionally helpful and friendly. A new kitchen provides excellent room-service meals. There are exercise and yoga classes (as well as special fitness packages), massages, and baby-sitting services, and arrangements can be made for car rental, guided land and water tours, and more. *Box 239, Road Town, tel. 809/495–4467, fax 809/495–4036. 10 units. Facilities: commissary, room service. AE, MC, V. $$–$$$*

Sebastian's on the Beach. The rooms are divided among three buildings, only one of which is on the beach—this is also the only building that has balconies in each room. These eight rooms are the best beachfront units on Tortola's north shore. Rooms in the other two buildings can be noisy. Decor in the guest rooms is typically Caribbean: beige tile floors, tropical oil paintings on white walls, and bright floral bedspreads. The restaurant here is excellent, and movies are presented nightly. *Box 441, Road Town, tel. 809/495–4212, fax 809/495–4466. 26 rooms. Facilities: restaurant, bar, beach, water sports, commissary. AE. $$–$$$*

Ole Works Inn. Nestled in the hillside across the road from one of Tortola's most beautiful beaches, is this rustic but appealing inn— owned by local recording star Quito Rhymer. A steeply pitched roof, wood, and island stonework add a contemporary flair to what was once an old sugar mill. Simply decorated rooms have ceiling fans, air-conditioning, and refrigerators. The Honeymoon Suite has an indoor swing for two. *Cane Garden Bay, tel. 809/495–4837, fax 809/495–9618. 8 rooms. No facilities: MC, V. $–$$*

Rhymer's Beach Hotel. With one of the Caribbean's most beautiful beaches right on the doorstep, the setting here couldn't be lovelier. The rooms are extremely basic but they are air-conditioned and have balconies, TVs, phones, and kitchenettes. But with the warm waters of Cane Garden Bay beckoning, who will spend much time indoors? The beach bar and terrace restaurant attract locals, daytrippers, and charter-boat types, so the atmosphere is always lively, though more so on evenings when local bands do their thing. Some days cruise ships send their passengers here (via taxi from Road Town)—you may wish to spend these days exploring the island. *Box 570, Cane Garden Bay, tel. 809/495–4639. 25 rooms. Facilities: restaurant, bar, beach, water sports. AE, MC, V. $–$$*

Private Homes and Villas The villa rentals companies listed below provide excellent alternatives for couples and families seeking greater seclusion. All villas boast fully furnished kitchens and maid service.

Rockview Holiday Homes (Box 203, Road Town, tel. 809/494–2550) represents the island's top-of-the-line properties. Homes offer accommodations for two to 10 people in one- to five-bedroom villas, decorated in soothing pastels. Many have swimming pools, Jacuzzis, and glazed terra-cotta courtyards. Standouts, both on Long Bay, are **Sunset House and Villas**, an exquisite hideaway whose first guest was Britain's Princess Alexandra (but you needn't be royalty to receive the royal treatment here) and **Equinox House**, a handsome three-bedroom estate set among lavish tumbling gardens. Rates vary, but range from expensive to very expensive in season. **Best Vacations Imaginable** (Box 306, Road Town, tel. 809/494–6186) handles numerous moderate to expensive properties including **Josiah's Bay Cottages**, tucked into a forest of almond and mahogany trees, and **Heritage Villas,** nestled on Windy Hill with sweeping views of the Carrot Bay, Long Bay, and Little Apple Bay area. The Tourist Board can suggest more inexpensive lodging in basic but clean efficiencies.

Campgrounds **Brewers Bay Campground.** Both prepared and bare sites are located on Brewers Bay, one of Tortola's prime snorkeling spots. Check out the ruins of the distillery that gave the bay its name. *Box 185, Road Town, tel. 809/494–3463. Facilities: beach, bar, restaurant, commissary, water sports, baby-sitters available.*

Nightlife

While the B.V.I. are not noted for swinging, Tortola has several cozy watering holes especially popular with yachties.

Bing's Drop In Bar (Fat Hog's Bay, East End, tel. 809/495–2627). This is a rollicking local hangout with a DJ nightly in season.

Bomba's Surfside Shack (Apple Bay, no phone). This unusually decorated little shack looks like a pile of junk during the day but is actually one of Tortola's liveliest night spots. Sundays at 4 PM there's always some sort of live music, and Wednesdays at 8 PM the Blue Haze Combo shows up. Also, every evening on the full moon, nearly everyone on Tortola surfaces to party through the night and dance to local bands.

Jolly Roger (West End, tel. 809/495–4559). An ever-changing array of local, American, and down island bands play everything from rhythm and blues to reggae to country to good old rock-and-roll, Tuesday, Wednesday, Friday, and Saturday at 8 PM.

The Pusser's Deli (Waterfront St., Road Town, tel. 809/494–4199). Thursday is "nickel beer night" and crowds gather here for pints of John Courage. Other nights try Pusser's famous mixed drink— "Painkillers"—and snack on their excellent pizza.

Pusser's Landing (Soper's Hole, West End, tel. 809/495–4554). The schedule at Pusser's varies nightly but you can usually count on some kind of live music (it could be reggae, rock, or a steel band) on Friday, Saturday, and Sunday evenings.

Quito's Gazebo (Cane Garden Bay, tel. 809/495–4837). B.V.I. recording star Quito Rymer sings island ballads and love songs (including many he has written himself), accompanied by the guitar and the gentle lapping of the surf, at this rustic beachside bar-restaurant on Cane Garden Bay. Shows are on Sunday, Tuesday, Thursday, and Friday nights at 8:30. Saturday a live band pumps out reggae.

Stanley's Welcome Bar (Cane Garden Bay, tel. 809/495–4520). It gets rowdy when crews stop by to drink and indulge in time-honored fraternity-type hijinks, such as piling up on the tire swing outside.

Virgin Gorda

Introduction

Virgin Gorda, with its mountainous central portion connected by skinny necks to southern and northern appendages—on a map they look like the slightest breeze would cause them to splinter—is quite different from Tortola. The island receives less rain, so some areas are more arid and home to scrub brush and cactus. The pace here is even slower than on its larger, sister island. One of the most effective ways to see Virgin Gorda is by sailboat. Paved roads are few and far between, alternative routes are limited, and most byways do not follow the scalloped shoreline. The main road also sticks resolutely to the center of the island, linking The Baths at the tip of the southern extremity with Gun Creek and Leverick Bay in the north, and providing exhilarating views from its higher points. The panorama of a craggy shoreline, scissored with grottoes and fringed by palms and the island's trademark boulders, possesses a primitive beauty. Goats and cattle own the right of way, and the unpretentious friendliness of the local people is winning. The island is small enough that a single day of touring will allow plenty of time to explore most of the sights.

Important Addresses and Numbers

Tourist Information The tourist board is in Virgin Gorda Yacht Harbour, Spanish Town (tel. 809/495–5182).

Emergencies Dial 999 for all emergencies.

Hospitals Virgin Gorda has two clinics, one in Spanish Town, or The Valley (tel. 809/495–5337), and one at North Sound (tel. 809/495–7310).

Pharmacies On Virgin Gorda, the Spanish Town pharmacy is **Medicure** (tel. 809/495–5479).

Getting Around

By Taxi Taxi service is available through **Mahogany Rentals and Taxi Service** (tel. 809/495–5469), **Speedy's Taxi Service** (tel. 809/495–5234), or **Andy's Taxi and Jeep Rental** (tel. 809/495–5252 or 809/495–5353).

By Car The taxi companies listed above also provide rentals. Mahogany is especially helpful.

By Moped **Honda Scooter Rental** (The Valley, tel. 809/495–5212) rents mopeds by the hour or the day.

Guided Tours

Guided tours on Virgin Gorda can be arranged through **Andy's Taxi and Jeep Rental** (tel. 809/495–5252 or 809/495–5353) or **Mahogany Rentals and Taxi Service** (tel. 809/495–5469).

Exploring Virgin Gorda

Numbers in the margin correspond to points of interest on the Virgin Gorda map.

❶ Virgin Gorda's main settlement, on the island's southern wing, is **Spanish Town,** a peaceful village so tiny that it barely qualifies as a town at all. Also known as The Valley, Spanish Town is home to a marina, a small cluster of shops, and a couple of car-rental agencies. At the **Virgin Gorda Yacht Harbour** you can enjoy a stroll along the dock front or do a little browsing in the shops here. The ferry slip is just north of town.

Time Out Settle down by the fountain on the cool patio of the **Bath and Turtle** (Virgin Gorda Yacht Harbour, tel. 809/495–5239), an English-style pub that opens onto the marina mall courtyard, and have a meatball hero, a pizza, or a chili-cheese dog with a mug of Courage draft beer or your favorite rum drink.

Having rented a vehicle (you'll find a Jeep the most satisfactory for negotiating some of the rougher terrain; remember that virtually none of the roads are marked, so be prepared to stop and ask for directions), turn right from the marina parking lot onto Lee Road and head through the more populated, flat countryside of the south for about 15 minutes. You'll pass the Fischer's Cove Beach Hotel on your right. Keep driving until the road ends at a round parking area; from ❷ here, a 35-yard trail takes you to **The Baths,** Virgin Gorda's most celebrated site. Giant boulders, brought to the surface eons ago by a vast volcanic eruption, are scattered about the beach and in the water. Boulders the size of small houses form remarkable swimmable grottos. Early morning and late afternoon are the best times to visit since The Baths and the beach here are usually crowded with day-trippers visiting from Tortola.

Time Out Just before the parking area for The Baths, there is a small bar called **Mad Dog's** (tel. 809/495–5830); you may want to pause for a cool drink and a BLT or a hot dog after making the climb back to the parking area. Piña coladas are the specialty.

If it's privacy you crave, follow the shore north for a few hundred yards to reach several other quieter bays—Spring, The Crawl, Little Trunk, and Valley Trunk—or head south to Devil's Bay. These beaches have the same giant boulders as those found at The Baths.

Back in the car, retrace your route along Lee Road until you reach the southern edge of Spanish Town. After passing the school and sports field on your right, take the next right and proceed to a "T" intersection, then make another right and follow Copper Mine Road, ❸ part of it unpaved, for a bumpy 10 minutes until you come to **Copper Mine Point.** Here you will discover a tall, stone shaft silhouetted against the sky and a small stone structure overlooking the sea. These are the ruins of a copper mine established here 400 years ago and worked first by the Spanish, then by English miners until the early 20th century. This is one of the few places in the B.V.I. where you won't see islands along the horizon. Retrace your tracks back to town and continue north to the extensive, beautifully cared-for property of **Little Dix Bay,** the elegant retreat that is the grandmother of all B.V.I. resorts. Much of its sloping 400 acres of verdant grounds looks like a golf course invaded by beautiful tropical trees.

Time Out You may want to pause for a drink at one of Little Dix's breezy beachside bars, the **Sugarmill** or the **Beachhouse,** while contemplating the long arc of the beach and the Dog Islands—Great Dog, George Dog, West Dog—lying offshore.

Back in the car and heading north again, you'll see on your left **Savannah Bay** and **Pond Bay,** two pristine stretches of sand that mark the thin neck of land connecting Virgin Gorda's southern extension to the larger northern half. The view from this scenic elbow, called ❹ **Black Rock,** is of the Sir Francis Drake Channel to the northeast and the Caribbean Sea to the southwest. The road forks as it goes uphill. The unpaved left prong winds past the Mango Bay Club resort (and not much else) to Long Bay and not quite to Mountain Point. To continue exploring, follow the road that bears right, which winds uphill and looks down on beautiful South Sound. You'll notice nary a dwelling or sign of mundane civilization up here, only a green mountain slope on your left and a spectacular view down to South Sound on the right. From here, too, you can also look back and get a wonderful, living sense of Virgin Gorda's stringy, crooked shape: Back there, looking flat and almost like a separate island, is the Valley, which you've just left. Because of this shape, Virgin Gorda is one of those places where you can get a bird's-eye (or map's-eye) view of things from right inside your car.

You may see a small sign on the left for the trail up to the 265-acre ❺ **Gorda Peak National Park** and the island's summit at 1,359 feet (sometimes the sign is missing, so keep your eyes peeled for a set of stairs disappearing into the trees). It's about a 15-minute hike up to a small clearing, where you can climb a ladder to the platform of a

Virgin Gorda

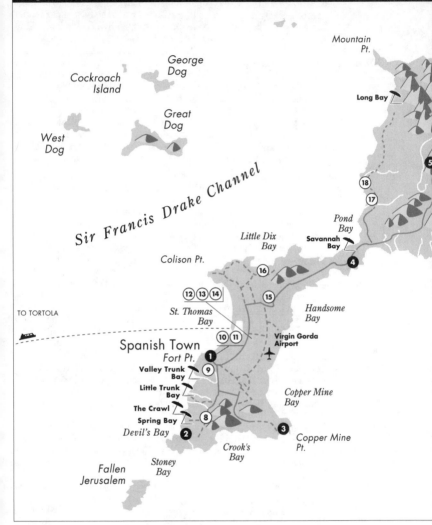

Exploring

The Baths, **2**

Black Rock, **4**

Copper Mine Point, **3**

Eustatia Sound, **7**

Gorda Peak National Park, **5**

Saba Rock, **6**

Spanish Town, **1**

Dining

The Bath and Turtle, **10**

Biras Creek, **22**

Chez Michelle, **11**

The Clubhouse, **23**

The Crab Hole, **13**

Drake's Anchorage, **24**

Little Dix Bay, **16**

Olde Yard Inn, **15**

Pusser's Leverick Bay, **19**

Teacher's Pet Ilma's, **14**

Lodging

Biras Creek Hotel, **22**

Bitter End Yacht Club and Marina, **23**

Drake's Anchorage, **24**

Fischer's Cove Beach Hotel, **9**

Guavaberry Spring Bay Vacation Homes, **8**

Leverick Bay Resort, **20**

Little Dix Bay, **16**

Mango Bay Resort, **17**

Olde Yard Inn, **15**

Paradise Beach Resort, **18**

Virgin Gorda Villa Rentals, **21**

The Wheel House, **12**

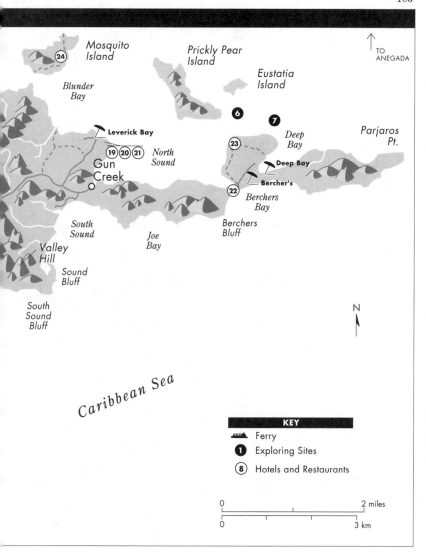

Mosquito Island

Prickly Pear Island

Eustatia Island

Blunder Bay

24

Leverick Bay

6

7

Deep Bay

Parjaros Pt.

19 20 21 North Sound

23

Deep Bay

Gun Creek

○

Bercher's

22

Berchers Bay

South Sound

Joe Bay

Berchers Bluff

Valley Hill

Sound Bluff

South Sound Bluff

N

↑ TO ANEGADA

Caribbean Sea

KEY

🚢 Ferry

❶ Exploring Sites

⑧ Hotels and Restaurants

0		2 miles
0		3 km

wood observation tower. If you're keen for some woodsy exercise or just want to stretch your legs, go for it. Unfortunately, the view at the top is somewhat tree-obstructed. A bit farther on, the road forks again. The right fork leads down to **Gun Creek** where launches pick up passengers for The Bitter End and Biras Creek, two of Virgin Gorda's most appealing hostelries.

The left fork will bring you to **Leverick Bay.** The **Leverick Bay Resort** is here, as well as a tiny beach and a marina, a Pusser's restaurant, a cluster of shops, and some luxurious hillside villas to rent, all a little like a tucked-away tropical suburb. (*see* Dining and Lodging, *below*). This is also where a launch picks up passengers for **Drake's Anchorage,** a resort on nearby Mosquito Island (*see* Dining and Lodging, *below*).

Time Out Stop by **Pusser's Beach Bar** for a snack and browse in the nearby stores before your return trip to your vacation headquarters.

Low-gear your way up one of the narrow hillside roads (you're not on a driveway, it only seems that way) to one of those topmost Leverick dwellings, where you can park for a moment. (Three of the highest, if you can find them, are called Seaview, Tamarind, and Double Sunrise.) Out to the left, across Blunder Bay, you'll see **Mosquito Island;** the hunk of land straight ahead is **Prickly Pear,** which has been named a national park to protect it from development. At the neck of land to your right, across from Gun Creek, is **Biras Creek Hotel** (*see* Dining and Lodging, *below*), and around the bend to the north of that you'll see the Danish-roof buildings of the **Bitter End Yacht Club and Marina** (*see* The Clubhouse in Dining, and Lodging, *below*). Between the Bitter End and Prickly Pear you should be able to make ❻ out **Saba Rock,** home of one of the Caribbean's best-known diving entrepreneurs, Bert Kilbride—a colorful character who knows where all the wrecks are and who is recognized and commissioned by the Queen of England as Honorary Keeper of the Wrecks. Once a dive shop, this stone building in the middle of North Sound is now the Pirates Pub and Grill, a very colorful watering hole. Locals and boaters will often give you a ride in a dingy from the dingy dock at Bitter End. Make it a point to visit the Rock at least once.

❼ That magical color change in the sea near Prickly Pear reveals **Eustatia Sound** and its extensive reef. Beyond that are Horseshoe Reef, Necker Island, and the flat coral island of Anegada some 20 miles north, where most of those wrecks *are* and where bare-boaters are not permitted to sail because of the perilous reefs. But you can easily take a boat to Biras Creek, Bitter End, or Drake's Anchorage. In fact, that's the only way you can get there.

Virgin Gorda for Free

Virtually all of Virgin Gorda's attractions are free of charge. A day spent roaming **Spanish Town, The Baths,** and the island's many **beaches** will cost only the price of your lunch. After all, who could fix a price tag on these breathtaking views?

What to See and Do with Children

Many of the same attractions that draw adults to Virgin Gorda will appeal to children as well. The grotto and the giant prehistoric boulders at **The Baths** are bound to captivate young minds, and hiking to the top of **Gorda Peak** should also keep active youngsters happily occupied.

Off the Beaten Path

The quaintly named islands of **Fallen Jerusalem** and **The Dog Islands** are easily reached by boat. Their seductive beaches and unparalleled snorkeling display the B.V.I. at their beachcombing, hedonistic best. Contact **DIVE B.V.I.** (Virgin Gorda Yacht Harbour, tel. 809/495–5513) for expert diving instruction, certification, and daytrips. Keen birdwatchers can call the **National Parks Trust** (tel. 809/494–3904) for information on visiting their protected nesting sites.

Shopping

On Virgin Gorda most boutiques are located within the individual hotel complexes. One of the best is the one in Little Dix Bay. Other properties—Biras Creek, the Bitter End, Leverick Bay, and nearby Mosquito Island's Drake's Anchorage—have small but equally select boutiques, and there's a more than respectable and diverse scattering of shops in the minimall adjacent to the bustling yacht harbor in Spanish Town.

Art **Olde Yard Inn Boutique** (The Valley, tel. 809/495–5544). This store carries locally crafted sculpture, pottery, jewelry, and paintings, as well as some clothing and gift items.

Clothing **DIVE B.V.I.** (Virgin Gorda Yacht Harbour, tel. 809/495–5513) sells men's and women's sportswear, sunglasses, and beach bags.

Island Silhouette in Flax Plaza (near Fischer's Cove Hotel, no phone). This is the place to go for resort wear and locally made tie-dye T-shirts.

Next Wave (Virgin Gorda Yacht Harbour, tel. 809/495–5623). This shop sells bathing suits, T-shirts, and canvas tote bags.

Pelican's Pouch Boutique (Virgin Gorda Yacht Harbour, tel. 809/495–5599). At the Pelican's Pouch you'll find a large selection of swimsuits plus cover-ups, T-shirts, and accessories.

Pusser's Company Store (Leverick Bay, tel. 809/495–7369). The Virgin Gorda branch offers its trademark line of rum products, gift items, and sportswear for men and women.

Food and Drink **Bitter End's Emporium** (North Sound, tel. 809/494–2745). The Bitter End resort is the place to look for such edible treats as local fruits, cheeses, and bakery goods.

Virgin Island Bakery (Virgin Gorda Yacht Harbour, no phone). Come here for freshly baked bread, rolls, muffins, and cookies, or sandwiches and sodas to go.

Gifts **The Palm Tree Gallery** (Leverick Bay, tel. 809/495–7421). This boutique features attractive handcrafted jewelry, paintings, and accessories.

The Reeftique (Bitter End, North Sound, tel. 809/494–2745). Reeftique carries a variety of gift items including island crafts and jewelry, clothing, and nautical odds and ends with the Bitter End logo.

Local Crafts **Virgin Gorda Craft Shop** (Virgin Gorda Yacht Harbour, tel. 809/495–5137). This shop features the work of island artisans, and carries West Indian jewelry and crafts styled in straw, shells, and other local materials. It also stocks clothing and paintings by Caribbean artists.

Sports and Outdoor Activities

Sailboarding **The Nick Trotter Sailing School** (Bitter End Yacht Club, North Sound, tel. 800/872–2392). Both beginner's and advanced courses are offered here.

Sailing See Sailing in the Virgin Islands, Chapter 4, for information.

Snorkeling/ See Diving and Snorkeling in the Virgin Islands, Chapter 3, for in-
Diving formation.

Sportfishing **Captain Dale** (Biras Creek, North Sound, tel. 809/495–7248) takes people out on *Classic*, his 38-foot Bertram.

Tennis **Biras Creek Hotel.** The hotel has two Astroturf courts. Intensive two-, three-, and five-day clinics are available. *North Sound, tel. 809/494–3555. Courts and lessons available to guests, and to nonguests for a fee. Lighted.*

Little Dix Bay. Peter Burwash International runs this crisp concession with seven hard surface courts. Resident tennis pro Jordan Sanchez gives private and group lessons; runs mixers, clinics, and tournaments; and the hotel offers tennis packages. Courts can be extremely busy on-season. *Just north of Spanish Town, tel. 809/495–5555. Available to hotel guests only. Lighted. Pro.*

Spectator Sports

Cricket matches can be seen at the Recreation Grounds in Spanish Town from February through April. Contact the tourist office (tel. 809/494–3134) for more information on specific game dates and times.

Beaches

The best beaches are most easily reached by water, although they are accessible on foot, usually after a moderately strenuous hike of 10 to 15 minutes. But your persistence is amply rewarded.

Anybody going to Virgin Gorda must experience swimming or snorkeling among its unique boulder formations. But why go to The Baths, which is usually crowded, when you can catch some rays just north at **Spring Bay** beach, which is a gem and, a little farther north, at the Crawl. Both are easily reached from The Baths on foot or by swimming.

Leverick Bay is a small, busy beach-cum-marina that fronts a resort, restaurant, and pool. Don't come here to be alone or to jog. But if you want a lively little place and a break from the island's noble quiet, take the road north and turn left while you're still up high, before the descent to Gun Creek. The view of Prickly Pear Island is an added plus and there's a dive facility right here to motor you out to beautiful Eustatia Reef just across North Sound.

It's worth going out to **Long Bay** (near Virgin Gorda's northern tip, past the Diamond Beach Club) for the snorkeling (Little Dix Bay resort has outings here). Going north from Spanish Town, go left at the fork near Pond Bay. Part of the route there is dirt road.

The North Shore has many nice beaches. From Biras Creek or Bitter End you can walk to Bercher's and Deep Bay beaches. Two of the prettiest beaches in North Sound are accessible only by boat: Mosquito Island's Hay Point Beach and Prickley Pear's Vixen Point Beach.

Savannah Bay is a lovely long stretch of white sand and though it may not always be deserted it seems wonderfully private for a beach just north of Spanish Town (on the north side of where the island narrows, at Black Rock). From town it's about 30 minutes on foot.

Dining

There are a number of excellent restaurants on Virgin Gorda. Hotels that are accessible only by boat will arrange transport in advance upon request for nonguests who wish to dine there. It is wise to make dinner reservations almost everywhere, and don't be put off if the restaurant also wants your order before you arrive. They just want to be sure they have the necessary ingredients. (And if they don't, they'll head to the store!)

Biras Creek. You come by boat (provided free) to this serene and elegant restaurant. Candlelit tables are set on a turret-like stonework terrace with the wild Caribbean on one side and calm North Sound on the other. The menu for the four-course prix-fixe dinner changes nightly, but always includes a choice of four entrées. There is an excellent wine list. *North Sound, tel. 809/494–3555 or 809/495–4356. Reservations advised. Dress: neat but casual (no shorts at dinner). AE, MC, V. $$$*

Chez Michelle. This picturesque dining room boasts a peaceful setting enhanced by stone walls, mahogany tables, and soft lamplight. The menu features Continental dishes prepared with a French flair: The Caesar salad gets an unexpected lift with garlic walnuts; try also the veal au poivre—veal scallops stuffed with hearts of palm in a cracked pepper sauce. *Spanish Town, north of the marina, tel. 809/ 495–5510. Reservations advised. Dress: casual. MC, V. No lunch; closed Sun. off-season. $$$*

★ **Drake's Anchorage.** Actually on Mosquito Island (ferry service available from Leverick Bay), this is a romantic candlelit setting right at the water's edge. Chef Erskine Husbands prepares Caribbean-accented fare, including dorado encrusted with bananas and bread crumbs, local lobster, and velvety chocolate mousse. *Mosquito Island, tel. 809/494–2254. Reservations advised. Dress: neat but casual. AE, MC, V. $$$*

★ **Little Dix Bay.** For an elegant evening out, you can't do better than this—the candlelit setting in the main pavilion is enchanting, the menu sophisticated, the service attentive. The dinner menu changes daily but there is always a fine selection of superbly prepared seafood, meat, and vegetarian entrées from which to choose. *Spanish Town, tel. 809/495–5555 (Ext. 174). Reservations advised. Dress: neat but casual (no shorts at dinner). AE, MC, V. $$$*

Olde Yard Inn. Civilized and charming, the dining room here is suffused with gentle classical melodies and the scent of herbs. A cedar roof covers the breezy, open-air room decorated with old-style Caribbean charm. The French-accented cuisine includes veal with shrimp and herbs, lamb chops with mango chutney, and chicken breast in a rum cream sauce, as well as grilled local fish and steaks. The key lime pie, cheesecake, and chocolate mousse are sure bets for dessert. *The Valley, north of the marina, tel. 809/495–5544. Reservations advised. Dress: casual. AE, MC, V. $$$*

Pusser's Leverick Bay. This two-level restaurant looks out over picturesque North Sound. The upstairs is more formal, although the menu is a combination of steak house and English pub. Below, the Beach Bar offers light fare all day and a nightly "theme." Thursday is $1 Heineken night. Tuesday is Pizza-and-Beer night. *Leverick Bay Resort, tel. 809/495-7369. Reservations accepted. Dress: casual. AE, MC, V. $$$*

The Clubhouse. The Bitter End's open-air restaurant is a favorite rendezvous for the sailing set, with huge buffets and fresh fish and lobster. It's a popular, crowded spot. *The Bitter End Yacht Club, North Sound, tel. 809/494-2746. Reservations accepted. Dress: casual. AE, MC, V. $$-$$$*

★ **The Bath and Turtle.** This informal patio tavern with a friendly staff is a popular spot where you can sit back and relax. Burgers, well-stuffed sandwiches, pizzas, pasta dishes, and daily specials round out the casual menu. Live entertainers perform on Wednesday and Sunday nights. *Virgin Gorda Yacht Harbour, tel. 809/495-5239. Reservations accepted. Dress: casual. MC, V. $$*

Teacher's Pet Ilma's. This restaurant in a small house offers delightful local atmosphere and delicious native-style family dinners, including local goat, fresh grouper or snapper, pork, and chicken. *The Valley, tel. 809/495-5355. Reservations required. Dress: casual. No lunch. No credit cards. $$*

The Crab Hole. This homey hangout serves West Indian specialties like callaloo soup, saltfish, stewed goat, curried chicken roti, rice and peas, and green bananas. *The Valley, tel. 809/495-5307. Reservations accepted. Dress: casual. No credit cards. $-$$*

Lodging

Virgin Gorda's charming hostelries appeal to a select, appreciative clientele. (Repeat business is extremely high here.) Visitors who prefer Sheratons, Marriotts, and the like may feel they get more for their money on other islands. But the peace and pampering offered on Virgin Gorda are priceless to the discriminating traveler.

Hotels and Inns **Biras Creek Hotel.** This enchanting 150-acre hideaway is so secluded that the only way to reach it is by launch. The hilltop, open-air bar and restaurant area is made of awesomely perfect stonework and offers stunning views of North Sound. Each guest cottage is a suite, with bedroom, bath, and living room. Perhaps its loveliest feature is the sensuous open-air walled shower in each bathroom. Guests can explore the grounds on foot or on bicycles provided by the hotel. There's a pool set right at the edge of the sea; tennis courts are lighted for night play; sailing, boardsailing, and snorkeling equipment is available. Beach aficionados will be disappointed with the rather grassy swimming beach. Guests are pampered here. The atmosphere is one of casual elegance. *Box 54, North Sound, tel. 809/494-3555, fax 809/494-3557. 34 rooms. Facilities: restaurant, bar, 2 beaches, tennis courts, marina, pool, water sports, hiking and biking trails. AE, MC, V. $$$$*

★ **Bitter End Yacht Club and Marina.** Stretching along the coastline of North Sound, the BEYC enjoys unique, panoramic views of the Sound, Leverick Bay, and nearby islands. Accommodations range from hillside or beachfront villas and chalets to live-aboard yachts, all of which include the basics, but are refreshingly no-frills. What's most inviting about this property, however, is the friendly, unpretentious welcome the resort extends to all its guests: Within days visitors and staff are on a first-name basis. Depending on your pace, your day can include as many or as few activities that you wish. The resort organizes daily snorkeling and diving trips to nearby reefs, windsurfing lessons, and excursion to local attractions, but the BEYC is most touted for its Nick Trotter Sailing School. Regarded as the best sailing instruction in the Caribbean, the school helps both seasoned salts and beginners sharpen their nautical skills. When the sun goes down, the festivities continue at either the elegant Carvery, where themed buffets are served on special occasions, or at the Clubhouse, an open-air restaurant overlooking the Sound. The hotel's character is the liveliest and most convivial in the B.V.I. *Box 46, North Sound, tel. 809/494–2746, fax 809/494–4756. 100 rooms. Facilities: 2 restaurants, bar, beach, marina, pool. AE, MC, V. $$$$*

★ **Little Dix Bay.** The luxury resort that first set the standards for understated elegance in the B.V.I. was taken over by Rosewood Resorts, refurbished, and re-opened in time for the 1994 winter season. Air-conditioning and telephones were added to the hexagonally shaped rooms, along with teal and terra-cotta fabrics and beautiful woven-wood furnishings. Returnees, of which there are many, and first-time visitors will be delighted at the results that have turned the rooms into peaceful retreats. There's a new Italian restaurant in the sugar mill; everything else is the same only better. The lawns are beautifully manicured; the reef-protected beach is long and silken; and the candlelight dining in an open peak-roof pavilion is a memorable experience. Tennis, sailing, snorkeling, water-skiing, and bicycling are included in the rate. Popular with honeymooners, and older couples who have apparently been coming back for years, Little Dix may leave the single traveler occasionally feeling slightly left out. Nonetheless, the accommodations are superb, the service thoughtful and attentive, and the setting unforgettable. *Box 70, tel. 809/495–5555, fax 809/495–5661. 102 rooms. Facilities: 3 restaurants, 2 bars, beach, water sports, hiking trails, marina, 7 tennis courts, boutique. AE, MC, V. $$$$*

Olde Yard Inn. Owners Charlie Williams and Carol Kaufman have cultivated a refreshingly unique atmosphere at this quiet retreat just outside Spanish Town. Classical music plays in the small bar; a large and varied collection of books lines the walls of the octagonal library cottage. The restaurant's French-accented menu is lovingly prepared and served with style in the high-ceiling dining rooms. The guest rooms are cozy and simply furnished. Arrangements can be made for day sails, and scuba diving excursions. Though the hotel is not on the beach (Savannah Bay and Pond Bay are only a 20-minute walk away), construction of a new pool should be completed by the time you read this. You may want to request one of the air-conditioned rooms; the hotel's location in the Valley means trade winds are less noticeable here. *Box 26, Spanish Town, tel. 809/495–5544, fax 809/495–5986. 14 rooms. Facilities: restaurant, bar, library, pool, horseback riding. AE, MC, V. $$–$$$$*

Fischer's Cove Beach Hotel. Set amid casually tended gardens this informal beachside hotel features rustic, simply furnished two-unit cottages, some of which are oddly shaped to catch the breezes off the sea. Dining at the Fischer's Cove Restaurant offers a choice of Continental cuisine or such West Indian classics as crispy conch fritters, red snapper, and fungi (pronounced FOON-jee), a polenta-like side dish. *Box 60, The Valley, tel. 809/495–5252. 22 rooms. Facilities: restaurant, bar, beach, water sports, discothèque. AE, MC, V. $$–$$$*

Leverick Bay Resort. This small hotel offers 16 hillside rooms decorated in pastels and with original artwork. All rooms have refrigerators, balconies, and gorgeous views of North Sound. Four two-bedroom condos are also available. A Spanish Colonial–style main building houses a restaurant and store operated by Pusser's of Tortola. A dive operation, a tennis court, a crafts shop, commissary, coin-operated laundry, and beauty salon are also on-site. The resort's office has books, games, and tennis rackets for guests to borrow. *Box 63, tel. 809/495-7421, fax 809/495-7367. 20 rooms. Facilities: restaurant, bar, small beach, marina, pool, tennis court, shopping arcade, water sports. AE, D, MC, V. $$-$$$*

The Wheel House. This hotel is easy on the pocketbook for those seeking a no-frills vacation headquarters. The cinder-block building offers rooms that are air-conditioned, but small; they've recently been repainted and redecorated with pastel-print bedspreads and curtains. The restaurant and bar can get noisy. It is conveniently close to the Virgin Gorda marina and shopping center. *Box 66, tel. 809/495-5230. 12 rooms. Facilities: restaurant, bar. AE, MC, V. $-$$*

Mosquito Island ★ **Drake's Anchorage.** Manager Albert Wheatley ensures that this small, secluded getaway offers true privacy and pampering you'd find in some of the more elegant resorts, but without the formality. Dinner attire here means changing from bathing suit to comfortable cottons. The three West Indian–style, waterfront bungalows contain 10 comfortably furnished rooms, including two suites. There are also two fully equipped villas for rent. There is a highly regarded restaurant, hiking trails, water-sports facilities, and four delightful beaches, and hammocks here and there—a truly peaceful, rejuvenating experience. *Box 2510, North Sound, Virgin Gorda, tel. 809/494-2254 or 800/624-6651, fax 809/494-2254. Facilities: restaurant, bar, 4 beaches, water sports, hiking trails, gift shop. AE, MC, V. $$$$*

Private Homes and Villas For those craving total seclusion, the following offer comfortable lodgings, with full kitchen and maid service.

Mango Bay Resort. Sparkling white villas framed by morning glory and frangipani, handsome contemporary Italian decor, and a gorgeous ribbon of golden sand that all but vanishes at high tide make this an idyllic family retreat. Even for Virgin Gorda it's a study in isolation. *Box 1062, Virgin Gorda, tel. 809/495-5672. 8 villas. Facilities: beach, water sports. No credit cards. $$$-$$$$*

Paradise Beach Resort. These one-, two-, and three-bedroom beachfront suites and villas are handsomely decorated in pastel colors and Caribbean style, and feature outdoor showers. Four-wheel-drive vehicles are included in the daily rate. *Box 534, Virgin Gorda, tel. 809/495-5871. 9 units. Facilities: beach, water sports. No credit cards. $$$-$$$$*

Virgin Gorda Villa Rentals. This company manages the adjacent Leverick Bay Resort, so it's perfect for those who want to be close to some activity. Many villas have private swimming pools; all are well-maintained and boast spectacular views. *Box 63, Virgin Gorda, tel. 809/495-7421. 21 villas, from studios to 3-bedroom. Facilities: access to restaurant, bar, marina, shopping center. AE, D, MC, V. $$$-$$$$*

Guavaberry Spring Bay Vacation Homes. Spending time in these unusual hexagon-shaped cottages perched on stilts makes you feel as if you are in a tree house, as you listen to the chirping birds and trees swaying in the breeze. These one- and two-bedroom units are situated on a hill, a short walk down to a tamarind-shaded beach and not far from the mammoth boulders and cool basins of the famed Baths, which adjoin this property. *Box 20, Virgin Gorda, tel. 809/495-5227. 16 units. Facilities: commissary, beach. No credit cards. $$-$$$$*

Nightlife

The Bath and Turtle (Virgin Gorda Yacht Harbour, tel. 809/495–5239). One of the liveliest spots on Virgin Gorda, this informal pub hosts island bands on Wednesday and Sunday evenings. The entertainment begins at 8 and goes until midnight. This is a good spot to rub elbows with local music aficionados as well as boaters.

The Crab Hole in The Valley (tel. 809/495–5307) has a disco with a local DJ on Saturday nights.

De Goose Restaurant and Nightclub (Spanish Town, tel. 809/495–5641) has live music on weekends. As a bonus, you can feast cheaply on authentic West Indian snacks like johnnycakes and souse.

Little Dix Bay (tel. 809/495–5555) and the Bitter End Yacht Club (tel. 809/494–2746) offer live entertainment several nights a week in season. Call for schedules.

Pirate's Grill on Saba Rock (tel. 809/495–9638) has a nightly jam session. Bring your own instrument or use one of theirs!

Pirate's Pub at Andy's Chateau (Fischer's Cove Beach Hotel, The Valley, tel. 809/495–5252). There's live music and the closest thing to a disco here Friday, Saturday, and Sunday nights.

Jost Van Dyke

Introduction

Named after an early Dutch settler, this small island northwest of Tortola is a worthwhile destination for those travelers who truly want to get away from it all. Mountainous and lush, the 4-mile-long island—home to only about 140 people—has one tiny hotel, two campgrounds, and less than a dozen informal eateries. With only a handful of cars, no paved roads, and small generators for electricity, visitors feel as if they've stepped back in time.

Exploring Jost Van Dyke

The best way to see Jost Van Dyke is by sailing around the island and dropping anchor wherever you see an attractive stretch of beach. Begin your tour in **Great Harbour,** a tiny settlement on the island's south shore just east of White Bay. Stroll through town, checking out the small cluster of buildings, including the church, the school, and the customs house. The island's popularity among boaters becomes apparent at the sight of the many gently rocking pleasure craft in the harbor. You'll notice a remarkably large collection of informal bars and restaurants, which have helped earn Jost its reputation as "Party Island" of the B.V.I. You can continue to walk east along the shore around Black Point to **Little Harbour,** where you will find several more bars and restaurants strung along both sides of the harbor.

Beaches

Jost Van Dyke's best spots for sunning are **Little Harbour** and **White Bay,** on the south shore. Just offshore, **Sandy Cay** is a gleaming scimitar of white sand, with marvelous snorkeling.

Dining and Nightlife

Restaurants on Jost Van Dyke are charming but very informal. Some serve meals family style, at long tables. The island is a favorite charter stop and you're bound to hear people exchanging stories about the previous night's anchoring adventures.

None of the following restaurants takes reservations unless specified, and in all cases, dress is informal.

Rudy's Mariner Rendezvous. This eatery at the western end of the beach specializes in lobster and other seafood dishes, and has live entertainment several nights during the week. *Great Harbour, tel. 809/495–9282. Reservations accepted at the customs office. No credit cards. $$*

Abe's Little Harbour. Specialties at this informal, popular spot include fresh lobster, conch, and spare ribs. During most of the winter season, there's a pig roast every Wednesday night. *Little Harbour, no telephone (use VHF Channel 16). Reservations accepted. No credit cards. $–$$*

Club Paradise Restaurant. The dinner menu at this casual beachfront establishment includes grilled local fish such as mahimahi, red snapper, and grouper; grilled steak; and barbecued chicken and ribs. Hamburgers, West Indian conch stew, and curried chicken are the luncheon fare. Be sure to try the excellent black bean soup. There's a pig roast with live entertainment every Wednesday night. *Great Harbour, tel. 809/495–9267. Reservations accepted. No credit cards. $–$$*

Foxy's Tamarind. One of the true "hot spots" in the B.V.I., and a "must stop" for yachters all over the world, it hosts the madcap *Wooden Boat Race* every August or September and throws big parties on New Year's Eve, April Fools' Day, and Halloween. This lively place features local dishes and the best barbecue, and it makes a rum punch that's all its own. Foxy himself plays the guitar and delights in creating calypso ditties about his guests. *Great Harbour, tel. 809/ 495–9258. Reservations advised. AE, MC, V. Closed for lunch. $–$$*

Harris' Place. Owner Harris Jones is famous for his Monday, Thursday, and Saturday Pig Roast Buffets and Monday night's Lobstermania. Harris' Place is a great spot to rub elbows with some of the local citizenry and the charter-boat crowd. There's live reggae music Thursday and Saturday. *Little Harbour, tel. 809/495–9302. AE, MC, V. $–$$*

Sydney's Peace and Love. Great lobster, barbecue, and (for the B.V.I.) a sensational jukebox. The cognoscenti sail here for dinner, since there's no beach—meaning no sand fleas, which are especially irksome in the evenings. *Little Harbour, tel. 809/495–9271. No credit cards. $–$$*

Happy Laury's. A great choice for a quick meal—snacks, fritters, fish, chicken, and chips. Try a Painkiller, the house-specialty tropical drink. Live entertainment is featured some nights. *Great Harbour, no phone (use VHF Channel 16). No credit cards. $*

Lodging

Sandcastle. This tiny, four-cottage hideaway, with a staff of five, is set on a half-mile of white-sand beach on remote White Bay. There's "nothing" to do here, except maybe relax in a hammock, read, walk, swim, and enjoy sophisticated cuisine by candlelight. Arrangements can be made for diving, sailing, and sport fishing trips. *White*

Bay, tel. 809/775–5262, fax 809/775–3590. 4 cottages. Facilities: restaurant, bar, beach. No credit cards. $$–$$$

Sandy Ground Estates. This collection of eight privately owned one- and two-bedroom houses is tucked into the foliage along the edge of a beach at the east end of Jost Van Dyke. Each one is architecturally different, and interiors range from spartan to stylish. The fully equipped kitchens can be pre-stocked if you supply a list of groceries (consider doing this—supplies are limited on the island), and there are four very casual restaurants within walking distance on the other side of the hill. *Sandy Ground, tel. 809/495–3391. Facilities: beach. No credit cards. $$–$$$*

Campgrounds

Tula's N & N Campground. This campground offers accommodations for those who wish to "rough-it" and for those who want a bit more comfort. Large ($35 per couple, per night) and small ($25 per couple) prepared sites include lean-tos and sheets and pillows. Bare sites ($15 per couple) are also available. *Little Harbour, tel. 809/774–0774 or 809/495–9302. Facilities: snack bar, restaurant, beach, commissary.*

White Bay Campground. On remote White Bay beach, this simple campground has bare sites ($15 per couple, per night) and equipped tent sites (tents with electricity and one lamp; $35 per couple). The owners will take you on nature walks and can arrange island tours and sailing and diving trips. *White Bay, tel. 809/495–9312. Facilities: informal restaurant, bar, beach.*

Peter Island

Introduction

A dramatic, hilly island with wonderful anchorages and beautiful beaches, Peter Island is directly south across the Sir Francis Drake Channel about 5 miles from Road Town, Tortola. Set amid the string of small islands that stream from the southern tip of Virgin Gorda, the island is an idyllic hideaway replete with white sand beaches, stunning views and, with the exclusive Peter Island Resort, a luxurious vacation lifestyle.

Exploring Peter Island

Peter Island Resort and Yacht Harbour is nestled against the water's edge of this mountainous and otherwise undeveloped island. It can be reached by sailing in on your own craft or, if you're not so fortunate as to have one, by launch from the Peter Island dock just east of Road Town, Tortola ($10 each way or free if you're coming for dinner). Once on the island, head out from the marina for the short hike to palm-fringed **Dead Man's Bay,** called one of the world's 10 most romantic beaches. Snorkeling is good at both ends of the beach and you'll find a bar and restaurant for lunch. Across the water is **Dead Chest,** the rocky island that purportedly inspired the sea chantey "Fifteen Men on a Dead Man's Chest." Legend holds that a band of pirates once fought to the death on the island for possession of a bottle of rum. If you feel like a bit of a hike, instead of heading down to Dead Man's Bay follow the road up, and when it levels off bear right and head down to the other side of the island and secluded White Bay.

Dining

★ **Tradewinds Restaurant.** Peter Island Resort's open-air dining room overlooking the Sir Francis Drake Channel provides an enchanting setting for some of the most elegantly prepared cuisine in the B.V.I. The à la carte menu offers a tempting variety of mostly Continental selections, with subtle Caribbean touches. Every Saturday night there is a delectable buffet. During or after dinner, dance under the stars to soft, rhythmic tunes performed by local musicians. *Peter Island Resort, tel. 809/494–2561. Reservations required. Dress: neat but casual (dress shirts, no shorts or jeans). AE, MC, V. No lunch. $$$$*

Deadman's Bay Bar and Grill. This more casual grill on the beach serves lunches of ribs, burgers, grilled fish, and a bountiful salad bar. Sunday lunch features a lavish West-Indian buffet and a steel band. A four-course, prix-fixe dinner, with a choice of grilled local fish, steak, chicken, or lamb chops, is served most evenings. Try one of the many delicious frozen tropical drinks. *Peter Island Resort, tel. 809/494–2561. Reservations required for dinner. Dress: neat but casual. AE, MC, V. $$$–$$$$*

Lodging

★ **Peter Island Resort and Yacht Harbour.** This resort is close to the last word in luxury in all the Caribbean. General Manager Jamie Holmes has made sure there is every imaginable living, dining, and recreational amenity, including a gourmet restaurant, stunning freshwater pool, tennis courts and resident pro, small sailboats, Sunfishes, kayaks, mountain bicycles, Windsurfers, Hobie Cats, an exercise room, a 20-station fitness trail, a dive shop, and a masseuse. The 50 guest rooms, in four-unit cottages tucked among beds of radiant tropical flowers, are either on the beach or near the pool. Beachfront units are beautiful stone-and-wood affairs that open out on one of the loveliest beaches anywhere. The bay here is palm fringed, and the calm water all shades of blue. The less expensive ocean view rooms, which are slightly smaller, look across the pool toward the hills and twinkling lights of Tortola. A spectacular hilltop villa, the *Crow's Nest*, rents for about $3,000 a day and includes four separate bedrooms, a living room, state-of-the-art kitchen, dining room, terrace, inner courtyard, fully stocked entertainment systems, domestic help, vehicles, and a private swimming pool overlooking the marina on one side and Dead Man's Bay on the other. This is a resort for people seeking elegant seclusion. Ten miles of walks and four beautiful beaches ensure a remarkable degree of privacy. Service is impeccable. *Box 211, Road Town, Tortola, tel. 809/494–2561 or 800/346–4451, fax 809/494–2313. 50 rooms, 2 villas. Facilities: 2 restaurants, 2 bars, 5 beaches, pool, 4 lighted tennis courts and pro, marina, 20-station fitness trail, 5-star PADI dive facility, helicopter pad. AE, MC, V. $$$$*

Anegada

Anegada lies low on the sea about 20 miles northeast of Virgin Gorda. Unlike the other islands of the chain, it is not volcanic but rather a coral and limestone atoll with no hills. Nine miles long and 3 miles wide, the island rises no more than 28 feet above sea level. In fact, by the time you are able to see it, you may have run your boat onto a reef. More than 300 other captains, unfamiliar with the waters, have done exactly that since the exploration days. The scores of shipwrecks that encircle the island as a result make it popular with scuba divers. The northern and western shores of Anegada have long stretches of stunning white-sand beach. The island's population of about 150 is clustered in a small village called The Settlement, and many of them are fishermen who will take visitors out bonefishing. Snorkeling, especially in the translucent waters around Loblolly Bay on the north shore, is a transcendent experience. It is possible to float in totally reef-protected calm water only several feet deep and several feet from shore and see one coral formation after another, each shimmering with a rainbow of colorful fish. Combine that with miles of whitest of white sand as fine as pancake batter and one lone beach bar serving wondrous home cooking and frosty beers, and you have a formula that should satisfy anyone's fantasy of being marooned on a desert island.

Exploring Anegada

Most of what's to see in Anegada is close to shore but underwater. A dirt road circumnavigates the island and several roads crisscross it. **Pat's Pottery** (tel. 809/495–8031) is about in the middle, via the main dirt road. Here you'll find bowls, plates, cups, candlestick holders, and original watercolors, all made locally.

Dining and Nightlife

There are somewhere between three to six restaurants open at any one time, depending on the season and also on whim. Check when you're on the island.

Anegada Reef Hotel. Seasoned yachters gather nightly at the bar here (bare-boat charters aren't allowed to head to Anegada without a trained skipper because of the dangerous reefs), to join conversations and dine with the hotel guests. Dinner is by candlelight and always features famous Anegada lobster, steaks, and chicken, all prepared on the large grill by the little, open-air bar. *Anegada Reef Hotel, tel. 809/495–8002. Reservations required for dinner. Dress: casual. No credit cards. $$*

Neptune's Treasure. Owners catch, cook, and serve the seafood, with lobster a specialty at this casual bar and restaurant. *Between Pomato and Saltheap points, tel. 809/495–9237. Reservations not necessary. Dress: casual. AE. $$*

Pomato Point Inn. This relaxed restaurant and bar is on a narrow beach, a short walk from the Anegada Reef Hotel. Entrées include steak, chicken, lobster, and fresh-caught seafood. Owner Wilfred Creque displays various island artifacts, including shards of Arawak pottery and 17th-century coins, cannonballs, and bottles. *Pomato Point, tel. 809/495–8038. Reservations advised. Dress: casual. $$*

Lodging

Anegada Reef Hotel. Those who stay here (and there are many devotees who return year after year) are truly in search of getting away from it all. This is the only hotel on the island, and it has only 16 simply furnished rooms. The hotel is on a narrow strip of beach, but beach lovers will want to spend their days on the beautiful deserted beaches on the other side of the island; you can be dropped off with a picnic lunch or be picked up and returned to the hotel for lunch. A bathing suit and something warmer for the evening are all the clothes you'll need. The outdoor bar is a great spot for a cool island drink or a cold beer, and the restaurant is one of the best spots for sampling Anegada's famous local lobster grilled or in cold salads. Snorkeling and diving are as good on Anegada as anywhere in the islands. Bonefishing in the flats is a favorite activity, and deep-sea fishing trips can be arranged. If you favor laid-back living with no schedules, this is the spot for you. *Anegada, tel. 809/495–8002, fax 809/495–9362. 16 rooms. Facilities: restaurant, bar, beach, gift shop, water sports. $$$–$$$$*

Campground

Anegada Beach Campground. The tents (8 by 10 feet or 10 by 12 feet) are put up in a marvelously serene setting. Sites cost $7 per person, per night. *The Settlement, Anegada, tel. 809/495–8038. Facilities: bar, restaurant, beach, gift shop, water sports, occasional entertainment.*

Other British Virgin Islands

Cooper Island, a small hilly island on the south side of the Sir Francis Drake Channel, about 8 miles from Road Town, Tortola, is a popular stop for the charter-boat crowd. There's a beach restaurant, a tiny hotel, a few privately owned houses (some of which are available for rent), and great snorkeling at the south end of Manchioneel Bay; a trail leads to a lookout affording a stunning view of Virgin Gorda.

Guana Island is very quiet and *very* private. Guana Island Club sends its private launch to pick up guests arriving at Beef Island. If you're not a guest, you'll have to rely on your own private boat to get here, and once you're onshore you'll be restricted to the beaches that ring the island. Guests of the resort, however, can make use of the numerous hiking trails throughout the island.

Marina Cay is a beautiful little island in Trellis Bay, not far from Beef Island and its airport. It can sometimes be seen from the air during the approach to the airport: a very dramatic sight, with large J-shape coral reefs engulfing the cay. With only 6 acres, this islet is considered small even by B.V.I. standards. Marina Cay Hotel, with 12 simple rooms, provides the only accommodations on the island, and is a favorite of yachtsmen who drop in to dine.

Dining

Cooper Island   **Cooper Island Restaurant.** Ferry service from Road Town is available only to guests of the hotel, but this restaurant is a popular stop for boaters. Come here for great ratatouille (it's a main course at lunch, an appetizer at dinner); grilled local fish, chicken, and steak; and conch Creole. For lunch, there are also hamburgers, conch fritters, and pasta salad. *Cooper Island, no telephone, (use VHF Channel 16). Reservations required. Dress: casual. AE, MC, V. $$–$$$*

Marina Cay   **Marina Cay Hotel.** Ferry service is available from Beef Island to the resort where this restaurant is located. The dinner menu ranges from fish and lobster to steak, chicken, and ribs. It has a salad bar as well, and every Friday it holds a beach barbecue. The restaurant and bar are favorites of local yachtsmen. There is live entertainment nightly. *Marina Cay Hotel, tel. 809/494–2174. Reservations advised. Dress: casual. AE, MC, V. $$–$$$*

Lodging

Cooper Island **Cooper Island Beach Club.** Two West Indian–style cottages house four no-frills units with a living area, a small but complete kitchen, and a balcony. This is a wonderful place to get away from it all and lead a somewhat back-to-basics existence: The only water available is rain collected in a cistern, and because of the limited amount of electricity, you won't be able to use a hairdryer, an iron, or any other electric appliance. If you want to mingle, the bar fills nightly with a new group of boaters. *Box 859, Road Town, Tortola, tel. 800/542–4624 or 413/659–2602. 4 rooms. Facilities: restaurant, beach, boutique, dive shop. MC, V. $$–$$$*

Guana Island **Guana Island Club.** Guana Island is owned entirely by the hotel, and as a result, the hotel is very private. Guests are met at Beef Island by the hotel's launch, the only organized access to the island. The hotel is situated on the top of a hill, from where it is a 10-minute walk to the beach. Fifteen rustic but comfortable guest rooms are spread among seven separate houses scattered along the hillside. The houses are decorated in Caribbean style, with rattan furniture and ceiling fans, and each has its own porch. Lack of facilities available to the public keep this island especially private. More than 50 species of bird can be observed on the island and the terrain is a verdant collection of exotic tropical plants ringed by six deserted beaches. *Box 32, Road Town, Tortola, tel. 809/494–2354, fax 914/967–8048. 15 rooms. Facilities: restaurant, wildlife sanctuary, tennis, croquet, hiking trails, water sports, boutique. No credit cards. $$$$*

Marina Cay **Marina Cay Hotel.** The tiny island's only hotel consists of 12 separate villas (only four of which are currently available), which fan out across the hillside, all with lovely views of the water and neighboring islands. Each has its own porch. *Box 76, Road Town, Tortola, tel. 809/494–2174, fax 809/494–4775. 12 rooms. Facilities: restaurant, bar, water sports. AE, D, DC, MC, V. $$–$$$*

Index

Personal Itinerary

Departure *Date*

Time

Transportation

Arrival *Date*   *Time*

Departure *Date*   *Time*

Transportation

Accommodations

Arrival *Date*   *Time*

Departure *Date*   *Time*

Transportation

Accommodations

Arrival *Date*   *Time*

Departure *Date*   *Time*

Transportation

Accommodations

Personal Itinerary

Arrival	*Date*	*Time*
Departure	*Date*	*Time*
Transportation		
Accommodations		

Arrival	*Date*	*Time*
Departure	*Date*	*Time*
Transportation		
Accommodations		

Arrival	*Date*	*Time*
Departure	*Date*	*Time*
Transportation		
Accommodations		

Arrival	*Date*	*Time*
Departure	*Date*	*Time*
Transportation		
Accommodations		

Personal Itinerary

Arrival	*Date*	*Time*
Departure	*Date*	*Time*
Transportation		
Accommodations		

Arrival	*Date*	*Time*
Departure	*Date*	*Time*
Transportation		
Accommodations		

Arrival	*Date*	*Time*
Departure	*Date*	*Time*
Transportation		
Accommodations		

Arrival	*Date*	*Time*
Departure	*Date*	*Time*
Transportation		
Accommodations		

Personal Itinerary

Arrival *Date*   *Time*

Departure *Date*   *Time*

Transportation

Accommodations

Arrival *Date*   *Time*

Departure *Date*   *Time*

Transportation

Accommodations

Arrival *Date*   *Time*

Departure *Date*   *Time*

Transportation

Accommodations

Arrival *Date*   *Time*

Departure *Date*   *Time*

Transportation

Accommodations

Addresses

Name	*Name*
Address	*Address*
Telephone	*Telephone*
Name	*Name*
Address	*Address*
Telephone	*Telephone*
Name	*Name*
Address	*Address*
Telephone	*Telephone*
Name	*Name*
Address	*Address*
Telephone	*Telephone*
Name	*Name*
Address	*Address*
Telephone	*Telephone*
Name	*Name*
Address	*Address*
Telephone	*Telephone*
Name	*Name*
Address	*Address*
Telephone	*Telephone*
Name	*Name*
Address	*Address*
Telephone	*Telephone*

Addresses

Name	*Name*
Address	*Address*
Telephone	*Telephone*
Name	*Name*
Address	*Address*
Telephone	*Telephone*
Name	*Name*
Address	*Address*
Telephone	*Telephone*
Name	*Name*
Address	*Address*
Telephone	*Telephone*
Name	*Name*
Address	*Address*
Telephone	*Telephone*
Name	*Name*
Address	*Address*
Telephone	*Telephone*
Name	*Name*
Address	*Address*
Telephone	*Telephone*
Name	*Name*
Address	*Address*
Telephone	*Telephone*

The only guide to explore a Disney World you've never seen before:

The one for grown-ups.

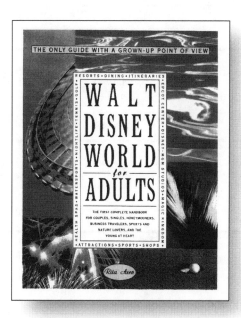

This is the only guide written specifically for the millions of adults who visit Walt Disney World each year <u>without</u> kids. Upscale, sophisticated, packed full of facts and maps, *Walt Disney World for Adults* provides up-to-date information on hotels, restaurants, sports facilities, and health clubs, as well as unique itineraries for adults. With *Walt Disney World for Adults* in hand, you'll get the most out of one of the world's most fascinating, most complex playgrounds.

At bookstores everywhere, or call **1-800-533-6478**.

Addresses

Name

Address

Telephone

Name

Address

Telephone

Name

Address

Telephone

Name

Address

Telephone

Name

Address

Telephone

Name

Address

Telephone

Name

Address

Telephone

Name

Address

Telephone

Name

Address

Telephone

Name

Address

Telephone

Name

Address

Telephone

Name

Address

Telephone

Name

Address

Telephone

Name

Address

Telephone

Name

Address

Telephone

Name

Address

Telephone

What's hot, where it's hot!

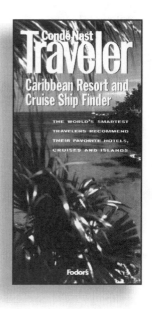

Condé Nast Traveler Caribbean Resort and Cruise Ship Finder
The World's Smartest Travelers Recommend Their Favorite Hotels, Cruises and Islands

Incorporating the results of the enormously influential *Condé Nast Traveler* survey with comprehensive Fodor's travel information — this brand new guide features 150 hotels and resorts, 30 cruise lines, 28 islands, and 60 pages of maps.

Cruises and Ports of Call 1995
Choosing the Perfect Ship and Enjoying Your Time Ashore

The most comprehensive cruise guide available offers all the essentials for planning a cruise: selecting the right ship, getting the best deals, and making the most of your time in port.

"A gold mine of information."
            —New York Post

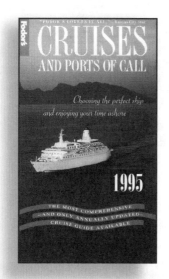

Fodor's Travel Guides

Available at bookstores everywhere, or call 1–800–533–6478, 24 hours a day.

U.S. Guides

Alaska

Arizona

Boston

California

Cape Cod, Martha's
Vineyard, Nantucket

The Carolinas & the
Georgia Coast

Chicago

Colorado

Florida

Hawaii

Las Vegas, Reno,
Tahoe

Los Angeles

Maine, Vermont,
New Hampshire

Maui

Miami & the Keys

New England

New Orleans

New York City

Pacific North Coast

Philadelphia & the
Pennsylvania Dutch
Country

The Rockies

San Diego

San Francisco

Santa Fe, Taos,
Albuquerque

Seattle & Vancouver

The South

The U.S. & British
Virgin Islands

USA

The Upper Great
Lakes Region

Virginia & Maryland

Waikiki

Walt Disney World and
the Orlando Area

Washington, D.C.

Foreign Guides

Acapulco, Ixtapa,
Zihuatanejo

Australia & New
Zealand

Austria

The Bahamas

Baja & Mexico's
Pacific Coast Resorts

Barbados

Berlin

Bermuda

Brittany & Normandy

Budapest

Canada

Cancún, Cozumel,
Yucatán Peninsula

Caribbean

China

Costa Rica, Belize,
Guatemala

The Czech Republic &
Slovakia

Eastern Europe

Egypt

Euro Disney

Europe

Florence, Tuscany &
Umbria

France

Germany

Great Britain

Greece

Hong Kong

India

Ireland

Israel

Italy

Japan

Kenya & Tanzania

Korea

London

Madrid & Barcelona

Mexico

Montréal &
Québec City

Morocco

Moscow &
St. Petersburg

The Netherlands,
Belgium &
Luxembourg

New Zealand

Norway

Nova Scotia, Prince
Edward Island &
New Brunswick

Paris

Portugal

Provence & the
Riviera

Rome

Russia & the Baltic
Countries

Scandinavia

Scotland

Singapore

South America

Southeast Asia

Spain

Sweden

Switzerland

Thailand

Tokyo

Toronto

Turkey

Vienna & the Danube
Valley

Special Series

Fodor's Affordables

Caribbean

Europe

Florida

France

Germany

Great Britain

Italy

London

Paris

Fodor's Bed & Breakfast and Country Inns Guides

America's Best B&Bs

California

Canada's Great Country Inns

Cottages, B&Bs and Country Inns of England and Wales

Mid-Atlantic Region

New England

The Pacific Northwest

The South

The Southwest

The Upper Great Lakes Region

The Berkeley Guides

California

Central America

Eastern Europe

Europe

France

Germany & Austria

Great Britain & Ireland

Italy

London

Mexico

Pacific Northwest & Alaska

Paris

San Francisco

Fodor's Exploring Guides

Australia

Boston & New England

Britain

California

The Caribbean

Florence & Tuscany

Florida

France

Germany

Ireland

Italy

London

Mexico

New York City

Paris

Prague

Rome

Scotland

Singapore & Malaysia

Spain

Thailand

Turkey

Fodor's Flashmaps

Boston

New York

Washington, D.C.

Fodor's Pocket Guides

Acapulco

Bahamas

Barbados

Jamaica

London

New York City

Paris

Puerto Rico

San Francisco

Washington, D.C.

Fodor's Sports

Cycling

Golf Digest's Best Places to Play

Hiking

The Insider's Guide to the Best Canadian Skiing

Running

Sailing

Skiing in the USA & Canada

USA Today's Complete Four Sports Stadium Guide

Fodor's Three-In-Ones (guidebook, language cassette, and phrase book)

France

Germany

Italy

Mexico

Spain

Fodor's Special-Interest Guides

Complete Guide to America's National Parks

Condé Nast Traveler Caribbean Resort and Cruise Ship Finder

Cruises and Ports of Call

Euro Disney

France by Train

Halliday's New England Food Explorer

Healthy Escapes

Italy by Train

London Companion

Shadow Traffic's New York Shortcuts and Traffic Tips

Sunday in New York

Sunday in San Francisco

Touring Europe

Touring USA: Eastern Edition

Walt Disney World and the Orlando Area

Walt Disney World for Adults

Fodor's Vacation Planners

Great American Learning Vacations

Great American Sports & Adventure Vacations

Great American Vacations

Great American Vacations for Travelers with Disabilities

National Parks and Seashores of the East

National Parks of the West

The Wall Street Journal Guides to Business Travel

At last — a guide for Americans with disabilities that makes traveling a delight

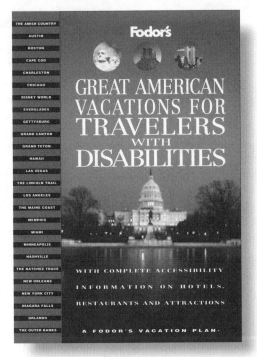

THE AMISH COUNTRY
AUSTIN
BOSTON
CAPE COD
CHARLESTON
CHICAGO
DISNEY WORLD
EVERGLADES
GETTYSBURG
GRAND CANYON
GRAND TETON
HAWAII
LAS VEGAS
THE LINCOLN TRAIL
LOS ANGELES
THE MAINE COAST
MEMPHIS
MIAMI
MINNEAPOLIS
NASHVILLE
THE NATCHEZ TRACE
NEW ORLEANS
NEW YORK CITY
NIAGARA FALLS
ORLANDO
THE OUTER BANKS

Fodor's

GREAT AMERICAN VACATIONS FOR TRAVELERS WITH DISABILITIES

WITH COMPLETE ACCESSIBILITY INFORMATION ON HOTELS, RESTAURANTS AND ATTRACTIONS

A FODOR'S VACATION PLAN·

This is the first and only complete guide to great American vacations for the 35 million North Americans with disabilities, as well as for those who care for them or for aging parents and relatives. Provides:

- Essential trip-planning information for travelers with mobility, vision, and hearing impairments
- Specific details on a huge array of facilities, along with solid descriptions of attractions, hotels, restaurants, and other destinations
- Up-to-date information on ISA-designated parking, level entranceways, accessibility to pools, lounges, bathrooms

 Fodor's At bookstores everywhere, or call **1-800-533-6478**